BASEBALL
IN
MEMPHIS

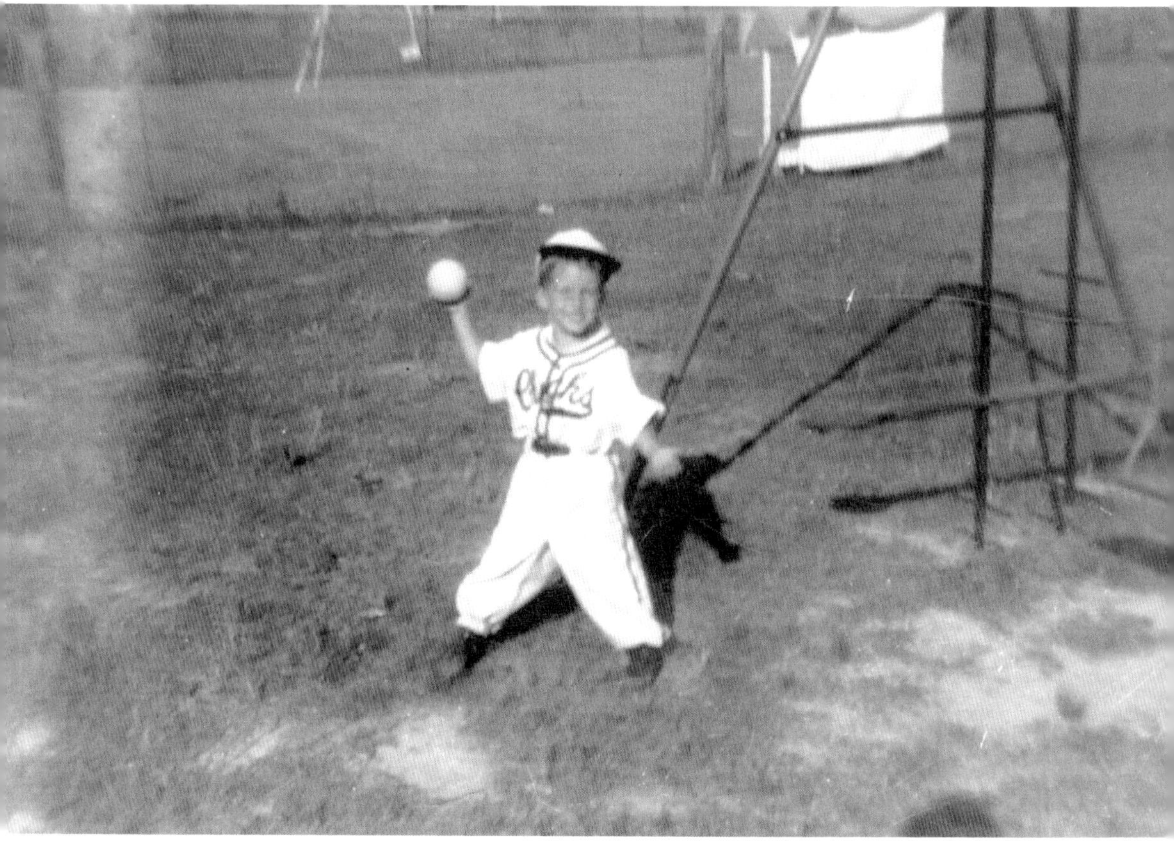

What happens when a small boy dresses up in his own Chicks uniform? Someone buys him a Ray Crone Spalding baseball glove. Crone was from Memphis and played for the Memphis Chicks in 1959. In the summer, the boy goes to sleep listening to Chicks and Cardinals baseball radio broadcasts coming from the next room, where his grandfather sleeps. As a teenager, the boy drifts from his love of baseball, but the Oakland A's dynasty of the early 1970s rekindles his passion for the sport. Later, as a young man, he goes to a baseball card show in Memphis, where an elderly gentleman, Al Price, is selling old scorecards of Southern Association teams. The young man must have the 1950s Memphis Chicks program with the majestic Chickasaw chief profiled on the cover. From that time on, the rediscovery of the history of baseball in Memphis would be part of his life and eventually culminate in the writing of this book. (Author's collection.)

FRONT COVER: Memphis Chicks pitcher Tom Flanigan (1954–1956) shows off his excellent pitching technique. (Author's collection.)

COVER BACKGROUND: The 1974 Memphis Blues pose for a team picture. (Courtesy of Memphis and Shelby County Room, Memphis Public Library and Information Center.)

BACK COVER: A wonderful aerial shot of downtown Memphis features AutoZone Park, the Pyramid, the Mississippi River, and the Hernando DeSoto Bridge. (Courtesy of Larry Inman/Memphis Redbirds.)

BASEBALL IN MEMPHIS

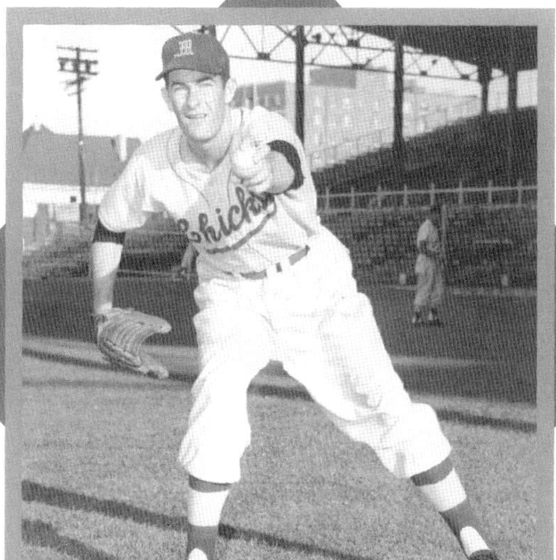

Clarence Watkins
Foreword by Jay Gauthreaux

ARCADIA PUBLISHING

ISBN 978-0-7385-9108-7

Published by Arcadia Publishing
Charleston, South Carolina

Printed in the United States of America

Library of Congress Control Number: 2011932734

For all general information, please contact Arcadia Publishing:
Telephone 843-853-2070
Fax 843-853-0044
E-mail sales@arcadiapublishing.com
For customer service and orders:
Toll-Free 1-888-313-2665

Visit us on the Internet at www.arcadiapublishing.com

This book is dedicated to Memphis baseball fans, whether you followed the Chicks, Red Sox, Blues, Redbirds, or all of the above. I hope this book strengthens your memories and revitalizes your interest. I hope it may also help create a new generation of fans interested in keeping the great history of the Memphis teams alive for the future.

To my wife, Carol, thank you for your patience during this time of preparation for the book and your help in placing my thoughts onto paper.

CONTENTS

FOREWORD

Going through the box scores was a treat for a young baseball fan growing up in New Orleans. Studying the stats, along with articles each week, provided an insight into the heroes who took the field. As a lifelong fan of the sport, I have a deep sense of appreciation for the players and teams who were part of the identity of the city.

In the "Bluff City" of Memphis, Tennessee, the history of baseball is strong in the ranks of high schools, colleges, and every level of minor-league baseball. The ballparks they played in served not only as a second home during the days of summer innocence, but as a church of hope as fans prayed for a Memphis win.

Memphis native and fellow SABR (Society of American Baseball Research) member Clarence Watkins can relate to these days in his new work, *Baseball in Memphis*. Clarence takes the reader on a historical tour through the good and bad days, from when a Memphis team first joined the old Southern League through today's Pacific Coast League teams. The images in Clarence's book show the ballplayers living out their dreams, earning a paycheck by chasing or hitting a round white sphere—which was better than milking cows or selling suits.

The city of Memphis identified with the players who graced the ballparks through the good and bad seasons in the Bluff City. This is why the history of baseball in Memphis is still special to fans who treasure those memories and to future fans who will start collecting theirs.

—Jay Gauthreaux

ACKNOWLEDGMENTS

The research for *Baseball in Memphis* has been a long and winding road. What started out as curiosity developed into an obsession. Only in the last two years did the idea of a book become a reality. Along the way, many people provided pieces to the great puzzle, and often the importance of this information was not understood until years later.

I must thank my fellow Southern Association researchers who have provided encouragement and important artifacts: Chris Drago, Jay Gauthreaux, Bill Plott, Skip Nipper, and Dan Creed. The staff at the Memphis Public Library in the Memphis Room was most helpful in locating long-forgotten manuscripts.

I also want to thank Jordan Johnson and Allison Rhoades from the Memphis Redbirds for their help with the Redbirds chapter. My thanks continue to Ben Powell for granting use of his photographs of AutoZone Park. Also, I want to thank my younger brothers Randy and Terry for filling in the gaps of Memphis baseball history when I moved away from Memphis.

In every Southern League city I have researched, I have always found a person who, in past years, kept the history of the team alive—even when fans no longer cared. I call this person the "flame keeper." For Memphis, the flame keeper is John Guinozzo. John first published his *Memphis Baseball Encyclopedia* in 1980 and has continued to print updates throughout the past 31 years. My thanks go to John for being the flame keeper for *Baseball in Memphis*.

And, finally, I want to thank Joe B. Scott, a great gentleman who treated me like an old friend from his days with the Memphis Red Sox. The two hours I spent with him in his home were "baseball heaven."

INTRODUCTION

At one of the book signings for *Baseball in Birmingham*, an incident occurred that made me want to write another book of baseball history. An elderly woman came into the bookstore with business other than buying one of my books. When she saw me at a table, she approached and asked what my book was about. After I gave her a brief summary, she told me about her memories as a child going to baseball games at Rickwood Field with her dad. Because her parents had no sons, and she was the youngest of several daughters, she got to go with him. She briefly paused before she said, "That was the only time I had my father all to myself!" It is my hope that writing this book about the history of Memphis baseball will evoke equally meaningful memories for baseball fans in Memphis.

Memphis was also a key player in the formation of the first Southern League in baseball. Before professional baseball in 1885, Memphis had an array of great amateur teams to fuel the love of the sport for its citizens. Teams such as the Red Sox, the Blues, and the Eckfords gave Memphis a strong foundation and knowledgeable fan base. During the absence of professional baseball before 1900, the Mighty Chickasaws claimed championships for the state and region, traveling to New Orleans, Nashville, Huntsville, and Selma to take on all rivals.

Prior to 1900, Memphis had several baseball parks, including Olympic, Citizen, Cycle, Chickasaw, and Red Elm Bottom. It is Red Elm Bottom that would evolve into Red Elm Park, and later into Russwood Park that we have such fond memories of. Let us take a walk back in time to become reacquainted with the heroes of the game: Ed Hurlburt, Dazzy Vance, Pete Gray, Doc Prothro, Johnny Antonelli, and Razor Shines. Baseball in Memphis was much more than a game.

The images and stories told in this book are only a small assortment of the history of baseball in Memphis; each team deserves its own book. No doubt, some very good and popular players do not appear in this text. Hopefully, this book will serve as the beginning of more research and publishing on the history of baseball in Memphis.

1

THE EARLY DAYS

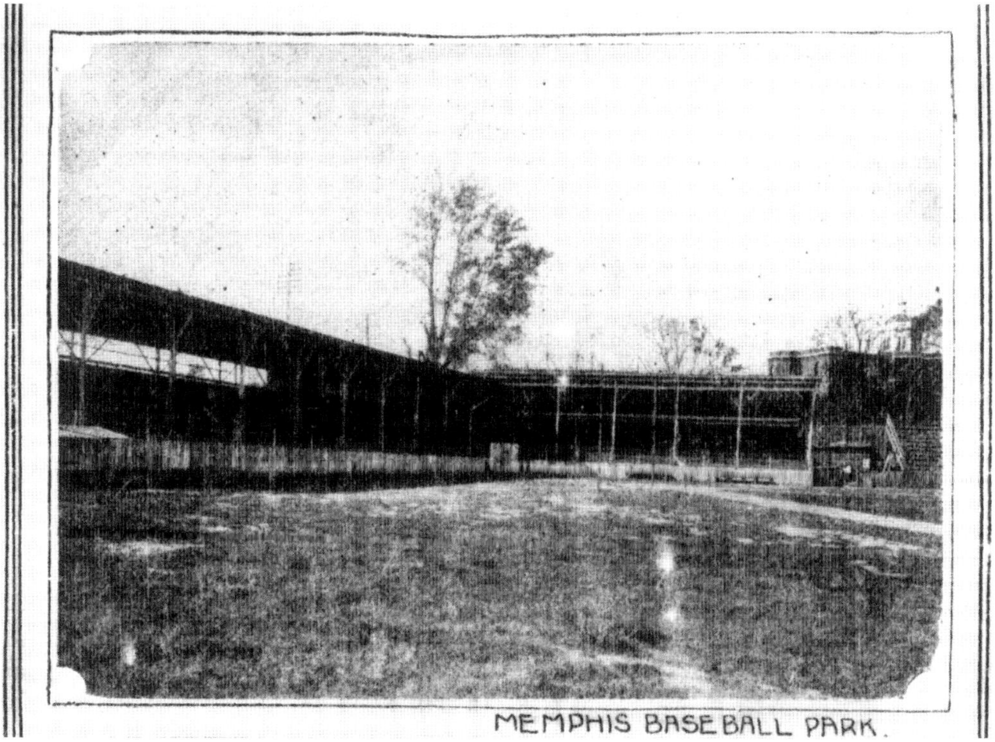

On the edge of Memphis, out on Madison Avenue, lay an ideal piece of bottomland called Red Elm Bottom—a favorite picnic spot for Memphians. Red Elm Bottom gently sloped down into a flat area of land fed by a small stream; this was the Elysian field of Memphis baseball. By 1896, a wooden ballpark had been built. After major renovations in 1915, the facility was renamed Russwood Park in honor of owner Russell E. Gardner. (Courtesy of Memphis and Shelby County Room, Memphis Public Library and Information Center.)

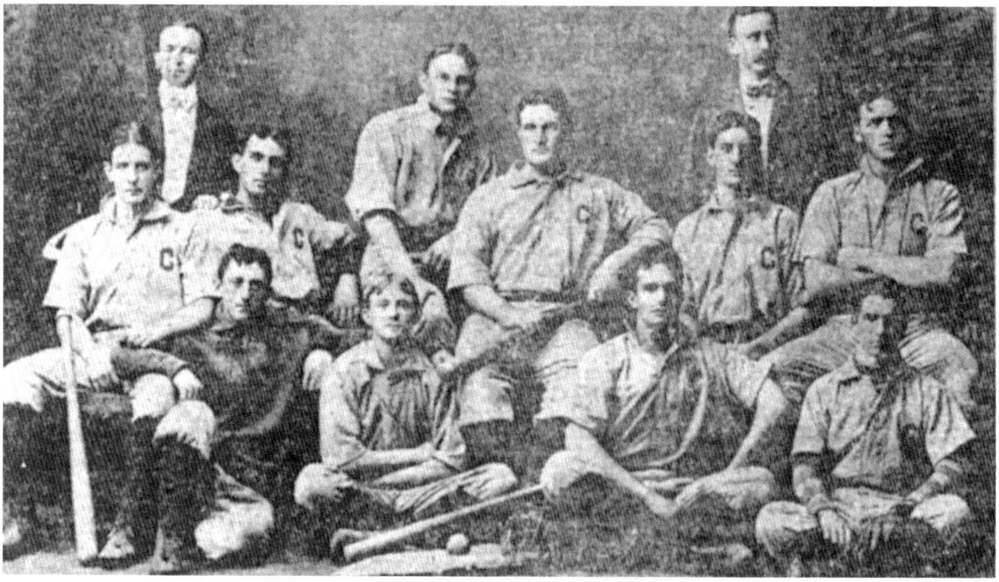

With the end of the original Southern League in 1897, Memphians did not lack for quality baseball. A group of college athletes, home for the summer, formed the Memphis Chickasaws, a team of seasoned players capable of defeating professional teams. On the far right in the first row is Joe Montedonico, the player who kept the scrapbook on the feats of the original Chickasaws. (Courtesy of Memphis and Shelby County Room, Memphis Public Library and Information Center.)

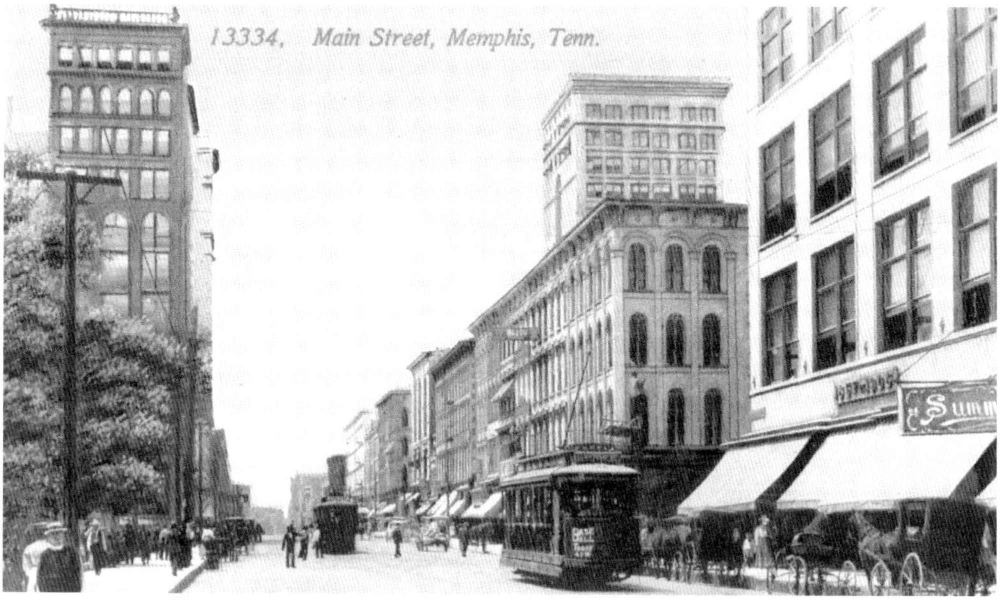

In a time before radio and television, alerting fans to upcoming games was important. No one enjoyed paying a dime for a streetcar ride to the baseball park only to find out there was no game that day. Listed in the 1913 program was the fact that a giant baseball was extended over the intersection of Main and Madison Streets to tell fans that there would be a game that day. Then, the streetcars advertised game-day notification, as seen in this 1910 postcard. (Author's collection.)

The full impact that Christian Brothers College and High School had on amateur baseball in Memphis may never be fully appreciated. In the 1890s, the Gideon Stars was the team to beat in the tri-state area. The team was coached by Brother Gideon (back row, wearing a bow tie). (Courtesy of Memphis and Shelby County Room, Memphis Public Library and Information Center.)

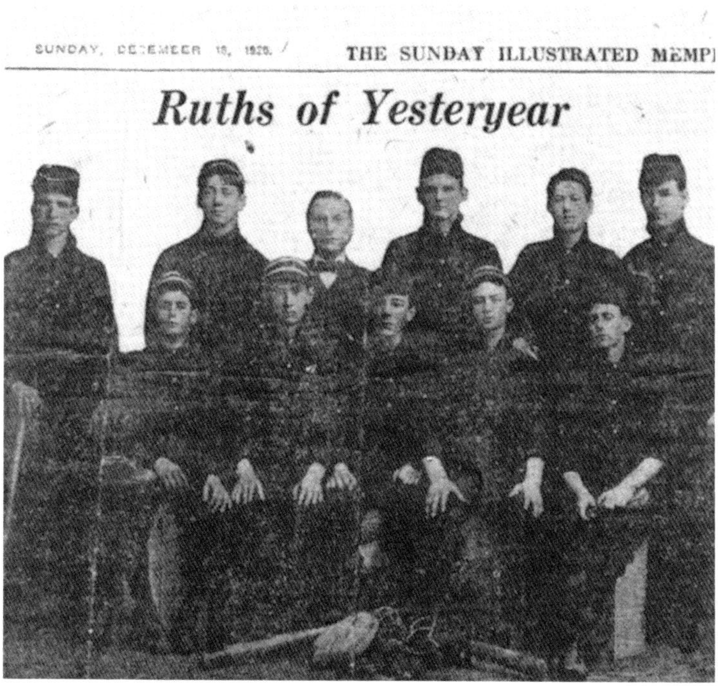

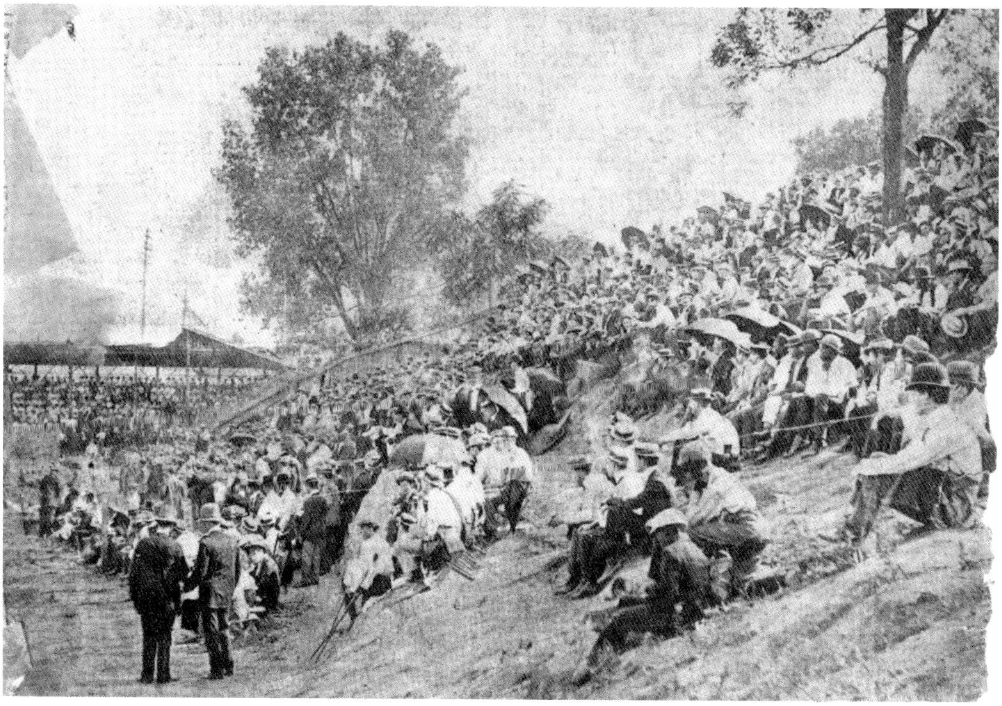

An early picture of Red Elm Park shows the natural slope of the land down to the bottom. This incline provided fans good views of the game. This photograph was taken before 1912, since the seven-story Baptist Memorial Hospital is not in the background. (Courtesy of Memphis and Shelby County Room, Memphis Public Library and Information Center.)

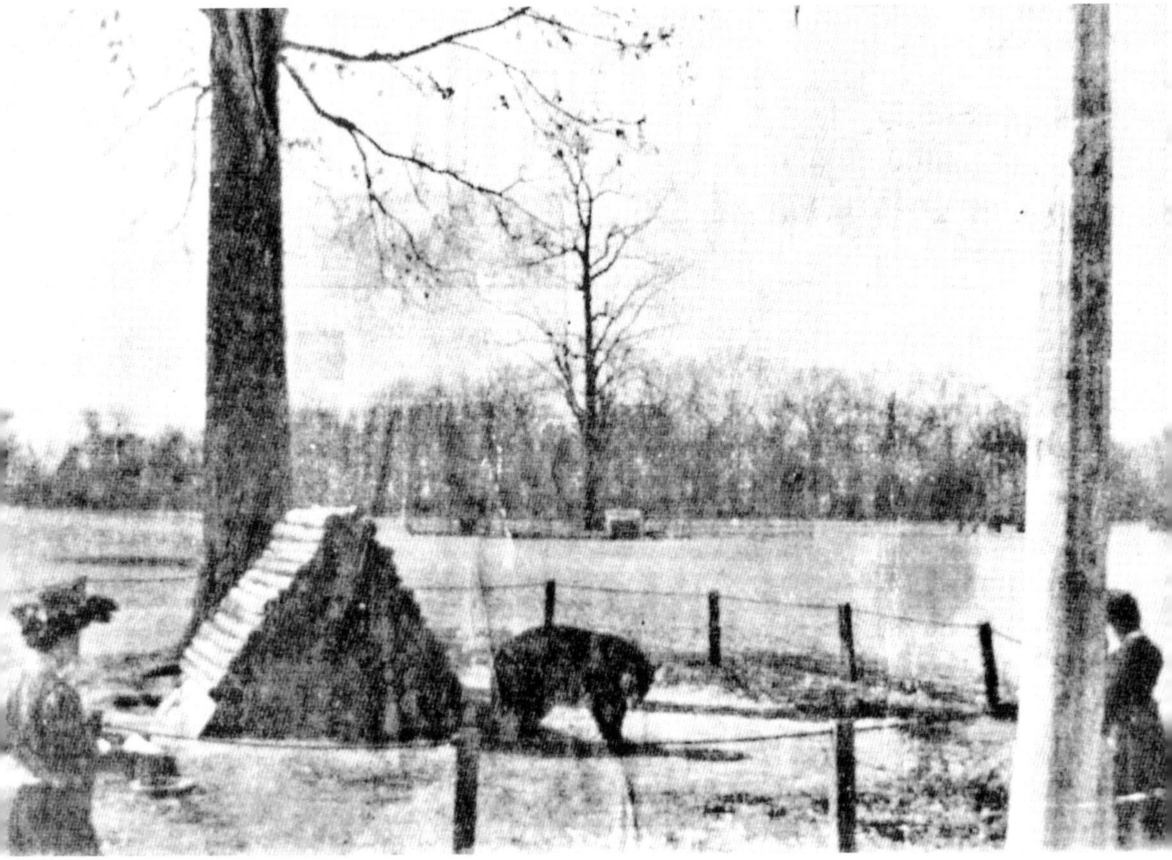

In 1905, Memphis businessman A.B. Carrathers accepted a black bear cub as partial payment for an order of shoes sent to Natchez, Mississippi. When the bear cub arrived, Carrathers gave it to the Memphis Turtles to serve as their mascot. The players named him Natch. It was not long before Natch became too hard to handle for both players and fans. He was returned to Carrathers to be staked out in his front yard, where he proceeded to destroy Mrs. Carrathers flower garden. Natch was then taken to the new Overton Park. A small enclosure was built, and he was muzzled and chained to a tree. People began coming to Overton Park to see Natch and feed him. Soon, people began leaving unwanted pets tied up near Natch. Colonel Galloway and others saw the need for a zoo in Memphis. In 1906, the Memphis Park Commission allocated $1,200 to build a zoo, with Natch the bear as its main attraction. Unfortunately, on January 15, 1908, someone broke into the zoo and poisoned Natch. (Courtesy of William Beardon.)

Many people remember "Moonlight" Graham from the movie *Field of Dreams.* This character was based on a real player, Archibald Graham, who played one game for the 1905 New York Giants. Unlike in the movie, Graham spent three more years in the minor leagues. In 1906, he played in 12 games for the Memphis club. In 1908, Graham completed his medical degree and served the people of Chisholm, Minnesota, for 45 years as told in the book *Shoeless Joe.* (Author's collection.)

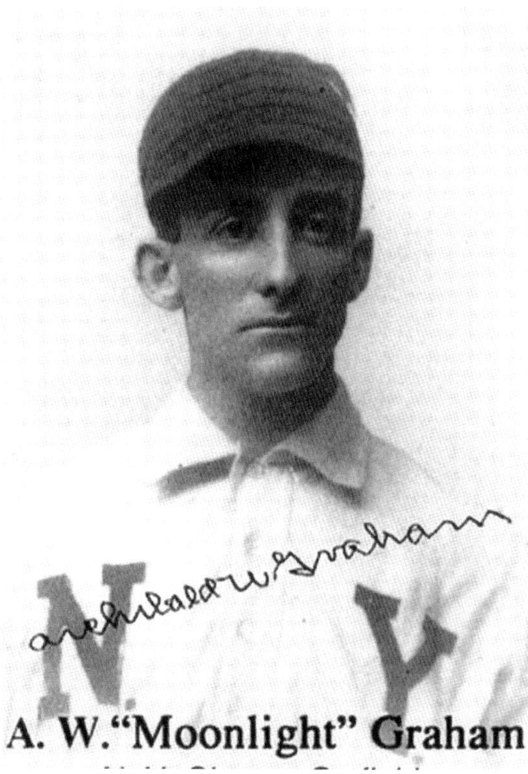

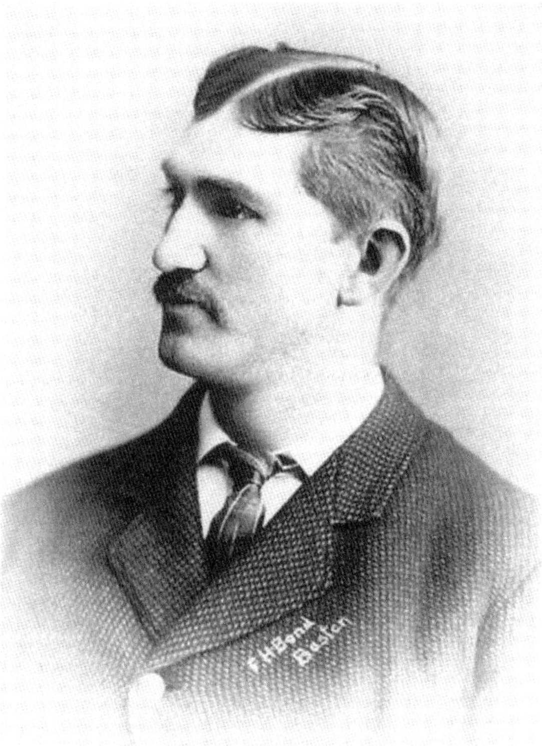

Tommy Bond was a pitcher for Hartford and Boston in the 1870s. Bond learned to throw a curveball from teammate Candy Cummings, the inventor of the pitch. Bond had three 40-game winning seasons from 1877 to 1879 with Boston. In Memphis, in the first year of the old Southern League in 1885, Bonds pitched three games for Memphis, winning two and losing one. Like Barry Force, Bond provided Memphis baseball with connections to the very foundations and the formative years of the sport. (Author's collection.)

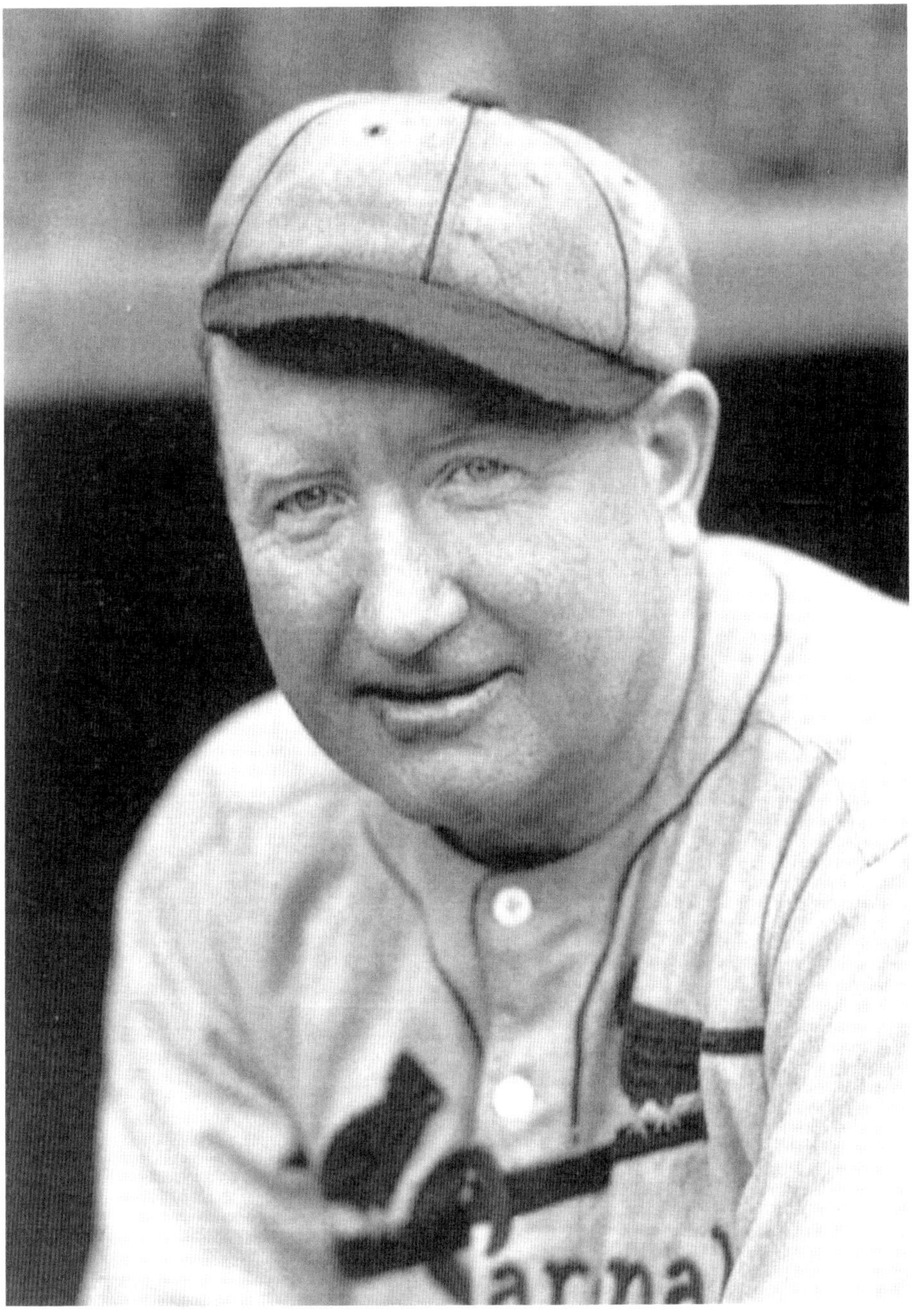

Dazzy Vance was one of the former Memphis players to be enshrined in the National Baseball Hall of Fame. Vance pitched for Memphis in 1917, 1918, and again in 1920. While living in Memphis, Dazzy taught a little girl next door how to pitch. That girl moved to Chattanooga and later struck out Babe Ruth and Lou Gehrig; her name was Jackie Mitchell. (Author's collection.)

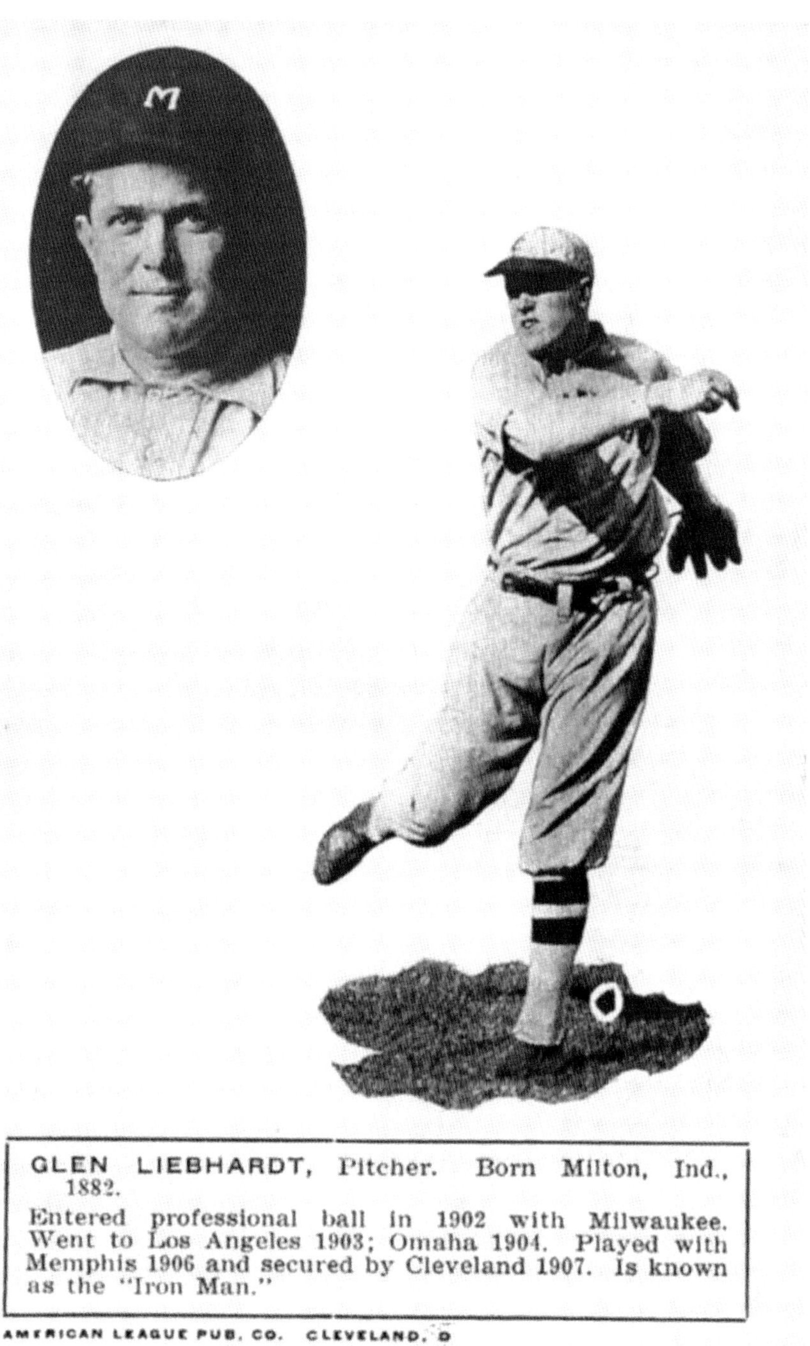

One of the most amazing years of pitching in professional baseball was Glenn Liebhardt's 1906 season with the Memphis Turtles. His record was 35 wins and 11 losses. He pitched a complete game in all except one. Liebhardt pitched both games of five doubleheaders, winning all but one game. The Turtles only won 79 games in 1906, with Liebhardt winning almost half. His excellent pitching earned him a late season call-up with the Cleveland Naps. (Author's collection.)

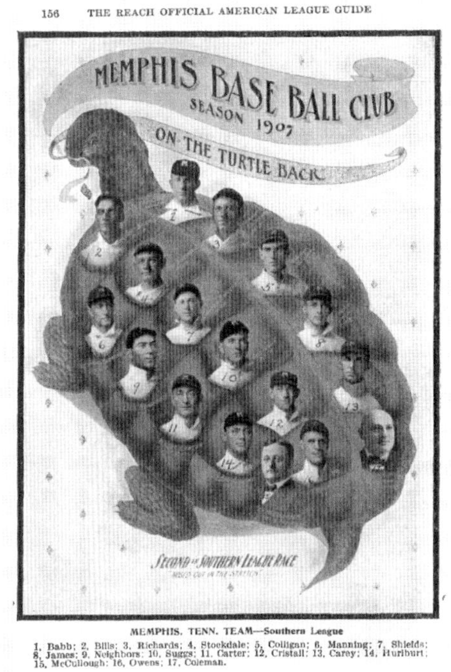
156 THE REACH OFFICIAL AMERICAN LEAGUE GUIDE

MEMPHIS, TENN. TEAM—Southern League

1, Babb; 2, Bills; 3, Richards; 4, Stockdale; 5, Colligan; 6, Manning; 7, Shields; 8, James; 9, Neighbors; 10, Suggs; 11, Carter; 12, Cristall; 13, Carey; 14, Hurlburt; 15, McCullough; 16, Owens; 17, Coleman.

So, what led to the Memphis baseball team being named the Turtles? The 1908 *Reach Baseball Guide* characterizes the team as crippled but finishing third. The playing field at Red Elm is described as a "turtleback field," which was common for baseball parks of the time. Without a sufficient drainage system under the field as seen today, the playing field had to gradually slope from the center to the outer edges. The slope at Red Elm was far more pronounced. (Author's collection.)

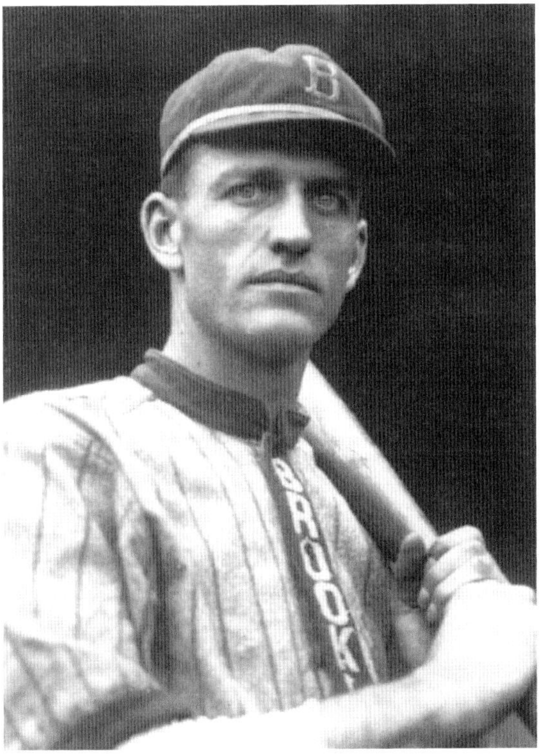

Jake Daubert played for the 1908 Southern Association champion Nashville Vols. He signed with the Memphis Turtles for the 1909 season, hitting a solid .314 average. One of the premier first basemen in the National League from 1910 to 1924, Daubert died unexpectedly in September 1924 from complications after an appendectomy—a Hall of Fame career cut short. (Author's collection.)

Max Carey was a slick-fielding first baseman for Memphis from 1907 to 1909. He was also one of the best base-stealers in the game. Carey spent most of his major-league career with the Pittsburgh Pirates. In the majors, he developed into a good hitter, batting over .300 in seven seasons. He was elected into the Baseball Hall of Fame in 1961. (Author's collection.)

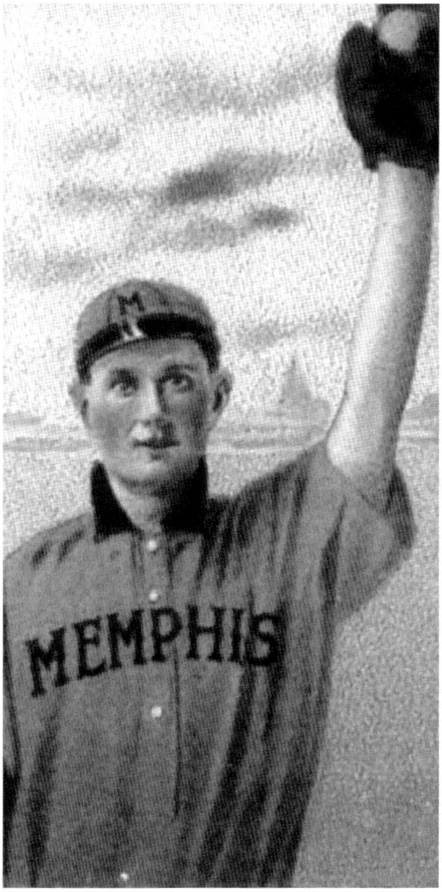

Charlie Frank's playing career included two tours of duty with Mobile and Memphis and two years with the St. Louis Browns as an outfielder. It was his managing of Southern League teams that made him famous. Frank (back row, second to the left) first came to Memphis to manage an independent team that would soon become a 1901 charter member of the Southern Association. After retirement, with severe heart problems, Frank moved to Memphis with his wife, Ann, to live his last few weeks among friends and relatives. (Author's collection.)

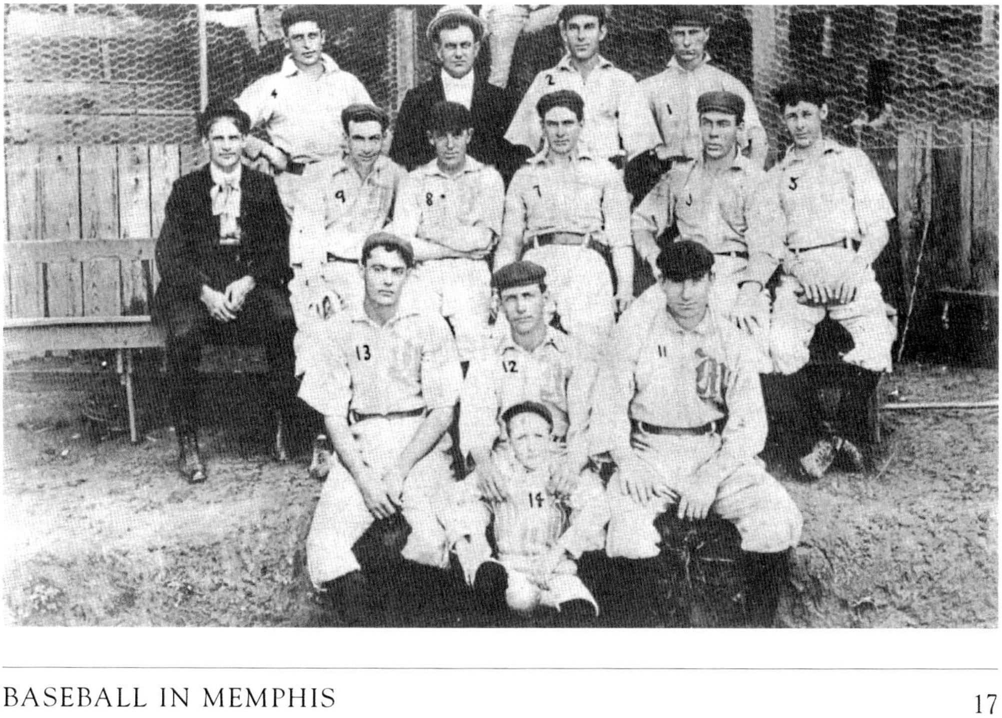

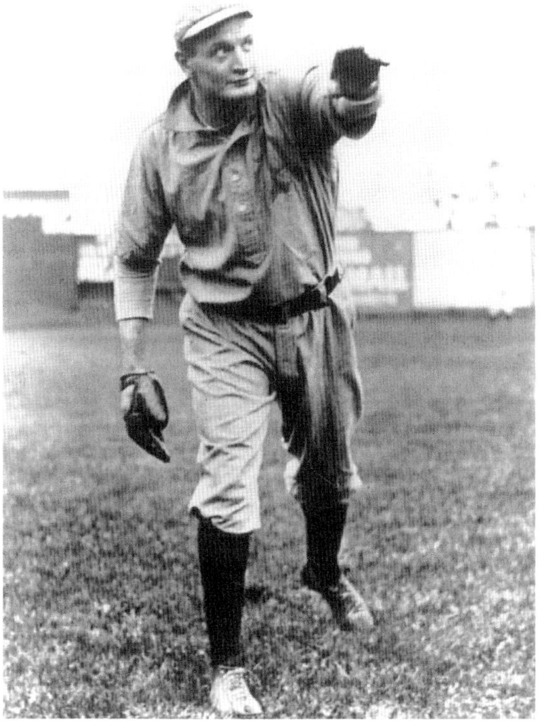

A real baseball fan will have heard the stories of Satchel Paige having his outfielders leave the field and then proceeding to strike out the side. Rube Waddell performed the same antic in an exhibition game against the Memphis Egyptians in 1906. In the ninth inning, he called time and sent the outfielders, shortstop, and second baseman to the dugout. Waddell then struck out Frank Manush to end the game. (Author's collection.)

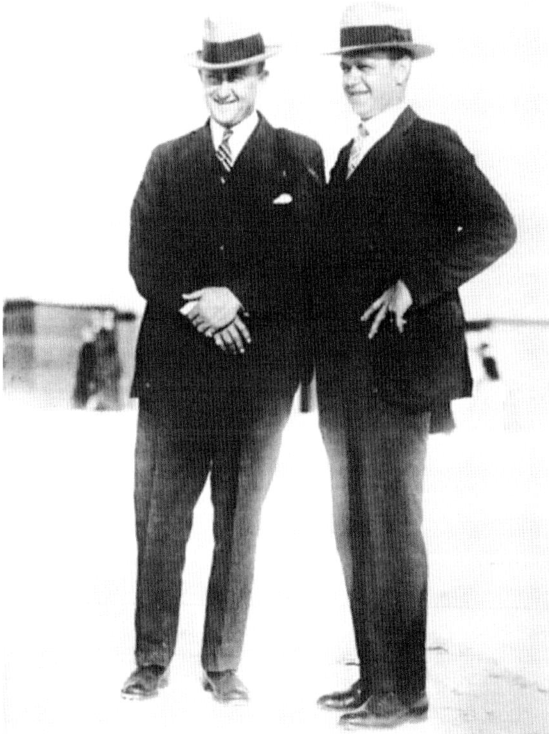

Paul Cobb was a good first baseman but could not hit like his older brother, Ty Cobb. Paul's brief stay in Memphis for five games produced a .357 average. A dispute over his contract led to his moving out west to play. John Paul (right) is seen here in the 1930s with his brother Ty after their playing careers were over. (Author's collection.)

Memphis baseball had several connections to the infamous Black Sox Scandal of 1919. One of these was Kid Gleason, the manager of the 1919 Chicago White Sox. In 1901, Gleason played in 10 games for the 1901 Memphis Leaguers. Gleason was a good manager and survived the scandal to manage and coach for many years after 1919. (Author's collection.)

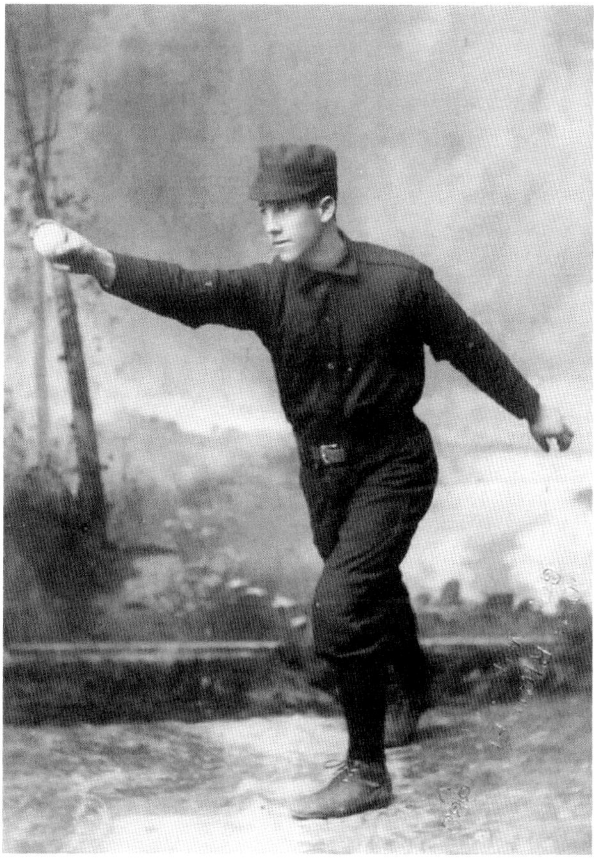

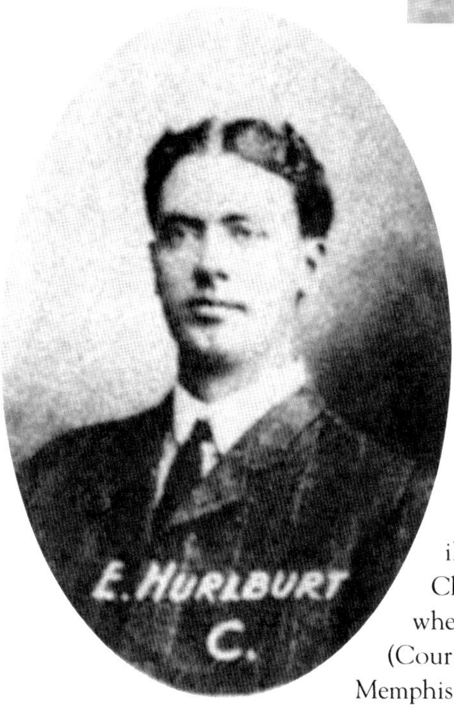

Ed Hurlburt played baseball with the original Memphis Chickasaws in the late 1890s. Hurlburt started a dry-cleaning business and was one of the first to introduce it in Memphis. He also served as a deputy sheriff. In 1918, after a night of confiscating illegal alcohol, he and his assistant, former teammate Charley Shields, were enjoying some of the evidence when a shotgun fell, discharging and killing Hurlburt. (Courtesy of the Memphis and Shelby County Room, Memphis Public Library and Information Center.)

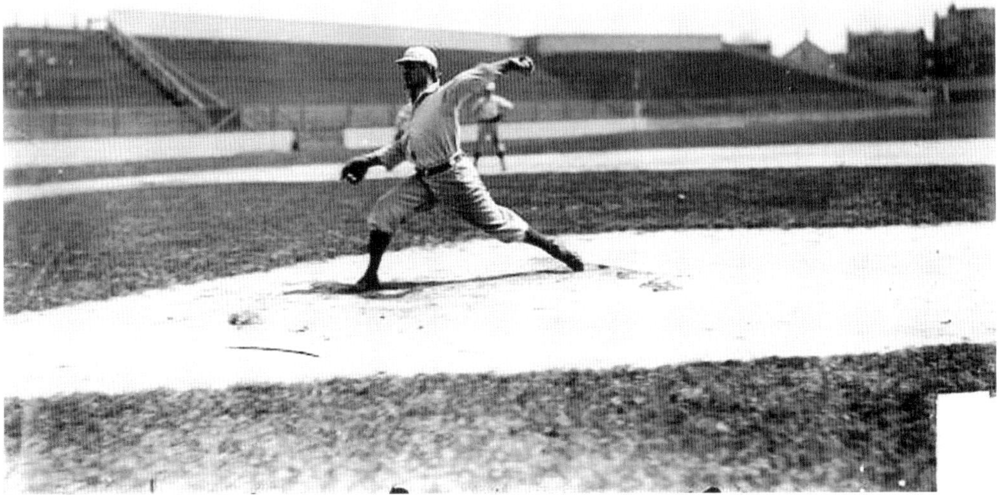

After a great year with Tacoma, Jim St. Vrain was sold to the Chicago Orphans (Cubs) in 1901. St. Vrain pitched poorly for Chicago and was told to report back to Tacoma. St. Vrain declared himself a free agent and signed with Memphis. His pitching for Memphis caused protests and the threat of forfeits and lawsuits. Finally, at the end of the season, the Southern Association did nothing, and St. Vrain's record stood. He registered an impressive 13-4 record for Memphis that year. (Courtesy of Jay Gauthreaux.)

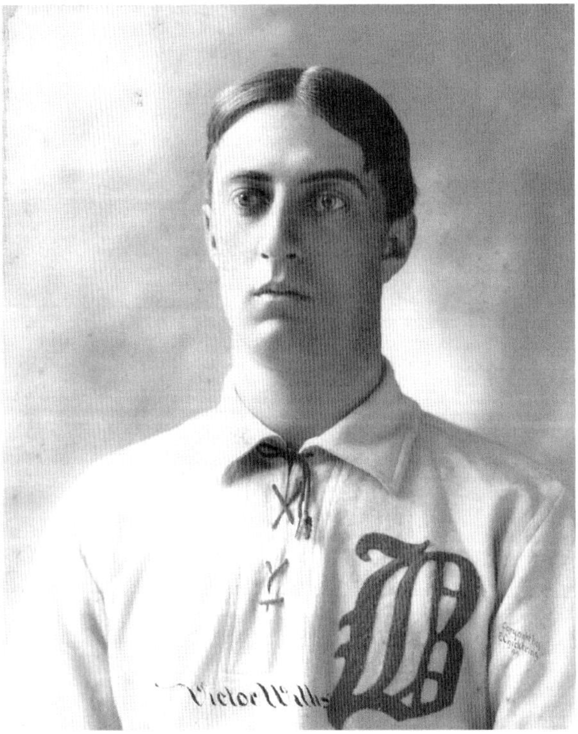

Vic Willis won over 240 games during a 13-year career. In 1912, after his major-league days were over, Willis may have pitched in a few games for the Memphis team. Some databases do not show Willis playing after 1910. (Author's collection.)

After a brief major-league career as a first baseman, Lew Whistler settled in the Southern Association as a manager: in 1901 with Chattanooga and 1903 with Montgomery. By June 1904, Whistler had taken over a Memphis team going nowhere. Then, Lew piloted the Egyptians to the league championship. In honor of Lew, the team was called the "Whistling Egyptians." (Author's collection.)

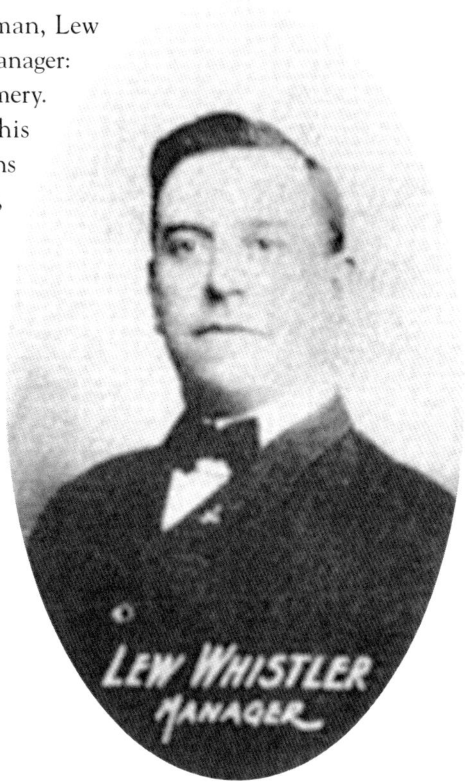

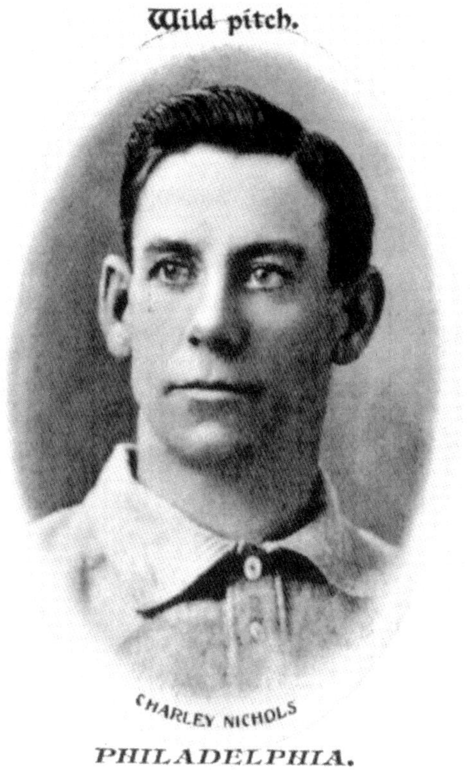

Charles "Kid" Nichols was the youngest pitcher to win 300 games, reaching the milestone at the early age of 32. Nichols ended his major-league career with 361 wins. He was voted into the Baseball Hall of Fame in 1949, just four years before his death in 1953. Early in his minor-league career, Nichols pitched for the 1888 Memphis Grays. He posted an 11-8 record in a shorter season. (Author's collection.)

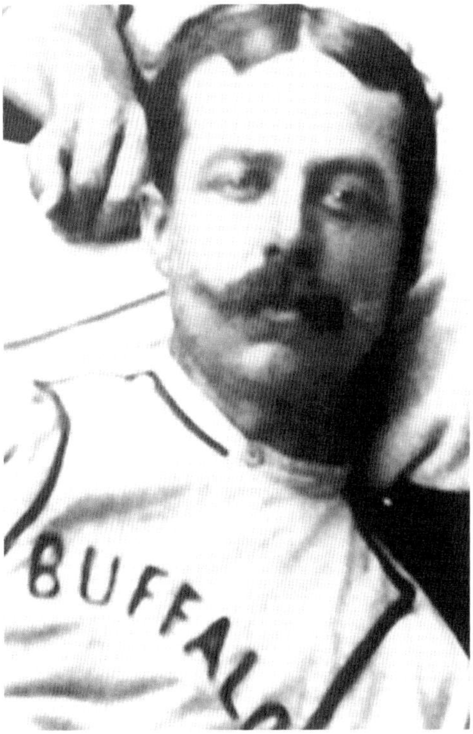

Davy Force learned to play baseball in New York City just after the Civil War. Force is best remembered for causing the demise of the old National Association, which led to the formation of the original National League in 1876. He signed with two different teams, causing a power struggle and the death of the National Association. At the end of a 22-year career, Force played the 1887 and 1888 seasons with Memphis. (Author's collection.)

146 BEACH'S OFFICIAL AMERICAN LEAGUE GUIDE.

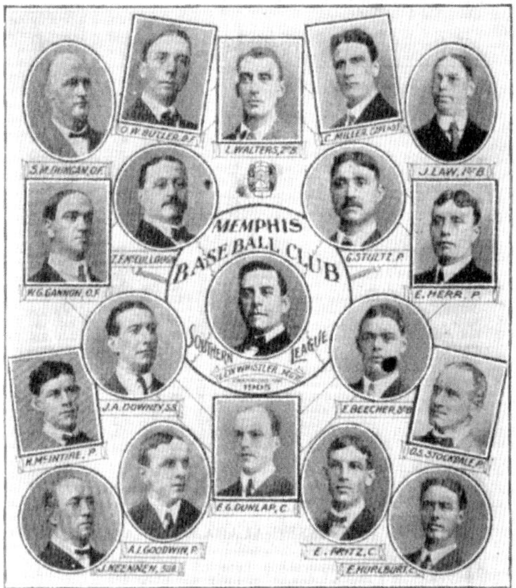

THE MEMPHIS TEAM.

Champions of the Southern League.

Personnel: Louis Whistler, manager; pitchers, Goodwin, McIntyre, Brown, Stockdale and Ehret; catchers, Hurlburt, Fritz, Law and Belt; first base, Fritz, Law and Whistler; second base, Keenan and Walters; third base, Keenan and Beecher; shortstops, Downey, Keenan and Beecher; outfielders, Dungan, Miller, Butler and Gannon.

In 1903, the Memphis team was named the Turtles. Back-to-back championships in 1903 and 1904 were a great start, but it would be 20 years before Memphis would produce another championship—and the name Turtles would be long forgotten. Both championship teams' pitching was anchored by Harry McIntire, who won a total of 39 games. (Author's collection.)

2

Russell E. Gardner

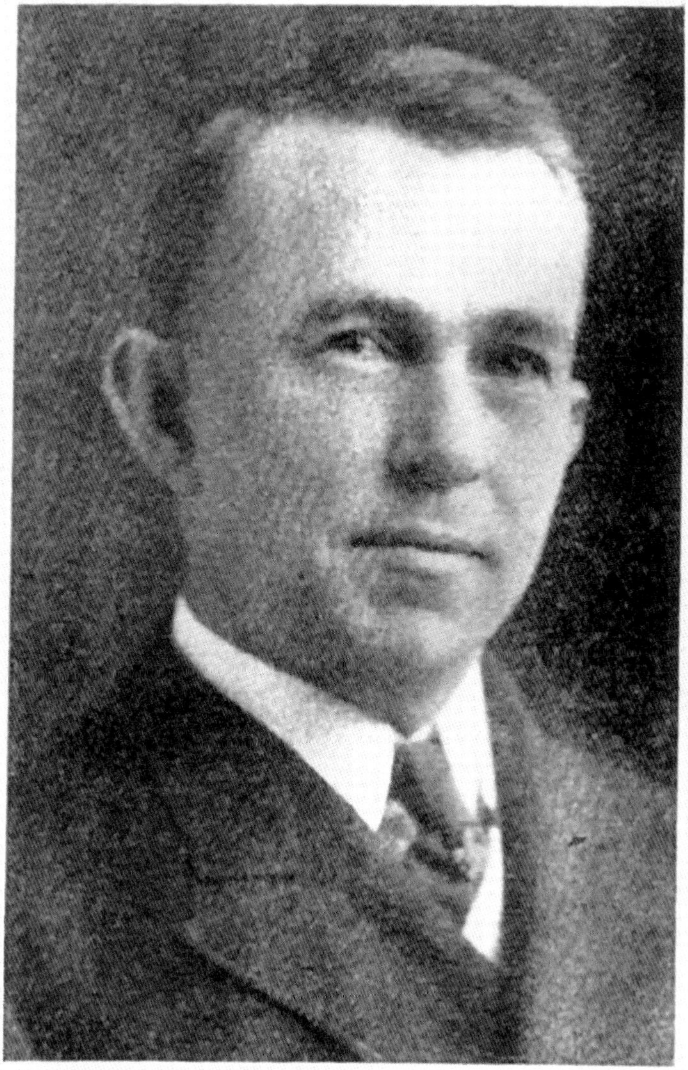

THE "RIGHT-AT-THE-TOP" FAN.

Russell E. Gardner was a self-made millionaire originally from west Tennessee. He made his fortune manufacturing horse-drawn buggies and, later, automobiles. For several years, Gardner made attempts to purchase the Memphis baseball organization. Finally, in the spring of 1915, he succeeded in buying the team from J.P. Coleman and immediately began making his mark on the club. (Author's collection.)

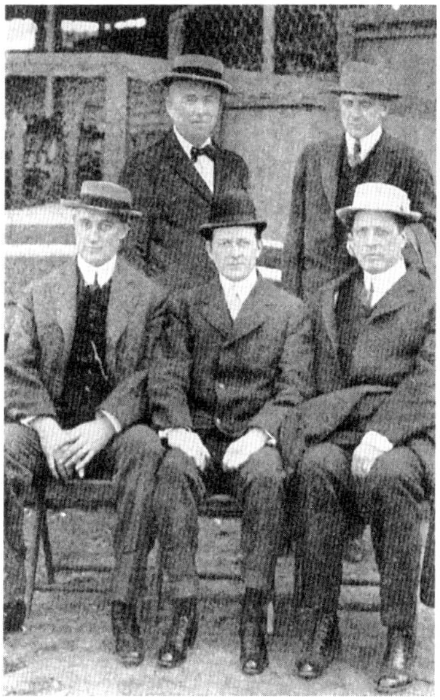

This photograph from the 1915 program reveals the future of the Memphis baseball club. Russell E. Gardner purchased the team and then returned to St. Louis to oversee his empire, but not before making some much-needed changes, including remodeling the ballpark. He also changed the name of the team to the Chickasaws and the ballpark to Russwood. Club president J.D. Martin soon became Southern Association president and left Gardner's son-in-law Thomas R. Watkins to learn the baseball business. Pictured here from left to right are (seated) J.J. Wade, John D. Martin, and J.M. Speed; (standing) Russell E. Gardner and Thomas R. Watkins. (Courtesy of Chris Drago.)

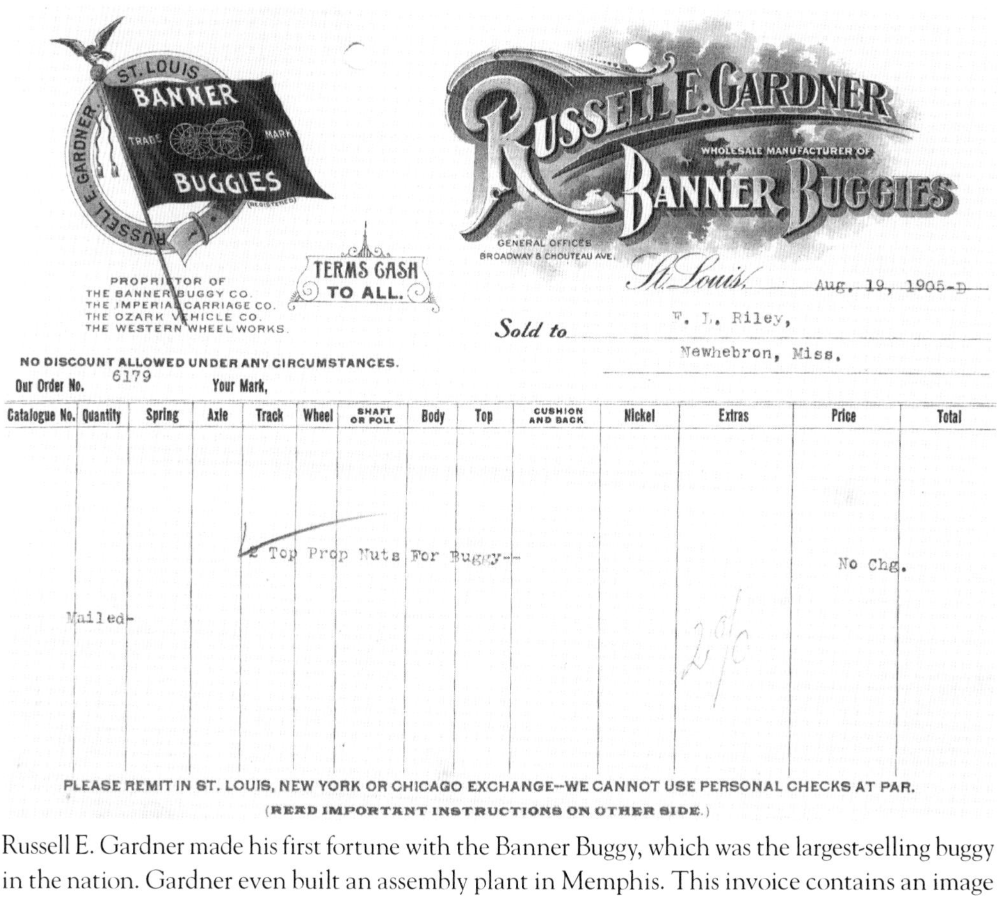

ST. LOUIS BANNER TRADE MARK BUGGIES (REGISTERED) RUSSELL E. GARDNER

PROPRIETOR OF
THE BANNER BUGGY CO.
THE IMPERIAL CARRIAGE CO.
THE OZARK VEHICLE CO.
THE WESTERN WHEEL WORKS.

TERMS CASH TO ALL.

RUSSELL E. GARDNER
WHOLESALE MANUFACTURER OF
BANNER BUGGIES

GENERAL OFFICES
BROADWAY & CHOUTEAU AVE.

St. Louis, Aug. 19, 1905-D

Sold to F. L. Riley,
Newhebron, Miss.

NO DISCOUNT ALLOWED UNDER ANY CIRCUMSTANCES.

Our Order No. 6179 Your Mark,

Catalogue No.	Quantity	Spring	Axle	Track	Wheel	Shaft or Pole	Body	Top	Cushion and Back	Nickel	Extras	Price	Total
				2 Top Prop Nuts For Buggy--								No Chg.	
Mailed-													

PLEASE REMIT IN ST. LOUIS, NEW YORK OR CHICAGO EXCHANGE--WE CANNOT USE PERSONAL CHECKS AT PAR.
(READ IMPORTANT INSTRUCTIONS ON OTHER SIDE.)

Russell E. Gardner made his first fortune with the Banner Buggy, which was the largest-selling buggy in the nation. Gardner even built an assembly plant in Memphis. This invoice contains an image of the famous buggy long forgotten by a nation consumed with cars. (Author's collection.)

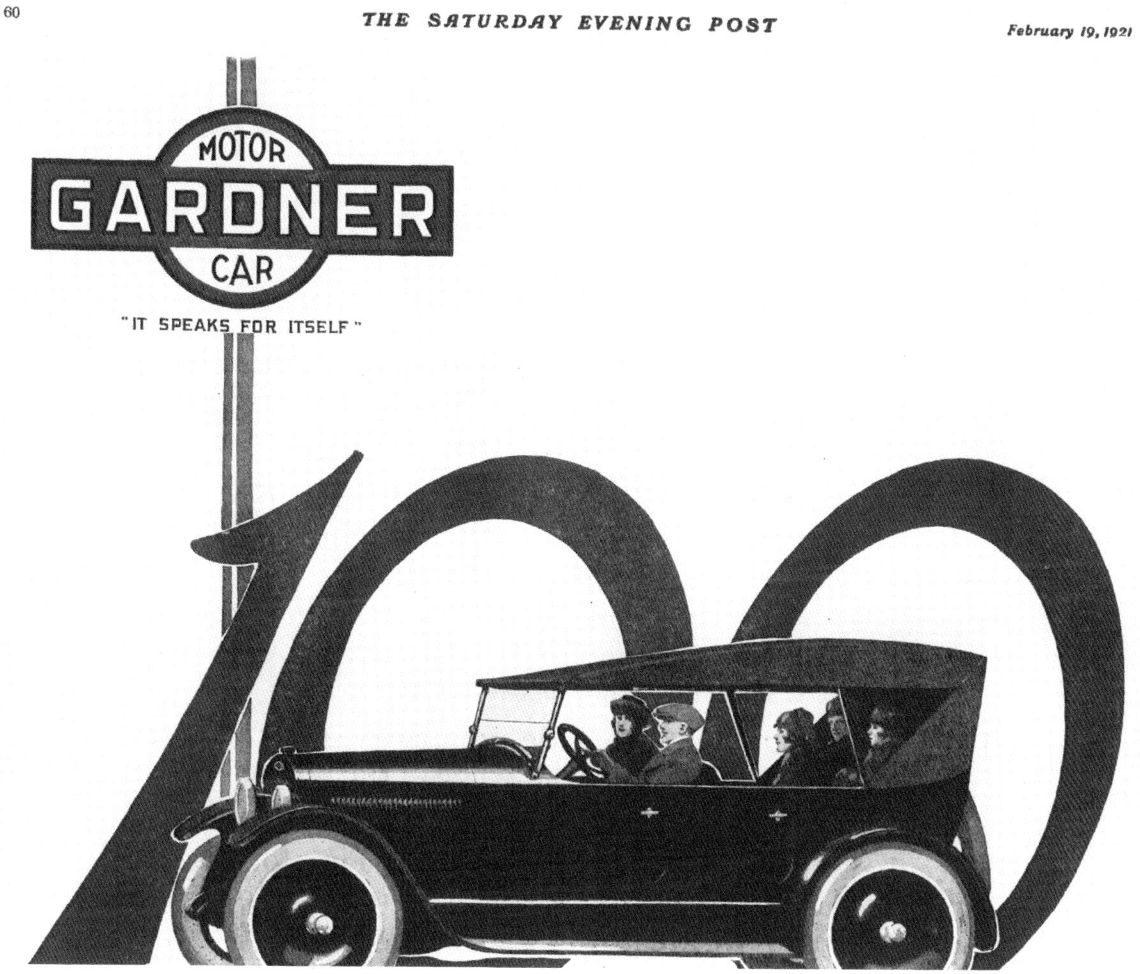

The Gardner automobile was a very good car. But Gardner was not the only automobile manufacturer in St. Louis. Several brands made their home in the Missouri city: Dorris, Ruxton, and the Moon. The city of St. Louis saw itself as a rival to Detroit as the automotive capital of the nation. The Great Depression would put an end to the automotive dreams of St. Louis and the Gardner Company, but maybe in a small way St. Louis would get its revenge in the 1933 World Series against Detroit. (Author's collection.)

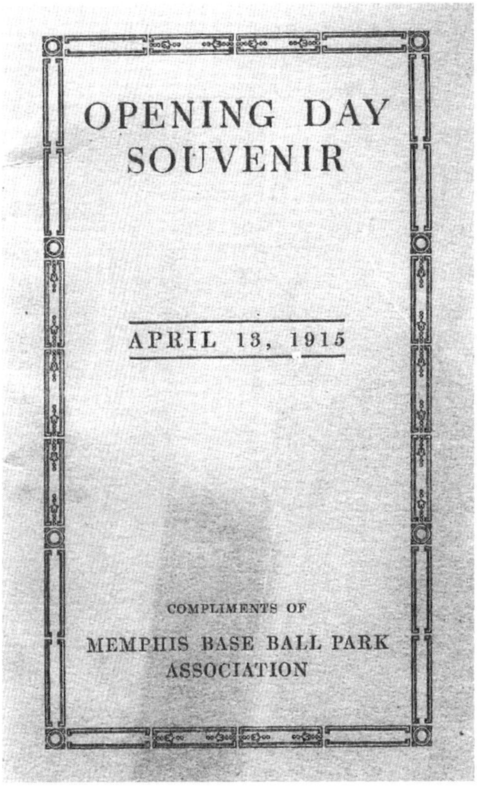
OPENING DAY SOUVENIR

APRIL 13, 1915

COMPLIMENTS OF

MEMPHIS BASE BALL PARK ASSOCIATION

This small pocket-size program was given to each fan who attended the first game under the new ownership of Russell E. Gardner. The first 10 pages contained information about the new ownership and management of the Memphis club; the rest of the program was a complete rule book for the game of baseball. (Courtesy of Chris Drago.)

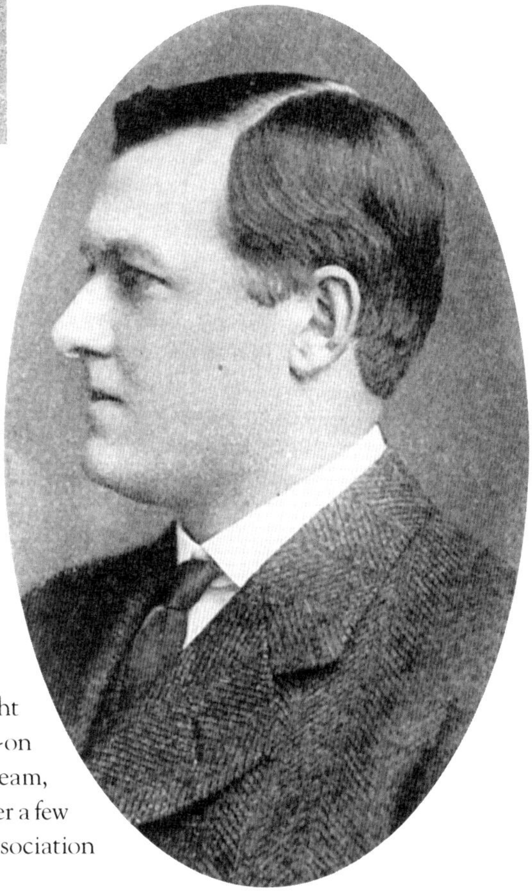

Russell E. Gardner told the press when he bought the team in 1915 that he would be a hands-on owner. But very shortly after purchasing the team, he appointed J.D. Martin as club president. After a few years, Martin took on the job as Southern Association league president. (Courtesy of Chris Drago.)

The Memphis team was headed in a new direction—up—therefore, a new manager was needed. Briscoe Lord, a former major leaguer and manager of the Mobile Sea Gulls, was brought in to change the image of the team. The season started off right with a 6-1 win over the Little Rock Travelers on April 13, 1915. (Courtesy of Chris Drago.)

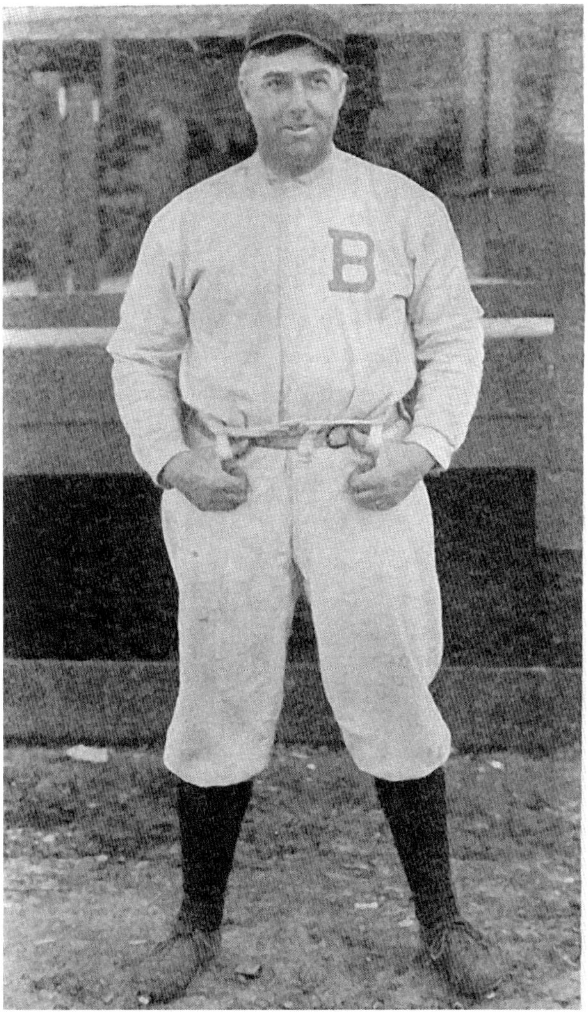

This early-spring team picture shows players and manager Briscoe Lord in a variety of different team uniforms and jackets; one player is still wearing a Turtles jersey. For some unknown reason, Tris Speaker (on the right, crouching in front), star outfielder for the Boston Red Sox, decided to get in the picture. (Courtesy of Chris Drago.)

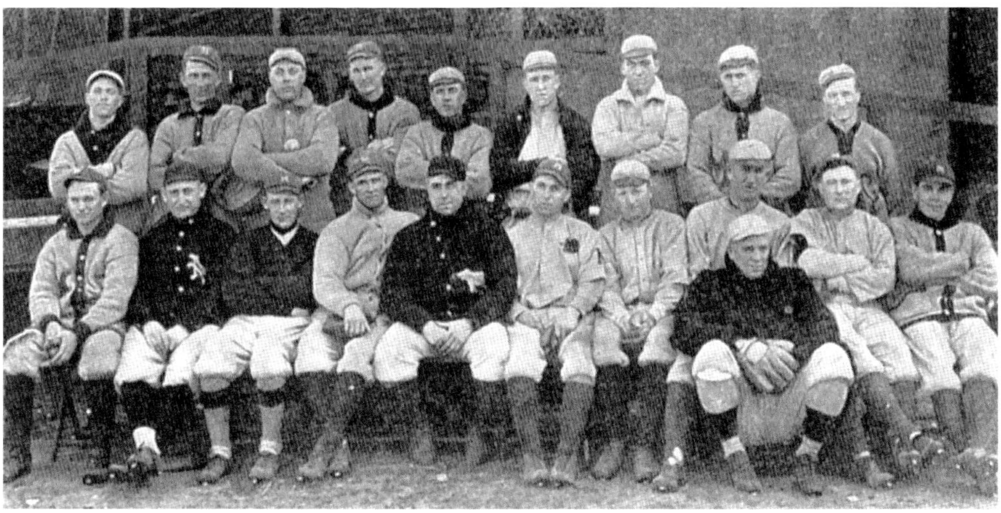

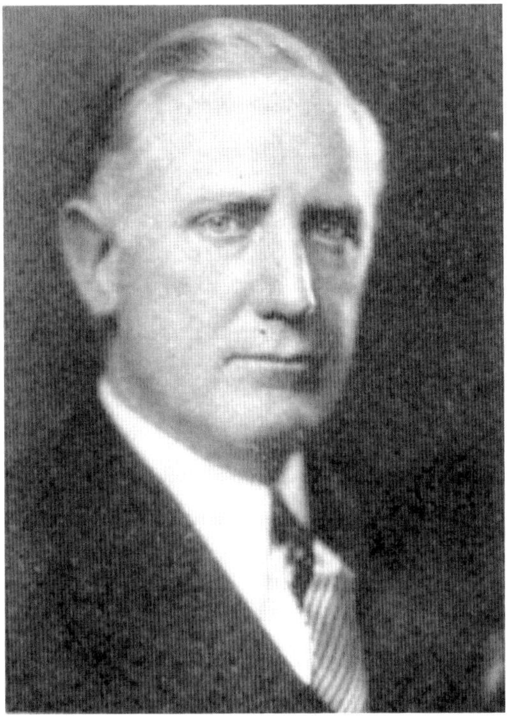

Thomas R. Watkins was a graduate of the University of Tennessee, where he excelled in football and track. Watkins married Elsie Gardner, daughter of Russell E. Gardner. Even though Watkins had very little experience in baseball, he learned the business side of the game very quickly and became an astute judge of talent. He earned the nickname "Trader Tom" because of his ability to find and develop local players to be traded or sold to major-league teams. (Courtesy of Chris Drago.)

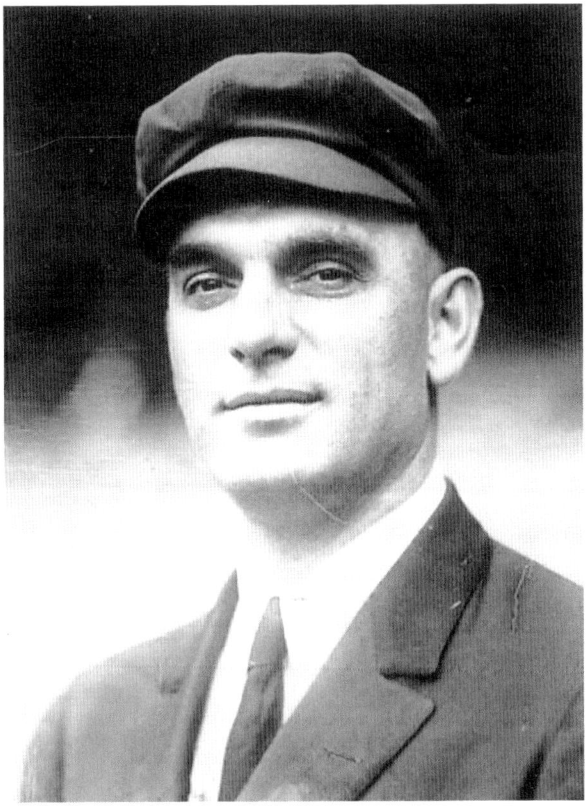

Briscoe Lord did not return as manager of the Memphis club for 1916. Dolly Stark started managing but was soon replaced by former Detroit Tigers player George Moriarity. Moriarity did not last the season and abruptly left the club due to illness. He tried a brief comeback in the major leagues in 1916 but retired in May. In 1917, he started a career as a major-league umpire. Officiating games until 1940, Moriarity was considered a very good ump. (Courtesy of Chris Drago.)

John McGraw signed Waite Hoyt at the age of 15 with the New York Giants organization. By the age of 18, Hoyt was pitching for the Memphis Chicks. Due to a paperwork blunder in the Giants front office, Hoyt was taken by the Boston Red Sox in 1919. On the morning of December 25, 1920, his father woke him up with news, calling it "an early Christmas present"—Hoyt had been traded to the New York Yankees. After retirement, he became the radio voice of the Cincinnati Reds. (Author's collection.)

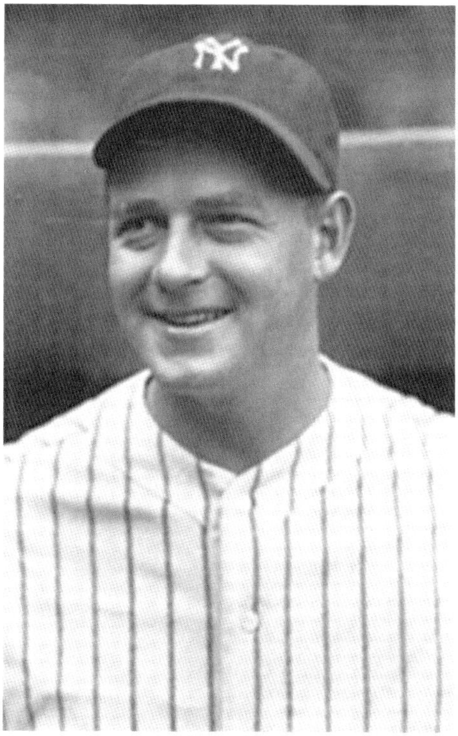

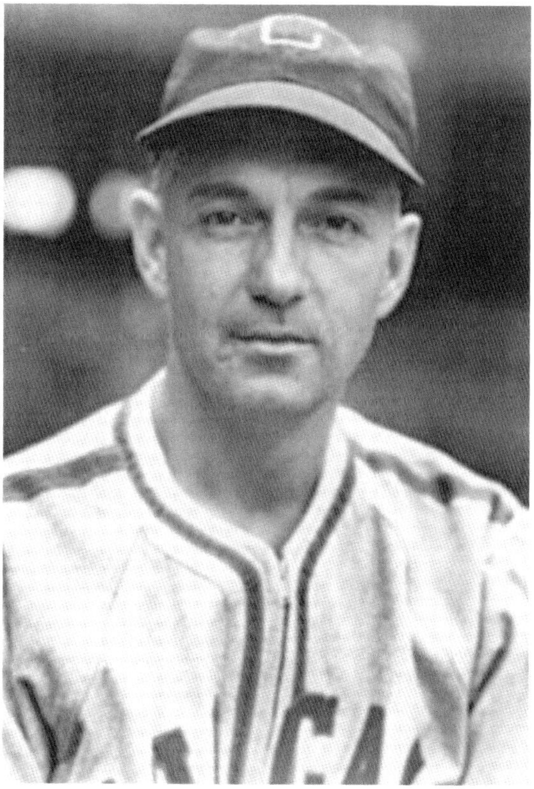

Muddy Ruel is given credit for coining the phrase "tools of ignorance" as a description of catcher's equipment. Ruel played for the Memphis Chicks in 1917 and 1918. He later became Walter Johnson's favorite catcher. Ruel was the catcher for the New York Yankees in 1920 when Carl Mays hit Ray Chapman, resulting in Chapman's death the next day. (Author's collection.)

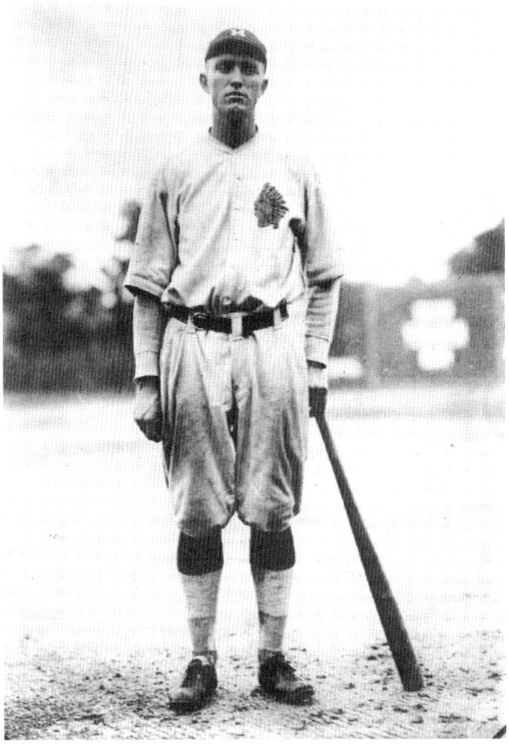

Sam Vick was from Batesville, Mississippi, just south of Memphis. He was the starting right fielder for the 1917 Memphis Chickasaws, finishing the season with an impressive .322 batting average. Thomas R. Watkins sold Vick to the New York Yankees. By 1919, Vick was the starting right fielder for the Yankees. During the off-season, the Yankees made a trade with the Boston Red Sox to obtain pitcher Babe Ruth, but the Yankees saw Ruth as their new right fielder. Vick would only play part-time for the Yankees in 1920 and 1921. He was then dealt to Boston, and his career continued to decline. By 1922, he was back in the minor leagues, never to play in the majors again. Vick was back with Memphis in 1923 and again in 1930, when he played his last year in the minors. (Author's collection.)

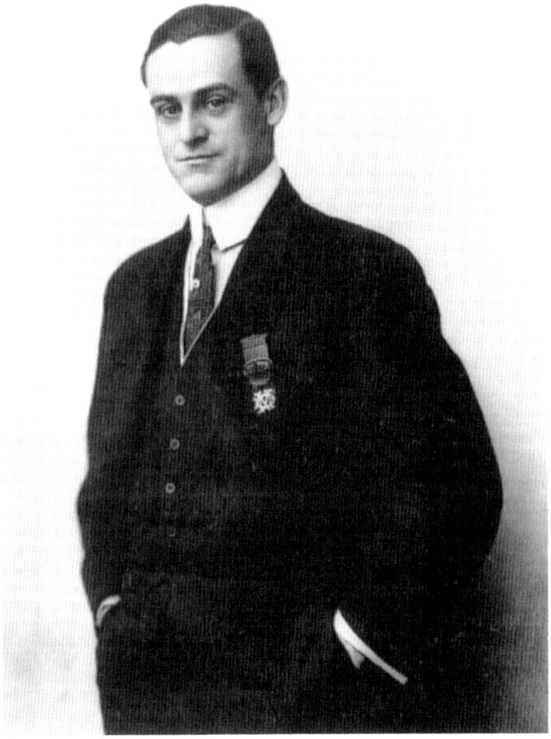

One of the first big decisions William R. Watkins had to make was finding a replacement for manager George Moriarity. Watkins went to St. Louis to hire Johnnie Miller, but he came back with Mike Donlen. Donlen had shown signs that he could have been a hall-of-fame player, but he lacked consistency. His time in Memphis was short. At the start of 1917, fans loved his flamboyant style, but their patience ran thin when he continually inserted himself in to pitch and lose the game. By mid-season, he was gone. (Author's collection.)

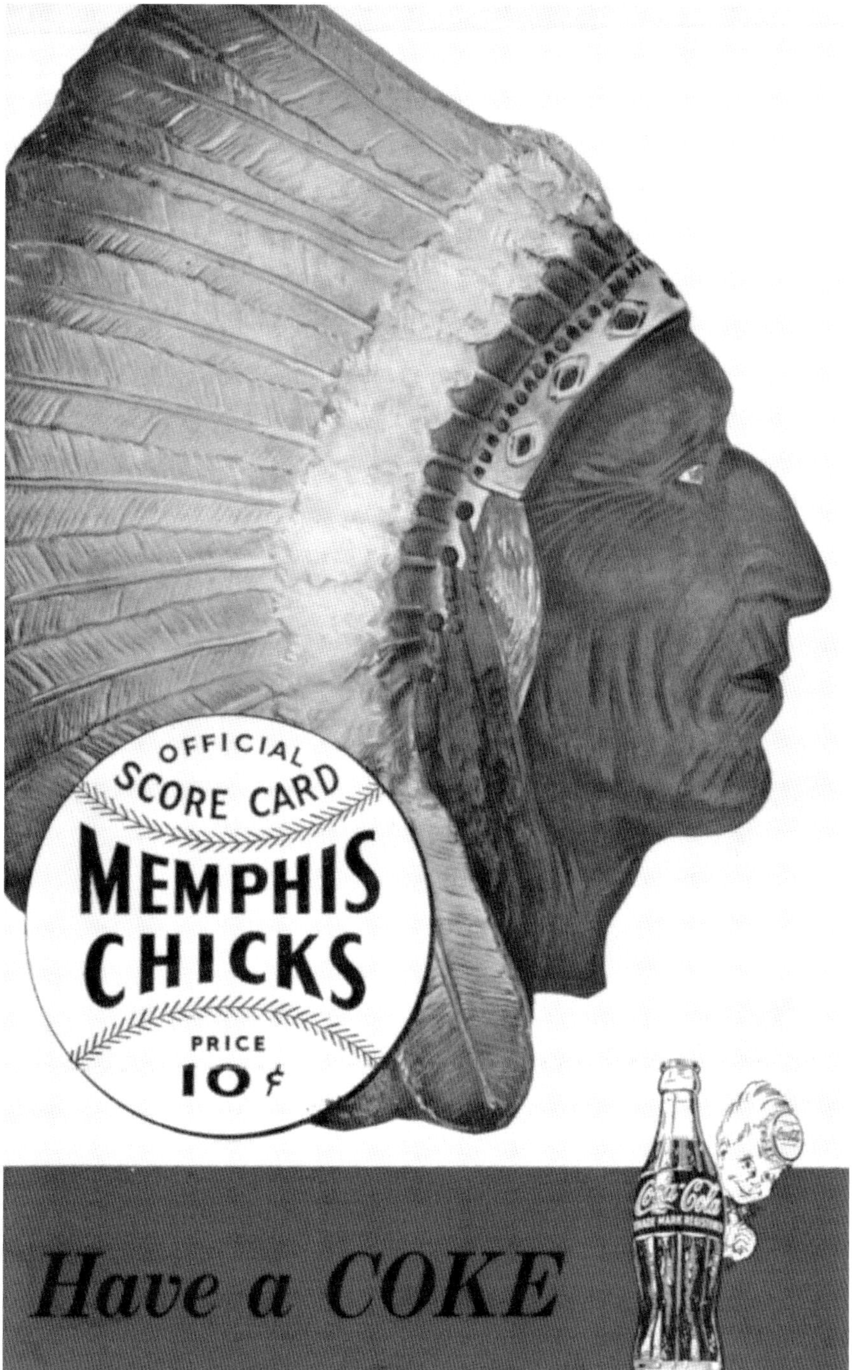

One of the first changes Russell E. Gardner made for the Memphis club was to find a replacement for the name "Turtles." A fan vote was taken and, overwhelmingly, "Chickasaws," the name of the local semipro team of the late 19th century, was selected. This program cover was used several years by the team and features the profile of a majestic Indian chief. (Author's collection.)

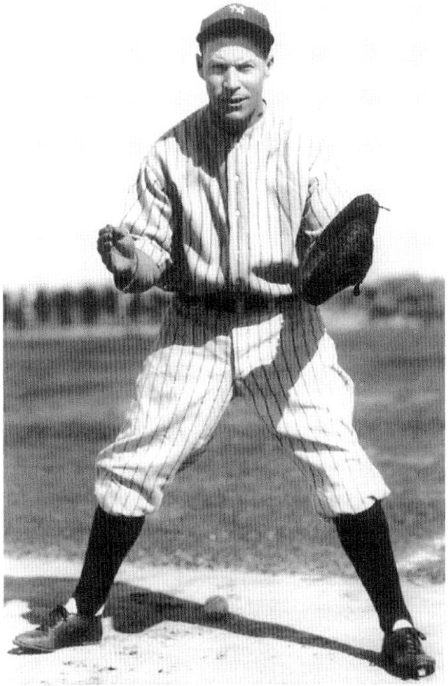

Bubbles Hargrave played in 64 games for the 1918 Memphis club. By 1921, he was starting for the Cincinnati Reds. Hargrave would hold that position for the decade. In 1926, he won the National League batting title with a .353 average. Hargrave was the first catcher to win a batting title. (Author's collection.)

Another connection with the 1919 Black Sox Scandal is pitcher Dick Kerr (left). In 1916, Kerr recorded a 24-2 record with the Memphis Chicks. After his playing days, he became a minor-league manager for the St. Louis Cardinals. In 1940, he managed the Daytona Beach team. Probably his greatest accomplishment in baseball was convincing a young, sore-armed pitcher to become an outfielder—the has-been pitcher was Stan Musial. At age 69, Kerr died at his home, which was a gift from Musial. (Author's collection.)

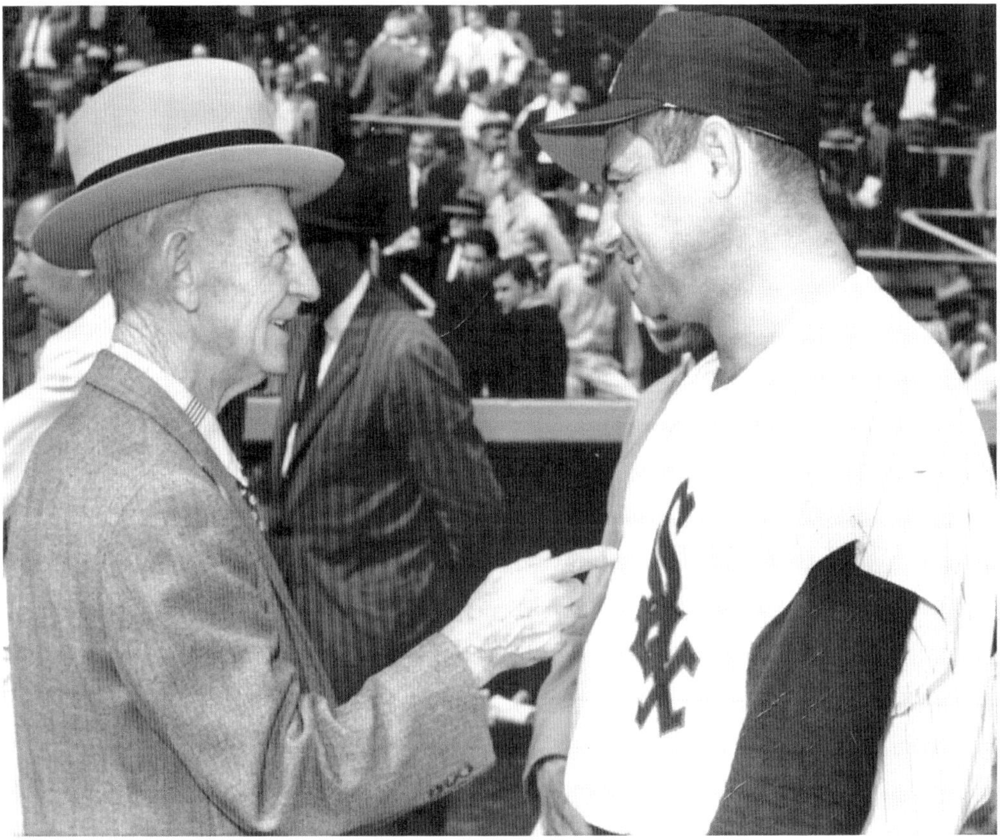

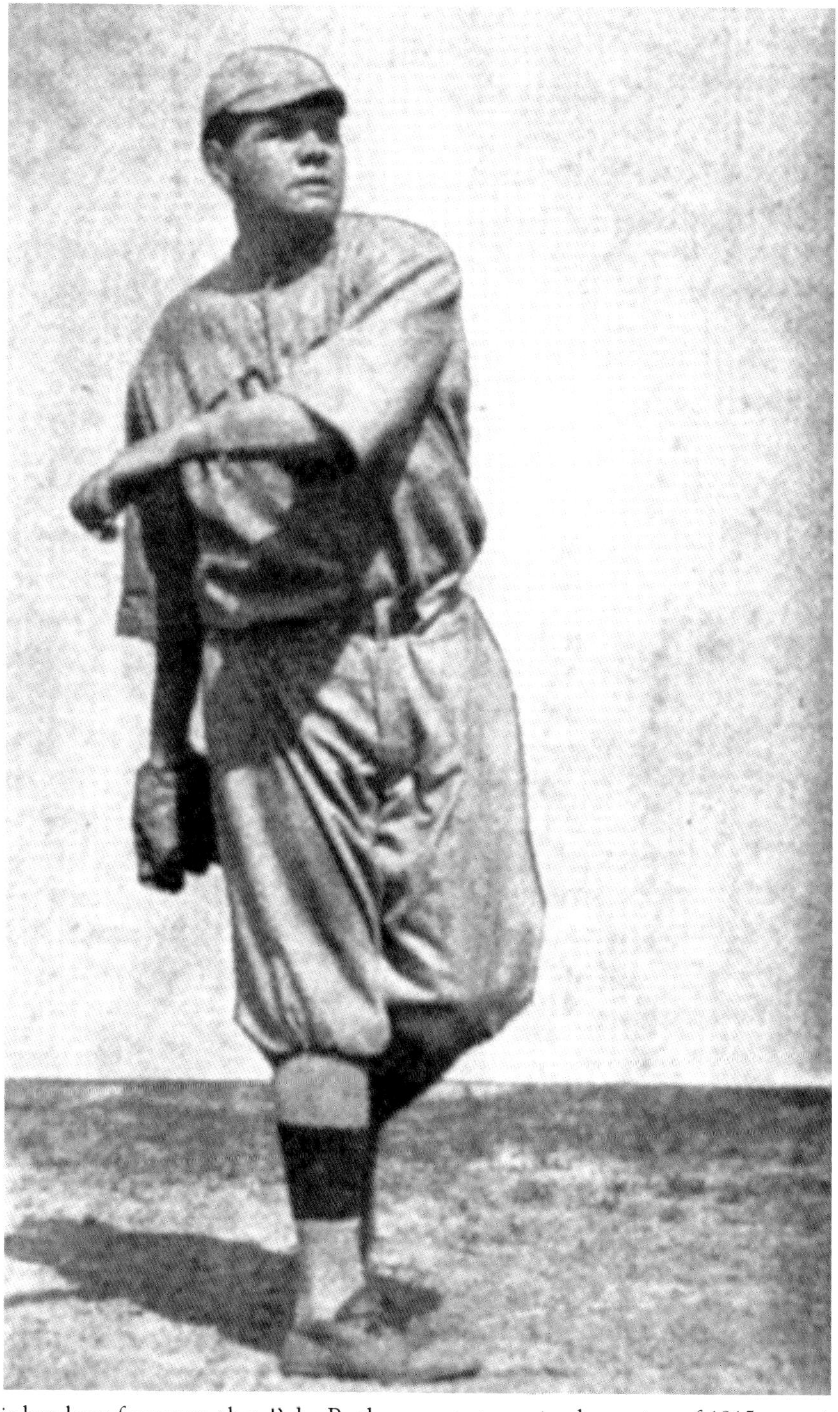

Memphis has long forgotten that Babe Ruth came to town in the spring of 1915 as a pitcher for the Boston Red Sox. Ruth pitched in the third game of the series, beating Memphis 10-5. His only mention in the paper was the box score. It would be very different when he returned in 1930. (Author's collection.)

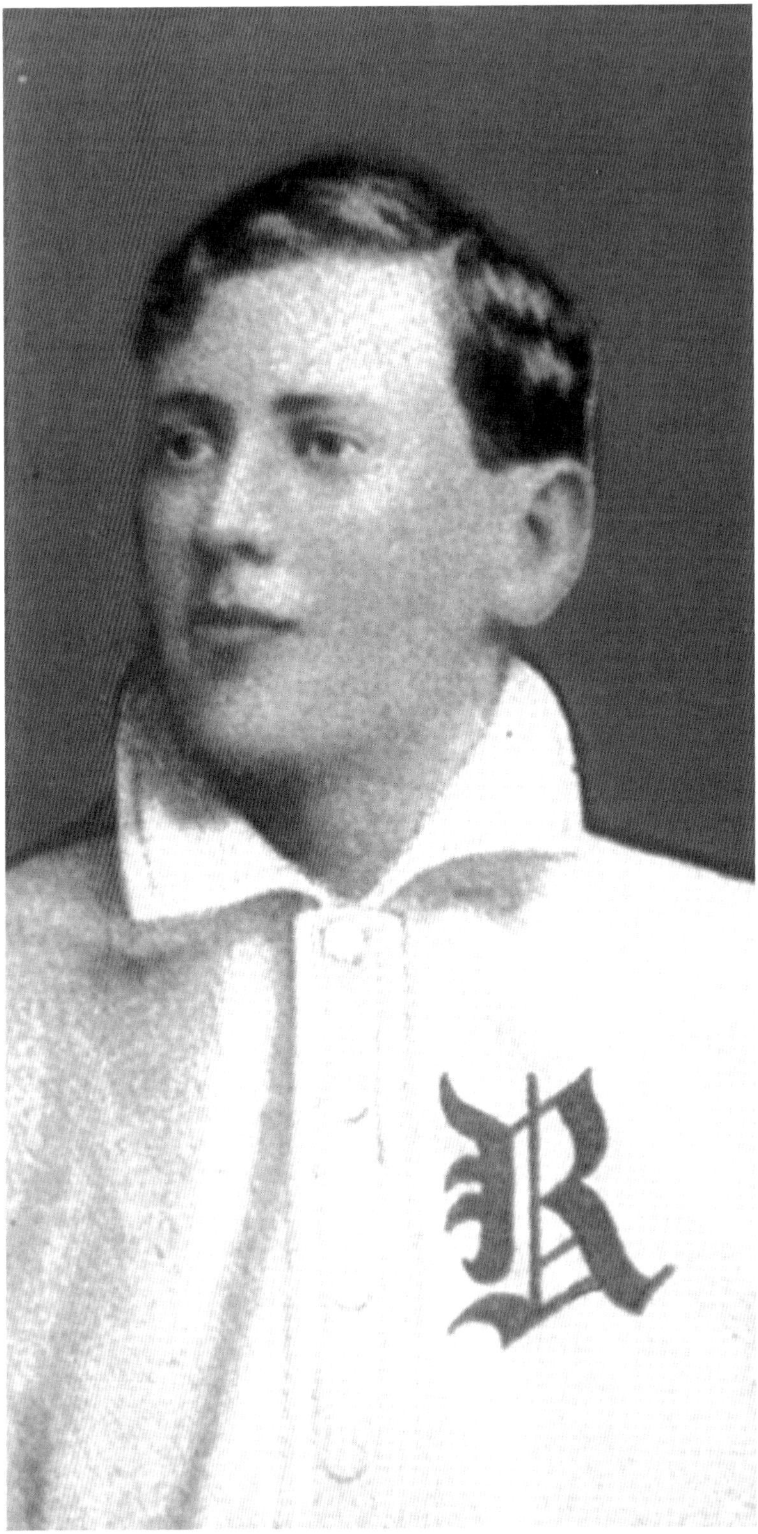

Cy Barger was a right-handed pitcher for the Memphis Chickasaws for four years (1916–1919); he also managed the team three of those years. Barger spent several years in the majors. His real name was Eros Boliras Barger, given to him because of the Greek god of love and South American hero Simon Bolivar. (Author's collection.)

3

THE GOLDEN AGE

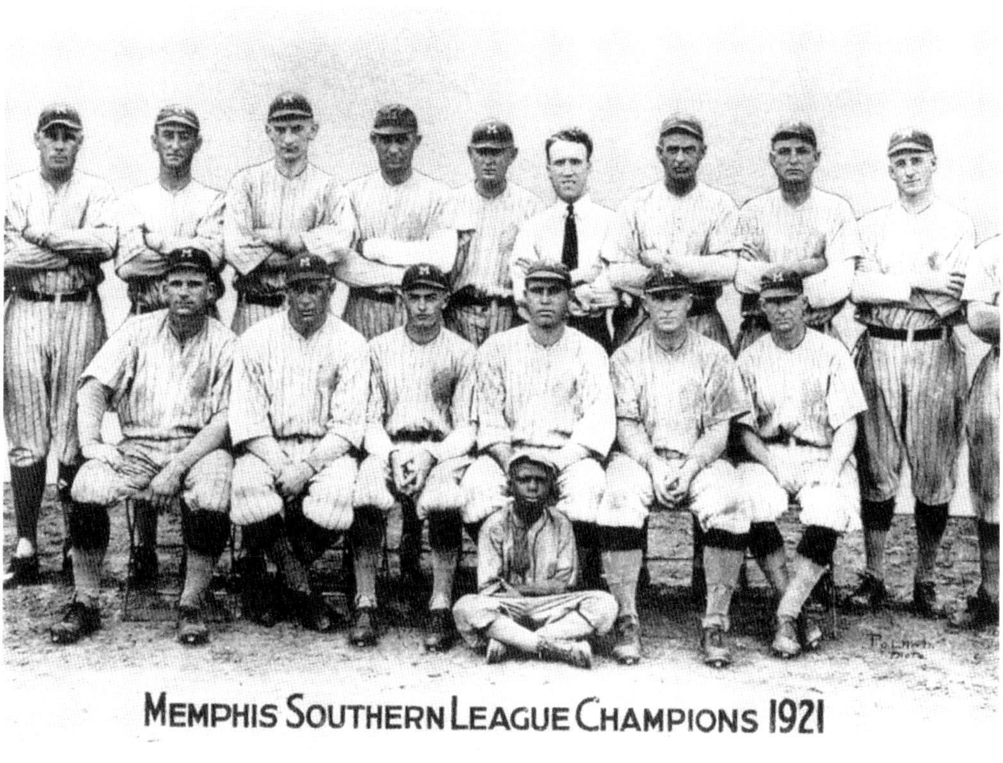

As part of the celebration of the 100th anniversary of minor-league baseball, a list of the top-100 greatest teams was compiled. Memphis was the only Southern Association team to place two teams on this prestigious list. Loaded with seasoned veterans, the 1921 team managed by Spencer Abbott won 104 games with a .680 winning percentage. Thomas R. Watkins was now a seasoned baseball general manager making all the right moves. Memphis also made the list in 1924. (Author's collection.)

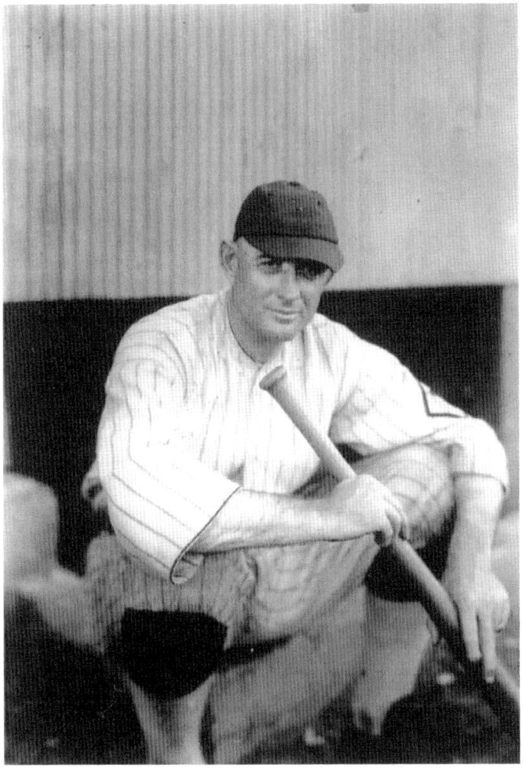

After back-to-back championship seasons managing the Tulsa Oilers, Spencer Abbott landed in Memphis as manager of the Chickasaws. With a new ballpark and a team loaded with talent, Abbott produced a 104-48 win-loss record—a .680 winning percentage. Abbott would continue to produce championships after leaving Memphis in 1923. (Author's collection.)

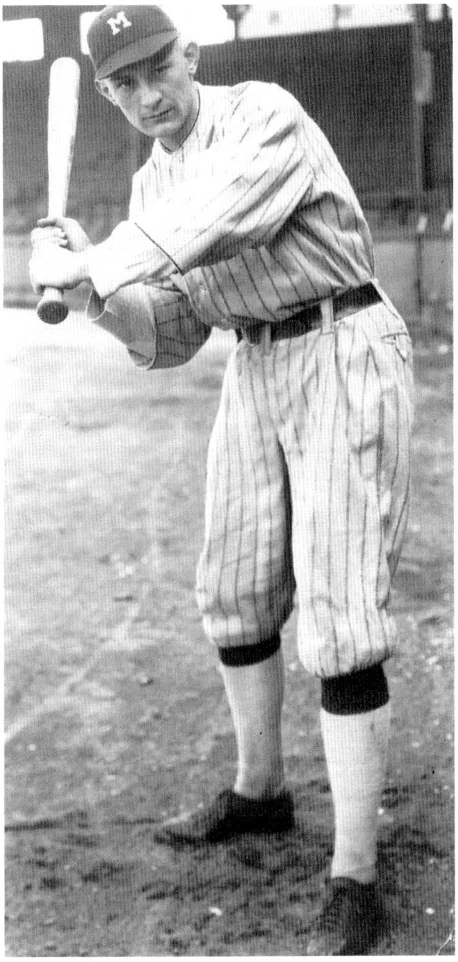

Bernie Hungling's baseball career spanned from 1916 to 1929. In 1921, he was the catcher for the Memphis championship team. Hungling batted .322 as a key cog of the Memphis hitting machine. His good play with the Chicks helped get him a brief stay with the Brooklyn team in 1923. (Author's collection.)

Babe Herman batted .339 for the 1923 Chicks. By 1926, Herman was with Brooklyn, where he would become one of the most feared batters in the late 1920s. Babe hit for the cycle a record four times. By 1938, with his batting average dropping and his continued miscues in the outfield, Herman moved to the Pacific Coast League, where he would play another six years. (Author's collection.)

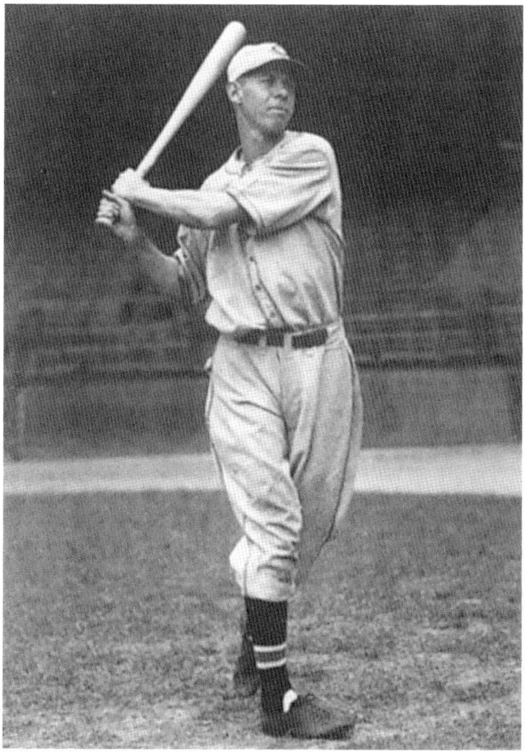

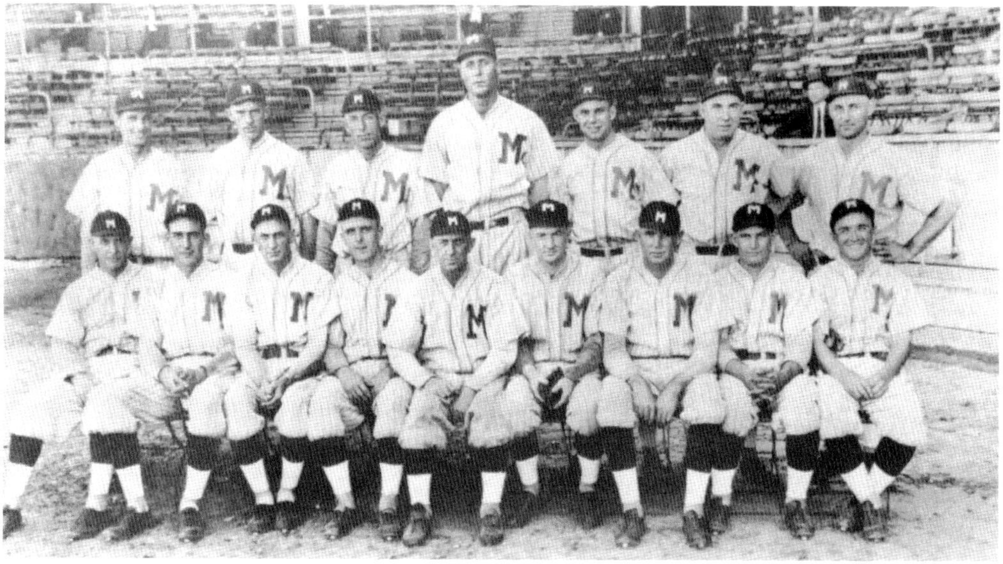

The second Memphis team to be ranked as one of the top-100 minor-league teams of all time is the 1924 team. Just three years after the 1921 championship, Memphis came back with a new manager and an entirely different group of players and won 104 games again. Roy Carlyle led the offense, and pitchers ? Rogers, Cy Warmouth, and Harry Kelley kept hitters off the bases. One of Johnny Dobbs's best jobs at managing was his long and successful career in the Southern Association. (Author's collection.)

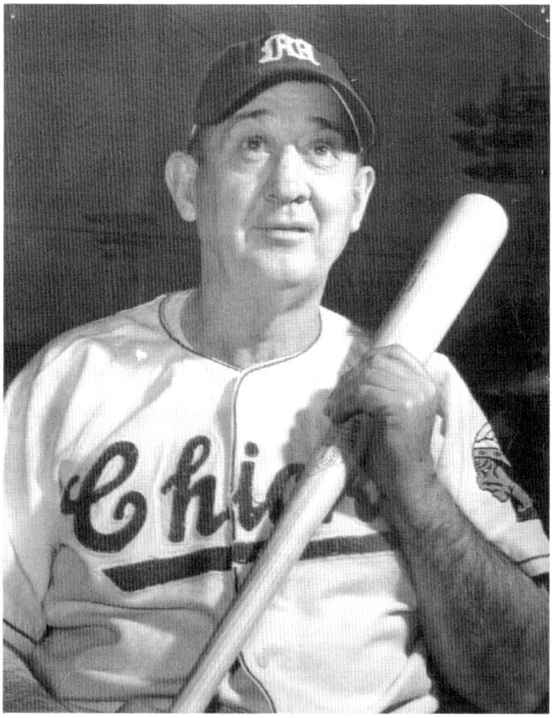

In 1948, Jack Onslow led the Memphis Chicks to a 92-win season. After six years of managing in the minors, Onslow, on the strength of his success in Memphis, was selected to manage the Chicago White Sox for the 1949 season. At age 60, Onslow was the oldest rookie manager in major-league history. (Author's collection.)

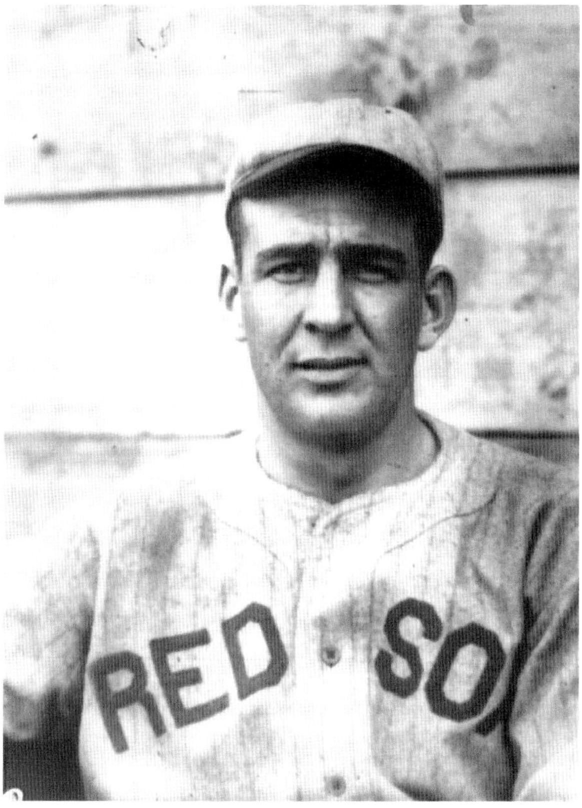

Minor league baseball was a tough business. Breaking into the major leagues sometimes took a lot more than talent. Former Memphis Chick Roy Carlyle was a good example of how difficult baseball could be. In 1924, Carlyle was a member of the Chicks championship team. He batted .368 and set four league records. Late in the 1926 season, the Red Sox traded Carlyle to the Yankees, where he hit .323 in 35 games. He found himself back in the minors the next year. (Author's collection.)

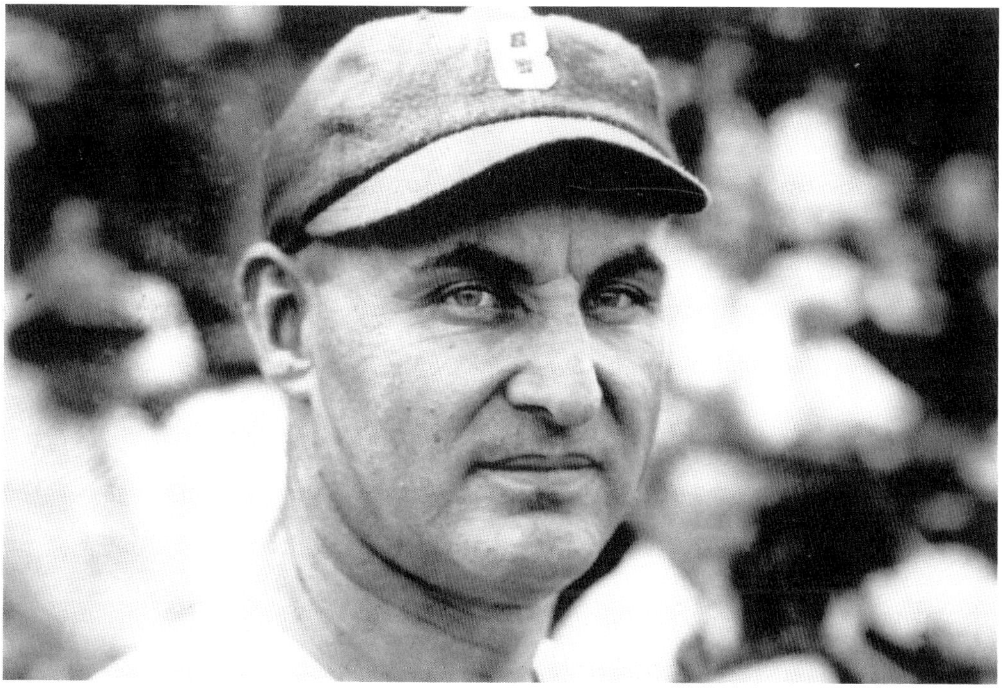

Clarence "Yam" Yaryan played 20 years in the minors as a catcher. He is considered probably the best hitting catcher of his time. Yaryan's 20-year career produced a lifetime .316 average. He did have two years in the majors with the Chicago White Sox in 1921 and 1922. Yaryan, with his .337 average, was a key factor in the Memphis Southern Association championship team of 1924. (Courtesy of the Friends of Rickwood.)

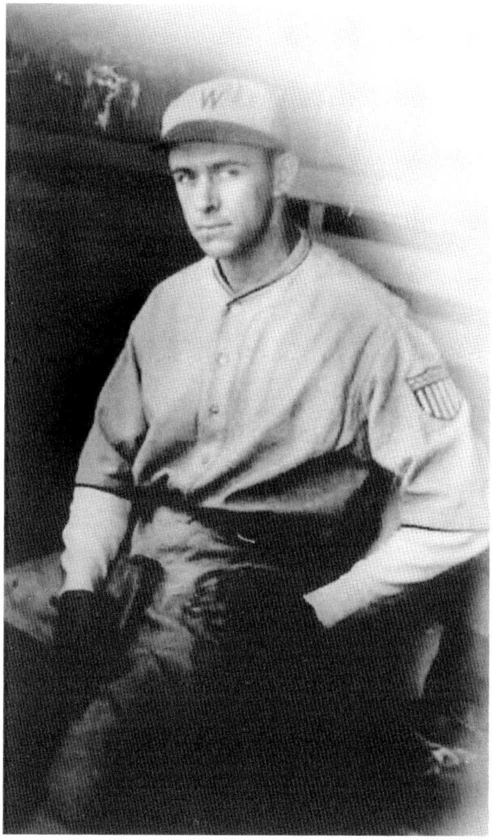

Hod Lisenbee's baseball journey is a truly amazing story of perseverance. Lisenbee did not start high school until age 21 due to having to work to help support his family. He then tried out for the Brookhaven, Mississippi, team, and two days later Lisenbee pitched a four-hit game against Vicksburg. His 17-9 record for Memphis in 1926 earned him a spot on the 1927 Washington Senators club. Lisenbee made his major-league debut at the age of 29. He would continue pitching professionally until 1949, when he was 51. (Author's collection.)

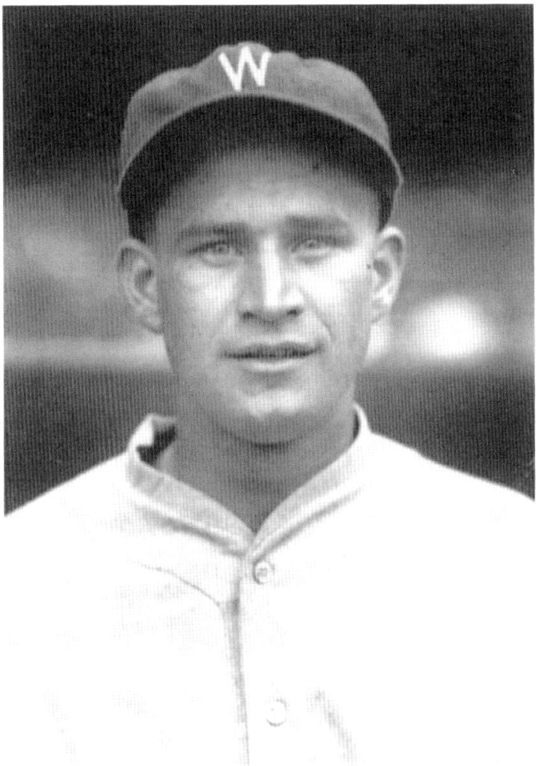

Harry Kelley, the little right-handed pitcher from Parken, Arkansas, holds just about every Memphis pitching record except saves (which was not a statistic back then). Kelley pitched in the major leagues for Washington and Philadelphia. His best year in the majors was 1936 with the Philadelphia A's. Kelley's feat of winning 20 games in three different seasons while with the Memphis Chicks may never be matched. (Author's collection.)

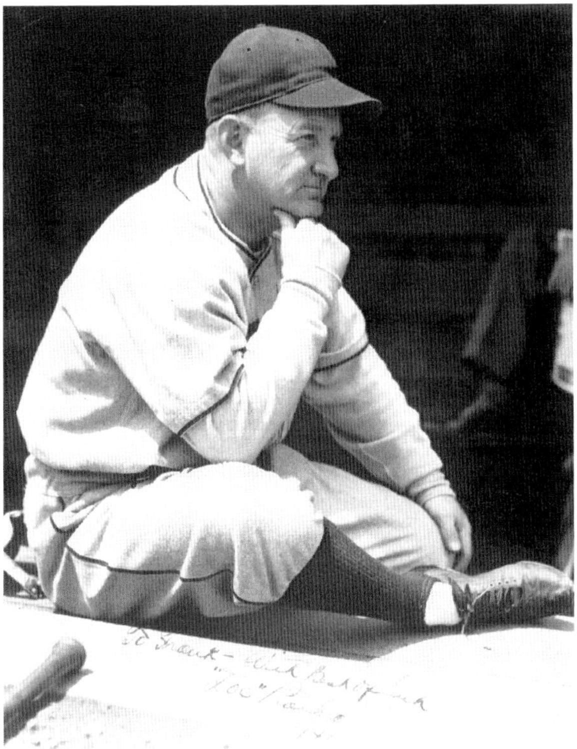

"Doc" James Thompson Prothro was born in Memphis in 1893. Doc went to dental school and set up practice in Dyersburg, Tennessee. He played for the Dyersburg semi-pro team when he was discovered by Washington scout Joe Engel. The Senators brought him straight to the majors. He came back to Memphis to play and manage from 1928 until 1934. In 1942, he returned just as manager and stayed until moving up to the front office after the 1947 season. (Author's collection.)

What Harry Kelley is to Memphis Chicks pitching Andy Reese is to hitting. Reese shared the record of longevity with the Chicks with Kelley; both played 10 seasons for Memphis. Reese holds eight career hitting records for the Chicks. He came to Memphis in 1926 hitting .307, and the next year he began a four-year major-league career with the New York Giants. In 1931, Andy returned to Memphis to play for the next nine years. In seven out of nine seasons, Reese hit well over .300 each year. He is one of the true all-time favorites of Chicks fans. (Author's collection.)

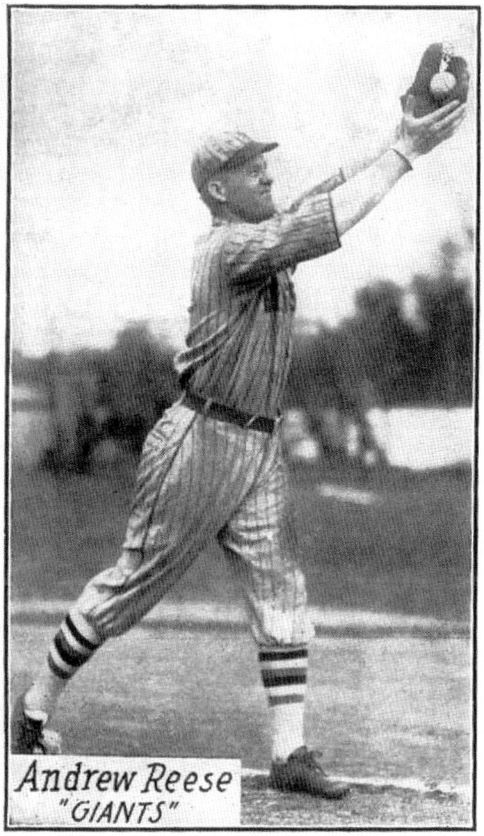

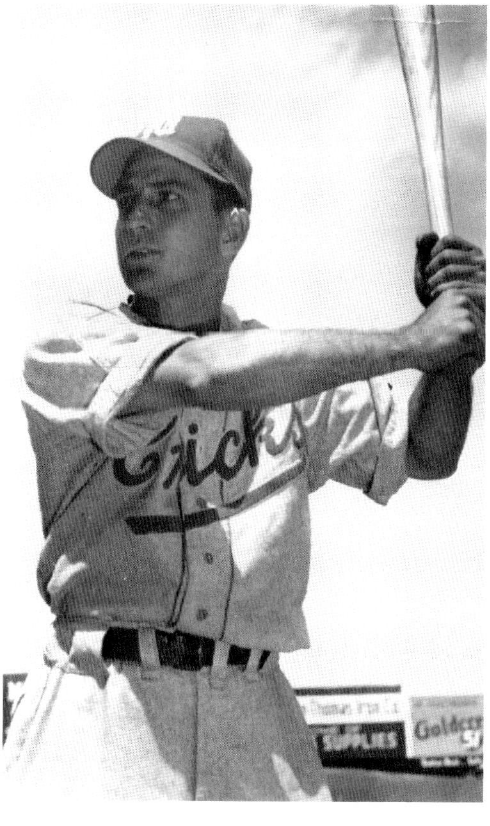

Pete Thomassie's first tour of duty with Memphis was in 1942. When he returned in 1945, Thomassie would have a career year. His .365 average and a string of 12 consecutive hits set a new league record. (Author's collection.)

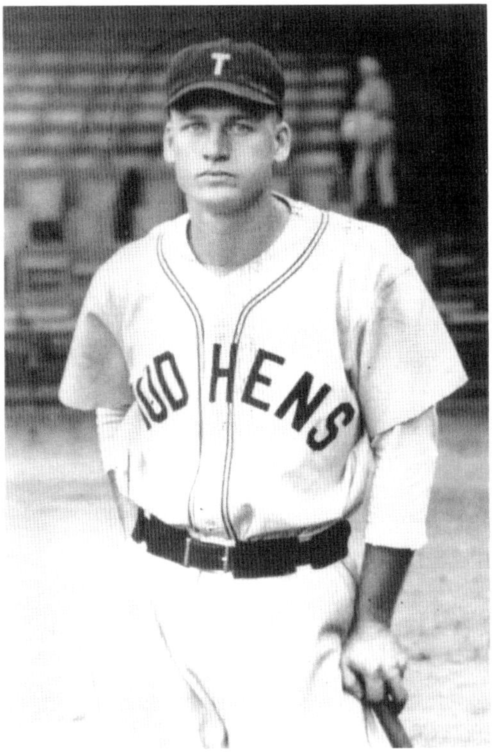

Bennie McCoy played half a season for the 1937 Memphis Chicks, batting .326; he was the property of the Detroit Tigers. Then, in a proclamation issued by Kenesaw Mountain Landis, McCoy and 90 other Detroit farmhands were made free agents. McCoy was a very good player but was stuck behind Charlie Gehringer. His free agency made McCoy a hot commodity. In 1940, Connie Mack signed him to a very lucrative contract with signing bonuses that had him earning more money in 1940 than the great Joe DiMaggio. (Author's collection.)

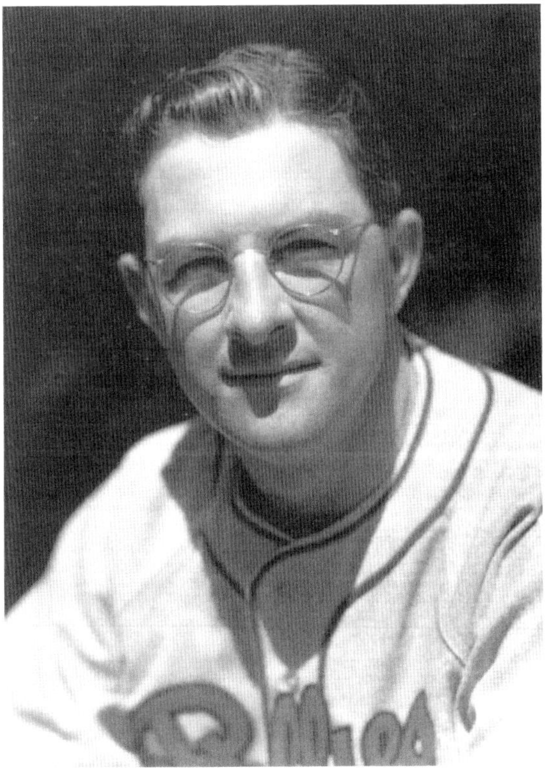

After an impressive 27-6 season in 1932, Walter Beck was promoted to the Brooklyn Dodgers. In a game in Philadelphia, Beck was having another bad outing. He saw Casey Stengel coming to the mound to take him out. In a moment of frustration, Beck turned and threw the baseball off the right-field wall. The boom of the ball hitting the metal sign awakened the right fielder, who turned and made a great throw to the catcher. For the rest of his baseball career, Walter was known as "Boom Boom" Beck. (Author's collection.)

Sam Leslie started the 1929 season with Selma in the Southeastern League. By the end of the year, he had batted .376 for the Chicks but unfortunately did not play enough games to qualify for the batting title. Leslie would play in the majors until 1938. After his baseball career was over, Leslie returned to his hometown of Pascagoula, Mississippi, to begin his second career in the local shipyards. (Author's collection.)

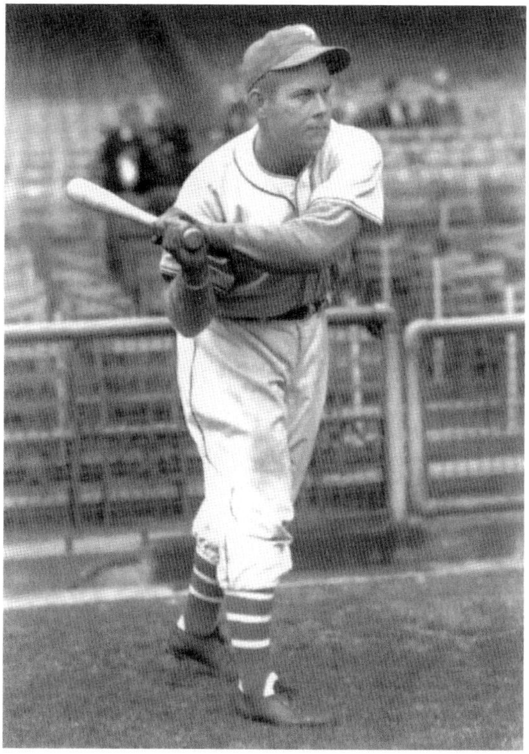

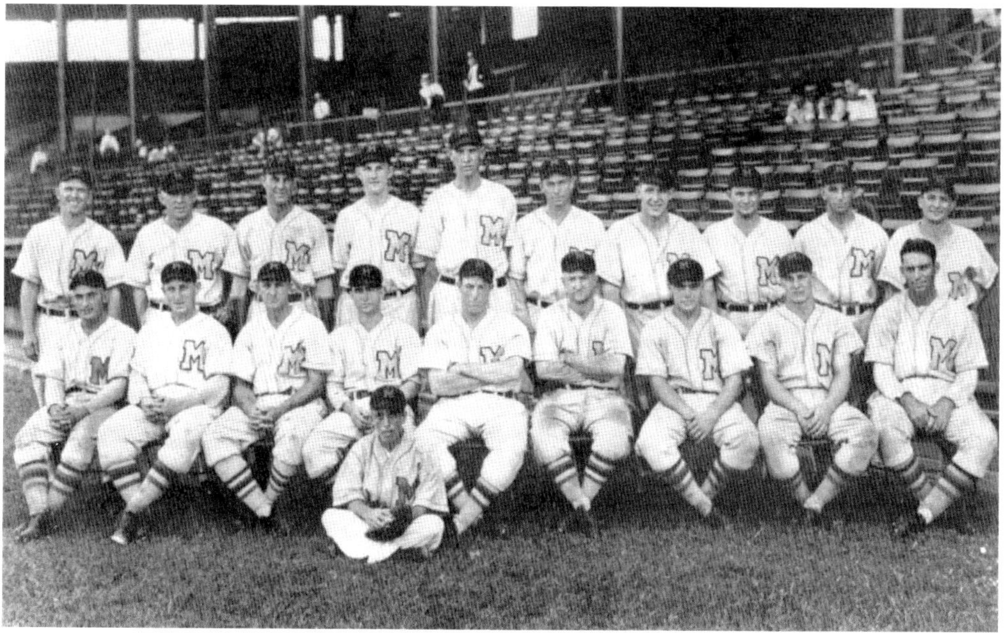

The golden era of Memphis baseball that began in 1921 found its conclusion in the 1930 season. Memphis would not have another first-place finish until 1953. The 1930 team, led by Doc Prothro, won 98 games. Joe Hutcheson led the league with a .380 average, Harry Kelley posted one of his 20-win seasons, and Sam Vick was back with his steady bat. (Author's collection.)

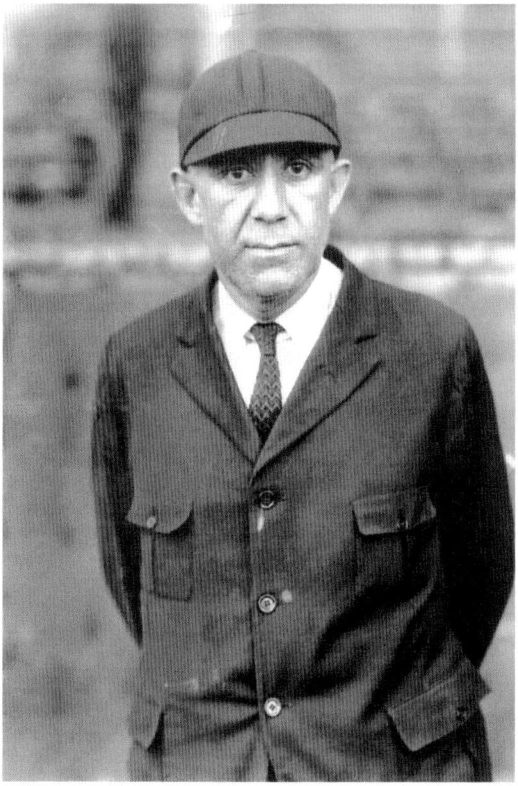

Harry "Steamboat" Johnson was a Southern Association umpire for 25 years. In 1935, he published his own autobiography about life as an umpire, entitled *Standing the Gaff*. Many stories were told about him selling his books before games. At one game in Memphis, fans angered by a close call by Johnson began throwing the books they had purchased at him. Johnson calmly picked up the books and resold them the next day in Nashville. Around 1925, Johnson moved his family to Memphis, where he lived until his death in 1951. (Author's collection.)

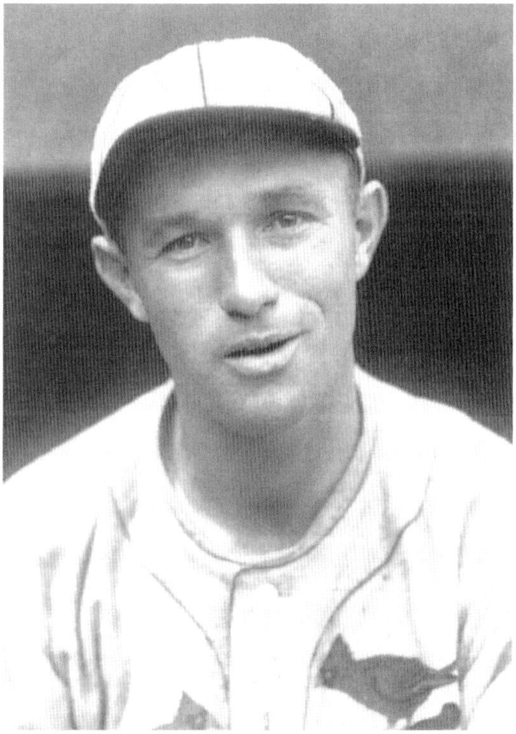

Andy High played for the Memphis Chicks from 1919 to 1921, and each year he steadily improved. His .321 average in 1921 was a key factor in the team's championship. Brooklyn bought him for the 1922 season. High would go on to spend 13 years in the majors. (Author's collection.)

4

CHICKASAWS TO CHICKS

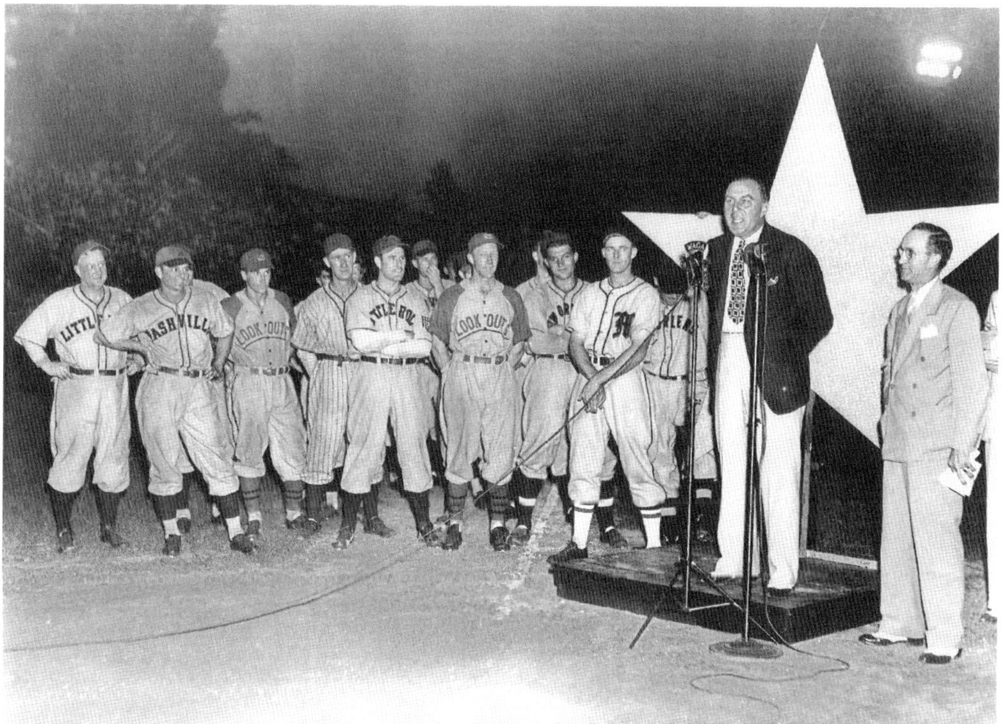

For many years, the Southern Association published a listing of its all-star team, but those chosen for the team had never actually played a game. In 1938, the first Southern Association All-Star Game was played in Atlanta, Georgia, at Ponce DeLeon Park. Memphis's sole starter was speedy outfielder Joe Grace, seen here to the left of the star. Also present on the far left is prodigal son Doc Prothro, manager of the Little Rock Travelers, who was elected as manager of the all-star team. (Courtesy of Dan Creed.)

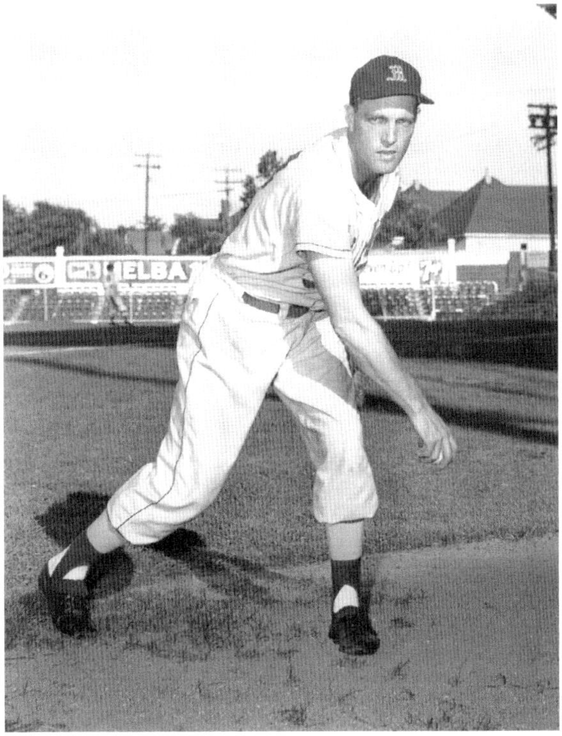

Millard "Dixie" Howell pitched for the Memphis Chicks from 1952 to 1954 and developed into a very effective relief specialist. His great relief pitching in 1953 helped Memphis win the championship. Howell would continue his good pitching for the Chicago White Sox for the next three years. Tragically, he died of a heart attack while running during spring training in Florida in 1960. (Author's collection.)

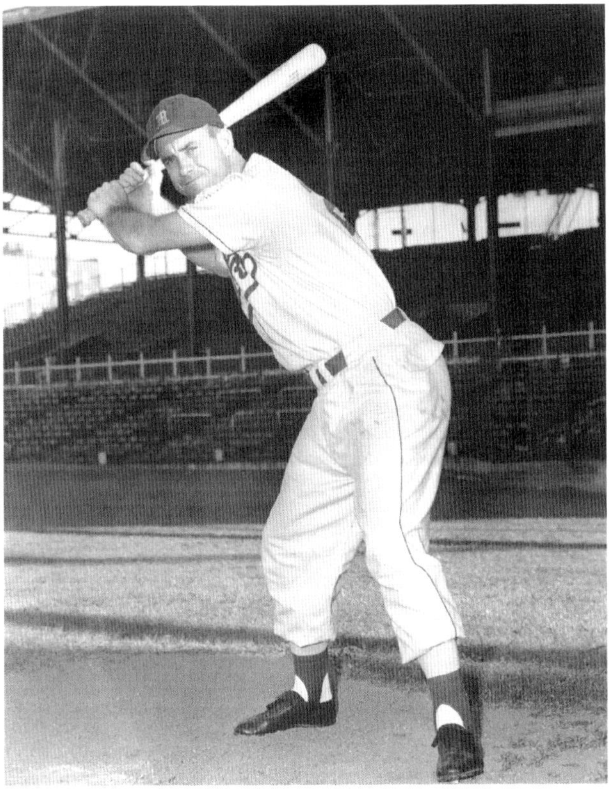

Ed White had six very good seasons with the Memphis Chicks; twice he led the team in batting. In the middle of his Chicks career, White played three games for the Chicago White Sox in 1955. His brief stay in the majors produced two hits and a .500 batting average. (Author's collection.)

Hugh Casey began his baseball career with the Atlanta Crackers at the age of 18, but it was his pitching for the 1938 Chicks that made Brooklyn take notice. Casey is best remembered for his wild pitch in the fourth game of the 1941 World Series, which led to the loss of the game. After several years in the Army during World War II, Casey came back to baseball and pitched effectively for two seasons. On July 3, 1951, he died of a self-inflicted shotgun blast in Atlanta. (Author's collection.)

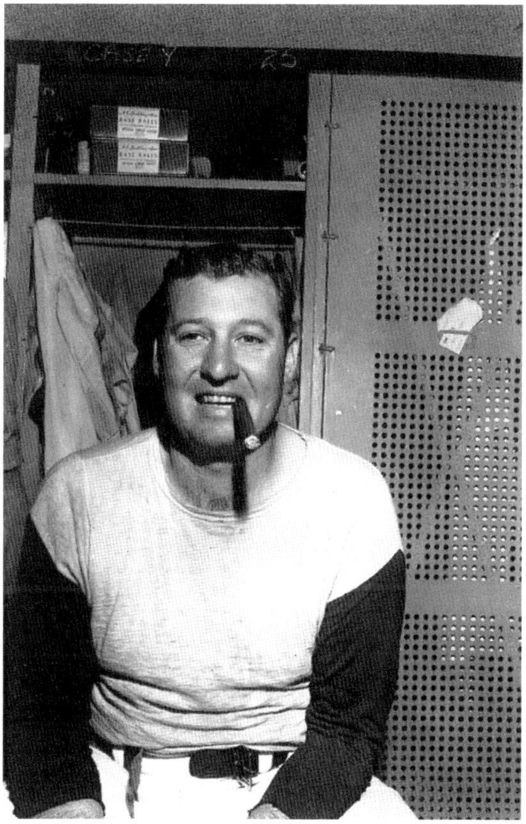

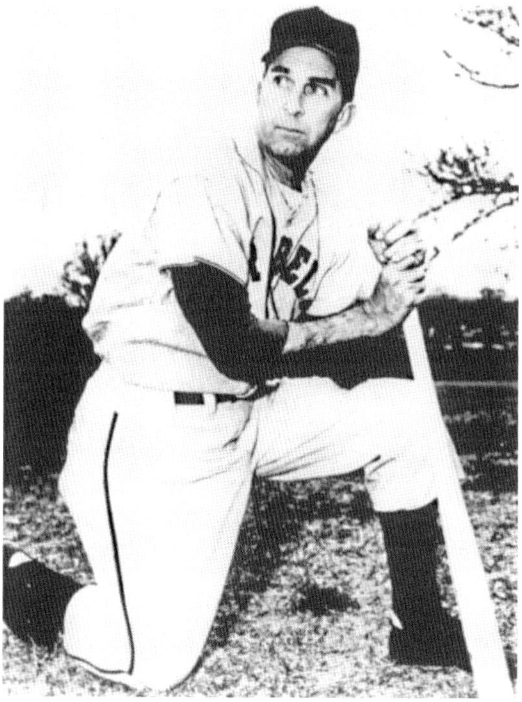

In 1933, Tom Watkins signed the all-sports star at Ole Miss, Tom Swayze, to play for Memphis. Swayze's professional career lasted only three years, including parts of two seasons with the Chicks. Swayze is best remembered for coaching the Ole Miss baseball team for 20 years, winning four SEC Championships. The baseball stadium at Ole Miss is named in his honor. (Author's collection.)

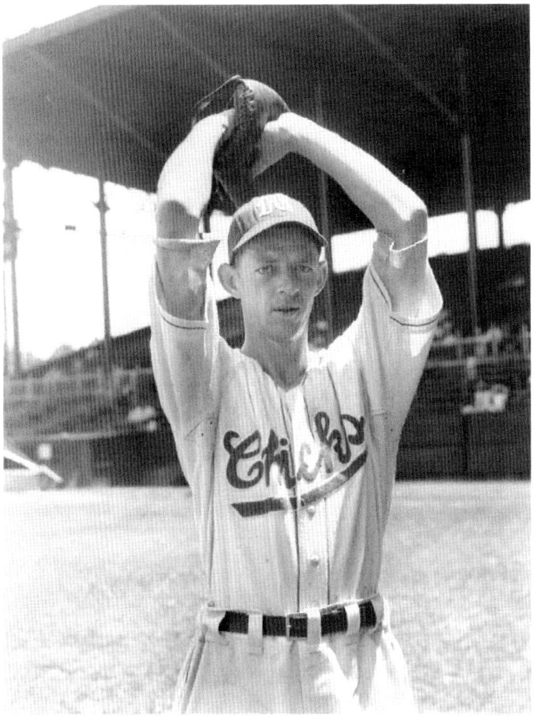

Despite losing records with the Chicks in 1942 and 1943, Weldon "Lefty" West pitched for the St. Louis Browns during the war years of 1944 and 1945. He actually pitched better in the major leagues than he did in Memphis. (Author's collection.)

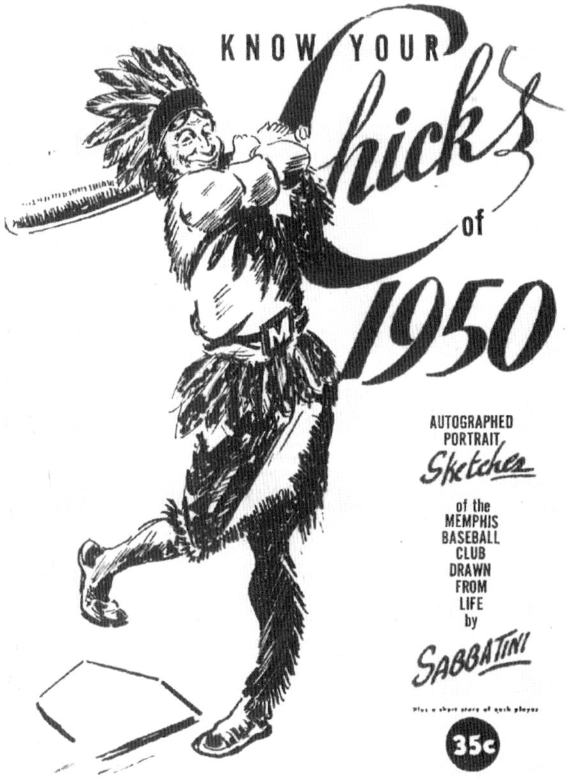

Starting in the late 1940s, local artist Paul Sabbatini began publishing a small pocket booklet called "Know Your Chicks." It contained drawings of each player by Sabbatini as well as other team information. Sabbatini tried to extend the program to other Southern Association teams and college football. These small Chicks artifacts are hard to find and very prized among Chicks memorabilia collectors. (Author's collection.)

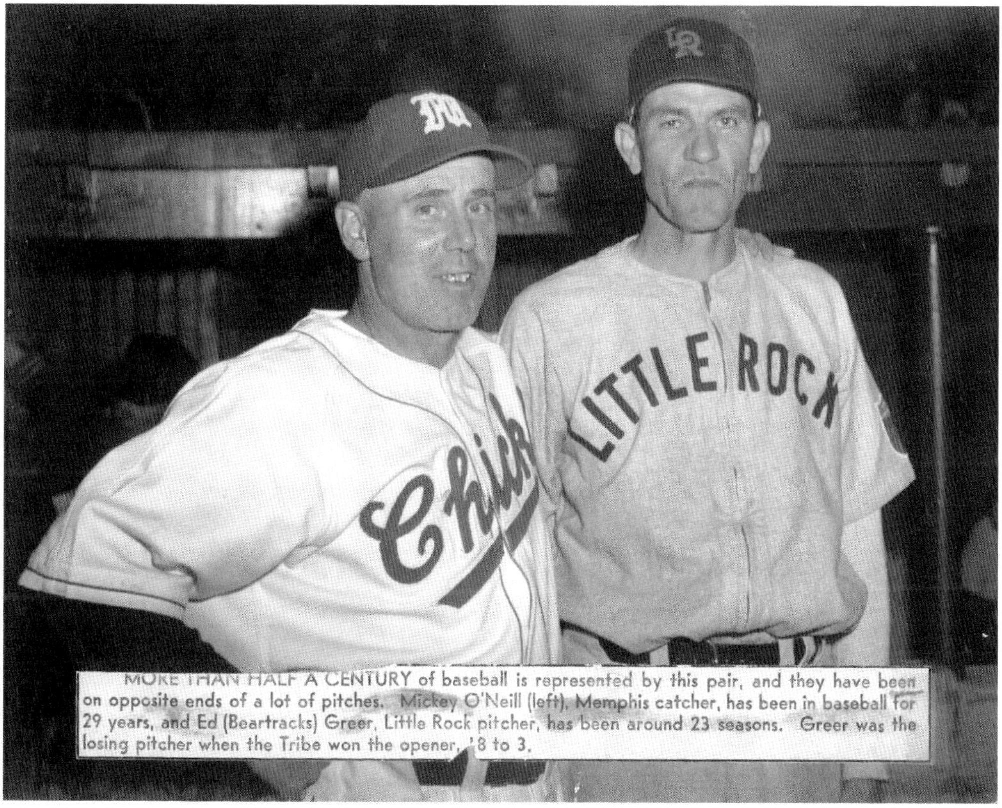

Memphis coach and part-time player Mickey O'Neil is shown here with Ed "Beartracks" Greer, a longtime minor-league pitcher. Greer was coming to the close of a 23-year career, all in the minor leagues. Twice Greer pitched for the Memphis Chicks, in 1935 and 1944–1945. (Author's collection.)

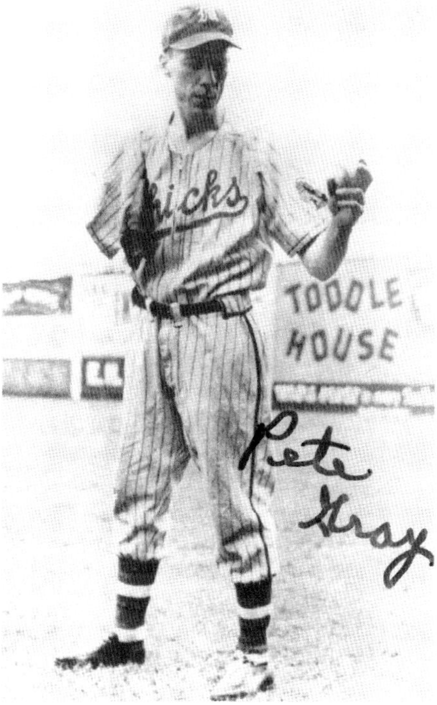

Arguably the most famous Memphis Chick was Pete Gray, the one-armed wonder who played for the Chicks in 1943 and 1944. Gray drew large crowds at Russwood as well as on the road; it was hard not to root for Pete. After his MVP season of 1944, he got to play in 77 games for the 1945 St. Louis Browns. In 1978, Pete returned to Memphis to be honored for his outstanding play for the Chicks. (Author's collection.)

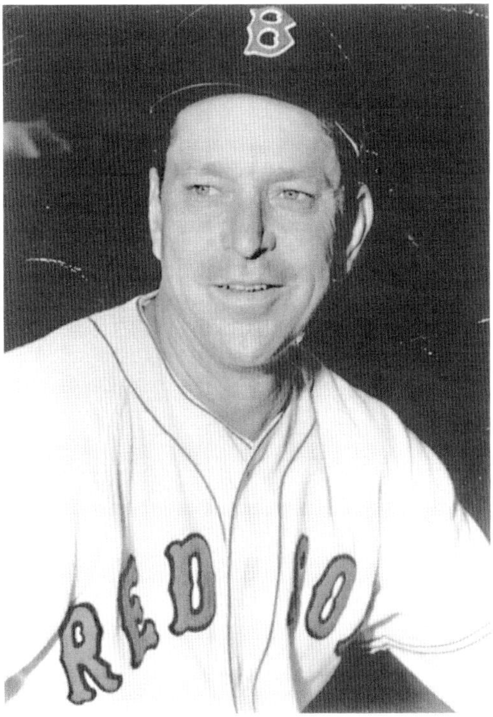

Ellis Kinder did not begin pitching professionally until the age of 24; he broke into the major leagues at the age of 31. After World War II, it was his breakthrough 19-6 season with Memphis that got him to the majors. Yet, it was his eight seasons with the Boston Red Sox that defined his career. As a starter in 1949, he had a 23-6 record. (Author's collection.)

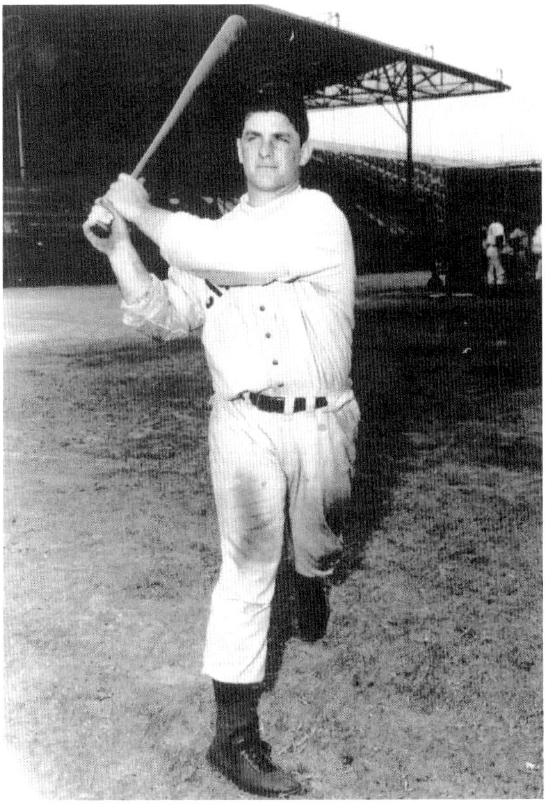

In 1946, Ted Kluszewski signed with Cincinnati for a $15,000 bonus. In 1947, Ted came to Memphis. As late as mid-August, he was hitting over .400. In a doubleheader in New Orleans, Ted hit a home run, three triples, two doubles, and two singles. He would win the Southern Association batting title in 1947 and make the Reds team in 1948. Ted was also with the Chicago White Sox, Pittsburgh Pirates, and Los Angeles Dodgers and played the last game at Russwood Park in 1960. (Author's collection.)

Al Lary won 15 games for the 1957 Memphis Chicks. He had two brothers who also pitched professionally. His younger brother Frank Lary is remembered as the "Yankee Killer" in the early 1960s. His other brother Gene pitched for several years for the Mobile Bears. While a hurler for the Chicago Cubs late in his career, Al gave up Willie Mays's 324th career home run—a grand slam. Al also is remembered as an outstanding football player for the University of Alabama. (Courtesy of Dan Creed.)

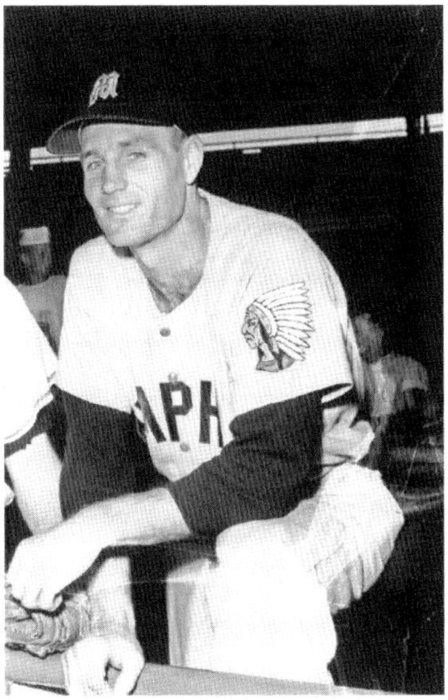

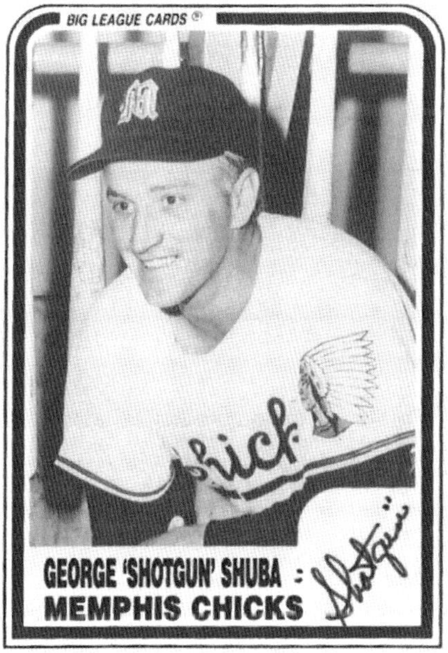

George Shuba spent several seasons in the Southern Association with New Orleans and Mobile before playing eight years with the Brooklyn Dodgers; this included three World Series appearances. George's nickname was "Shotgun" due to his ability to hit line drives to all fields. He was also known as a clutch pinch hitter. Shuba spent his last year in professional baseball with the Memphis Chicks in 1957. He received much-deserved recognition in Roger Kahn's baseball classic, *The Bears of Summer*. (Author's collection.)

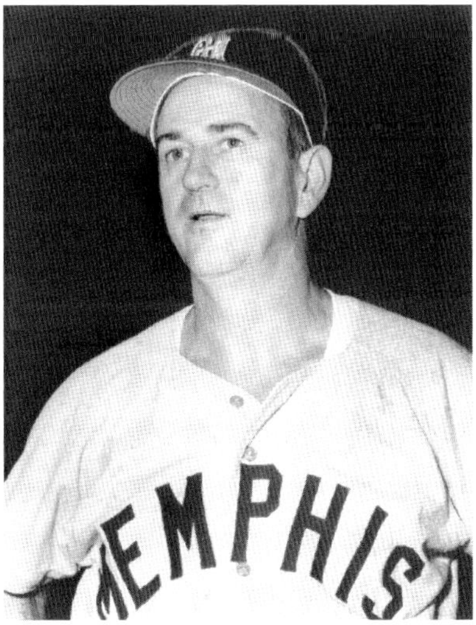

Luke Appling was the shortstop for the Chicago White Sox from 1930 to 1950. He played one year in the minors for the Atlanta Crackers. His lifetime batting average of .310 helped earn him a place in Cooperstown in 1964. Appling twice managed the Chicks, from 1951 to 1953 and again in 1959. The Chicks finished in first place in 1953 under Appling. (Author's collection.)

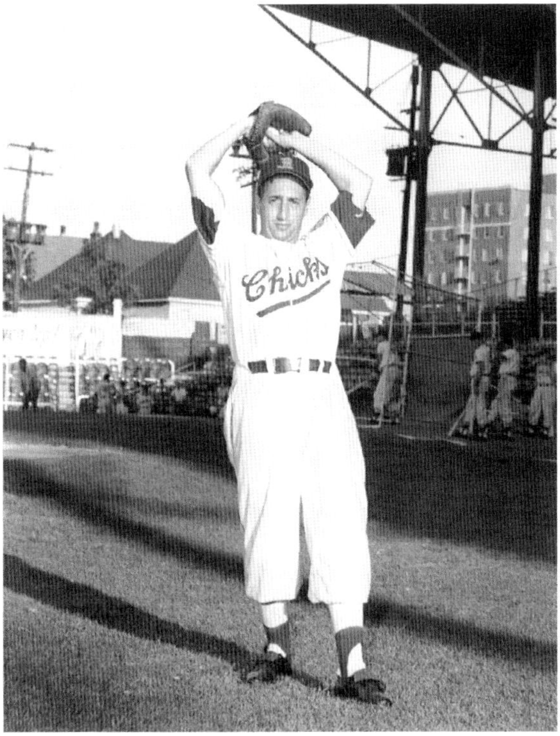

Marvin Rotblatt pitched for the Memphis Chicks in five different seasons. He is most remembered for his outstanding 1950 record of 22 wins. Rotblatt had three late-season tryouts with the Chicago White Sox. The Chicks made the playoffs in 1950 due primarily to Rotblatt's stellar mound work. (Author's collection.)

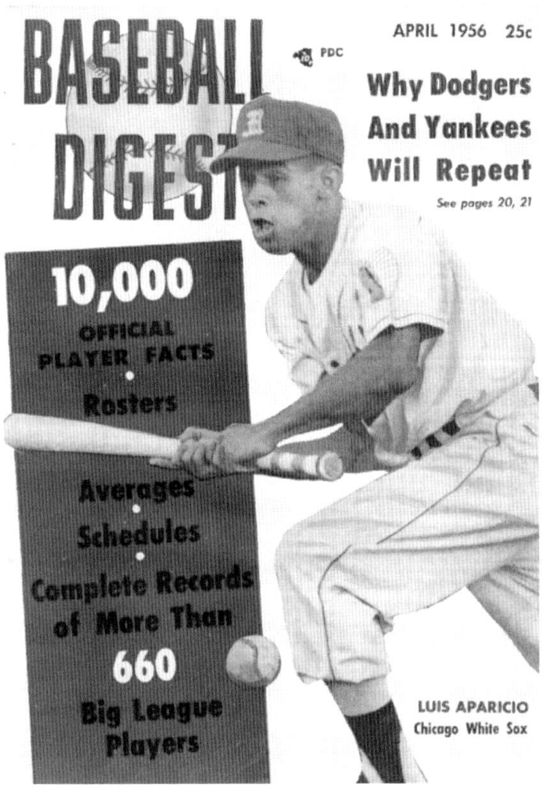

After a very good season for the Chicks in 1955, the Chicago White Sox organization traded shortstop Chico Carresquel to Cleveland to make room for Luis Aparicio to be the starting shortstop in 1956. (Author's collection.)

The Memphis club always used pictures of very regal and stoic Indians on its programs. In 1958, the Chicks began to use the cartoonish image of Chief Wahoo, the mascot of the Cleveland Indians, on their programs. Gratefully, when the Chicks returned in 1978, this style did not continue. (Author's collection.)

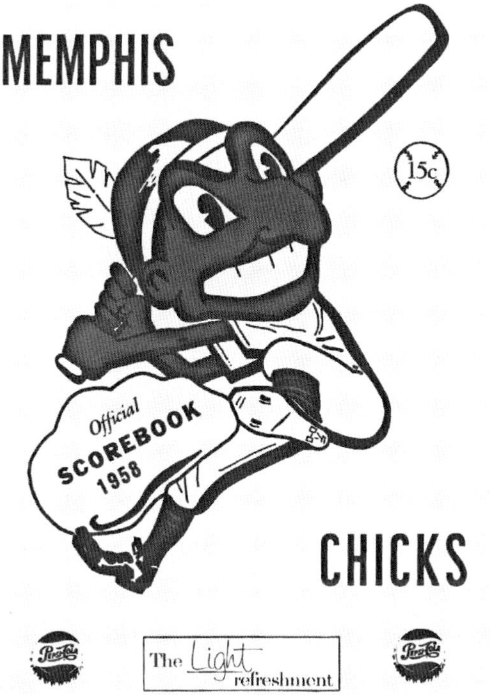

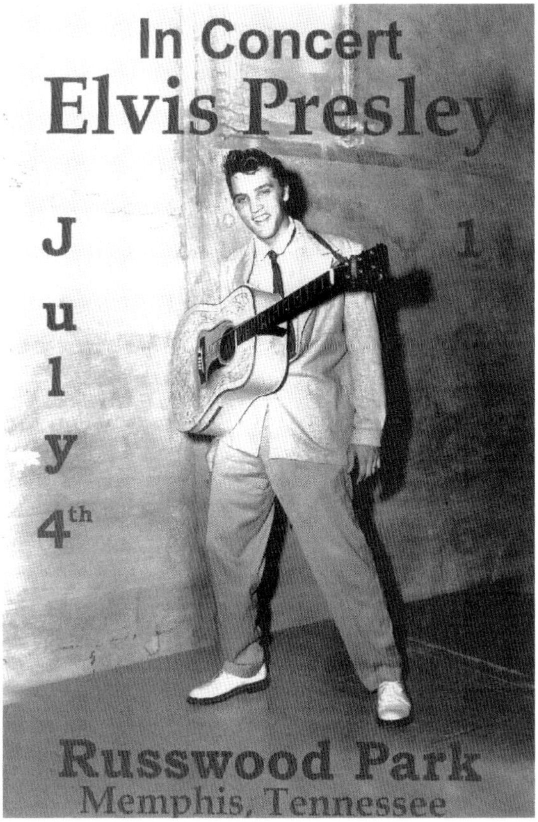

On the Fourth of July in 1956, Elvis Presley performed at Russwood Park as the headliner for a charity event for the Cynthia Milk Fund. Elvis was just then taking the nation by storm. On July 1, he had performed on the Steve Allen Show. The next day, he recorded "Don't Be Cruel" and "Hound Dog." On July 3, Elvis boarded a train for Memphis to perform at Russwood Park. (Author's collection.)

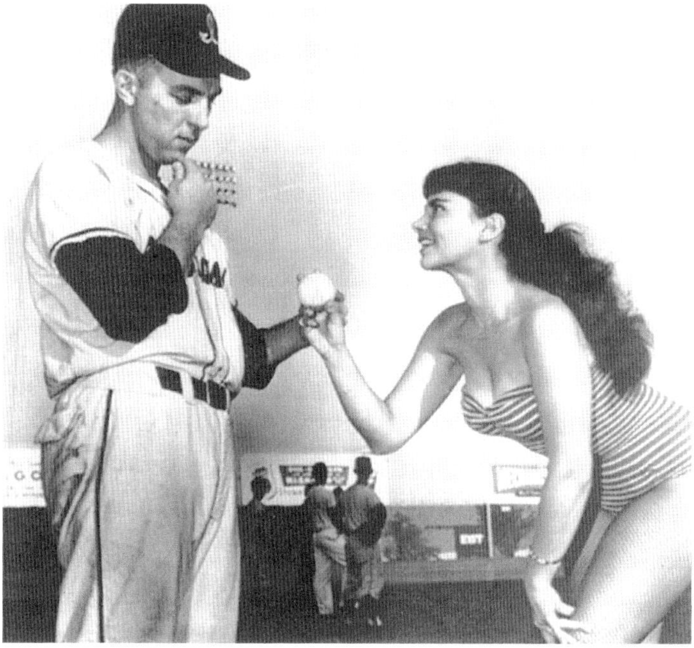

Don Rudolph pitched for the Memphis Chicks in 1955 and 1956. At his next stop in Indianapolis, Rudolph met and married an exotic dancer named Patti Waggen. She is shown here giving her husband some advice on pitching. It must have helped; by 1963, Rudolph was the opening-day starter for the Washington Senators. Tragically, Rudolph was killed in a truck accident at the age of 37 in 1968. (Author's collection.)

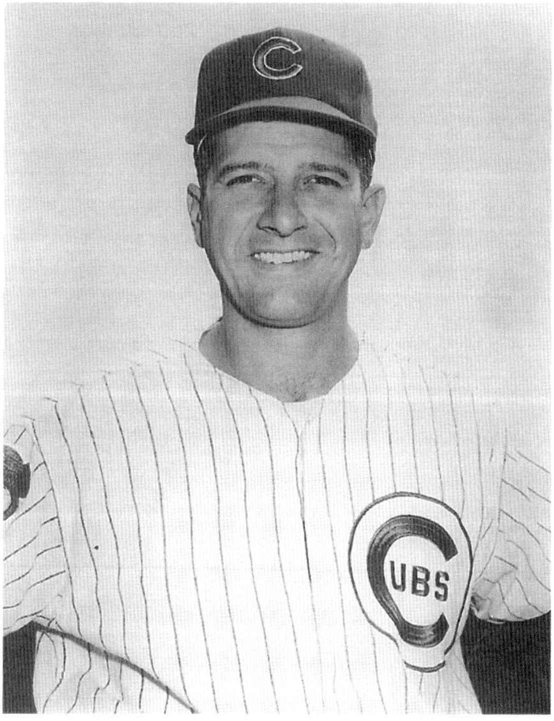

Alex Grammas is a native of Birmingham, Alabama. After college, Grammas signed a professional contract and spent 1950 and 1951 with the Memphis Chicks. In 1950, he was joined on the team by his brother Pete. Grammas had a 10-year career in the National League. After his playing days were over, he coached and managed several teams. He may be best remembered as Sparky Anderson's third-base coach in both Cincinnati and Detroit. (Author's collection.)

5

The Fire

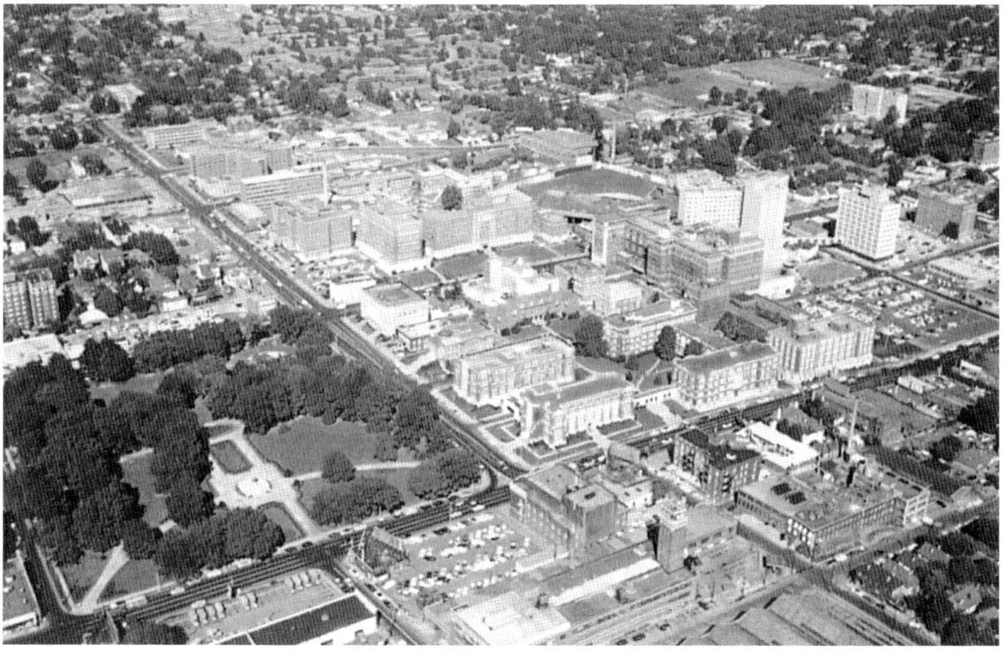

This postcard of the Medical Center of Memphis reveals the approaching future of Russwood Park—it is almost surrounded by hospitals. This late-1950s aerial shot shows Russwood wedged in between John Gaston Hospital and Baptist Hospital's new East Wing. In the upper right-hand corner is Hodges Field, the high school football stadium where the Chicks played their first home game after the fire. Hodges Field experienced the fate that awaited Russwood had that park not burned in 1960. Hodges Field was torn down to make way for a hospital. (Author's collection.)

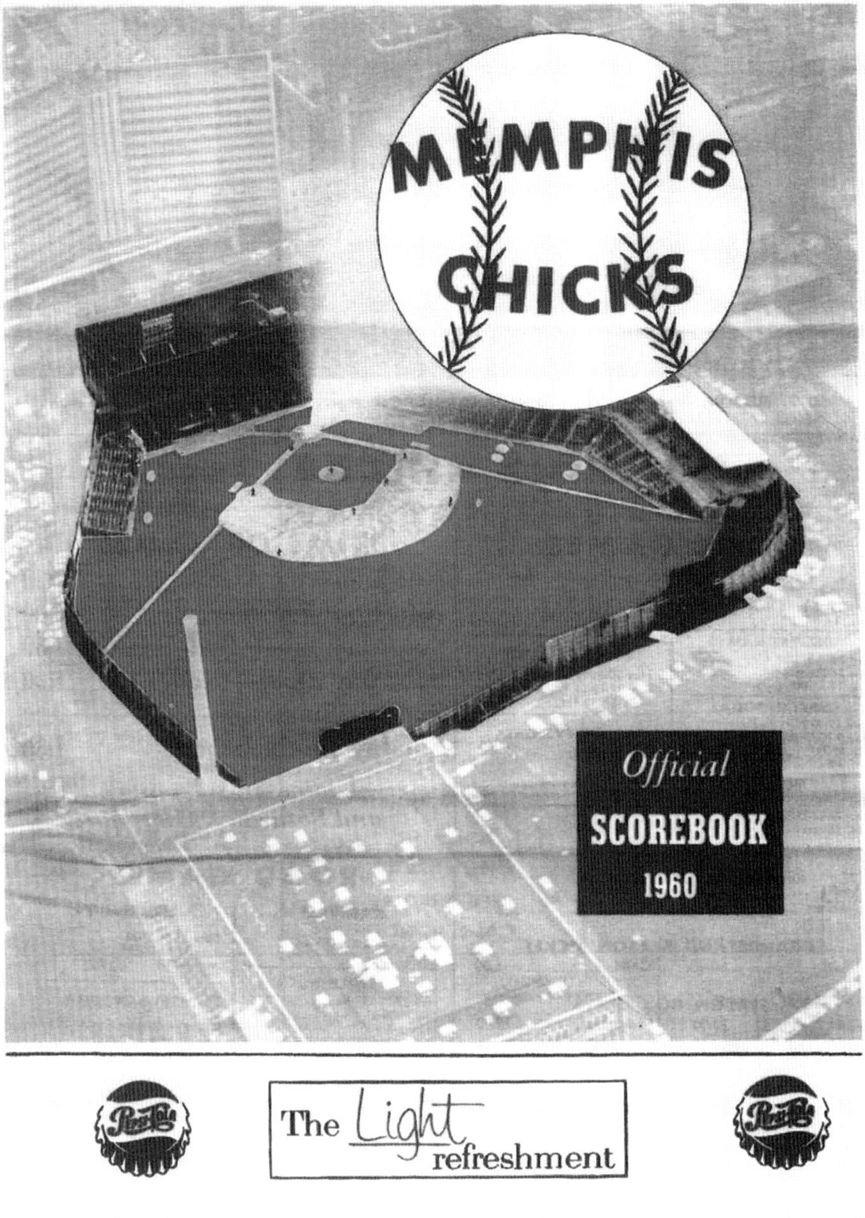

Unknown to the fans and players of April 16, 1960, the exhibition game between the Chicago White Sox and the Cleveland Indians turned out to be a Chicks reunion of sorts. No less than 12 former Chicks were on the rosters of both teams. Also, there were 22 former Southern Association players on both teams. Almost half of the two teams that day had played at Russwood in Southern Association games. Memphis was looking forward to the 1960 season. Two hometown boys were on the team: Tim McCarver and Phil Gagliano. Memphis was now the Double-A farm team of the St. Louis Cardinals. This program cover from 1960 gives fans a last look at Russwood Park. (Author's collection.)

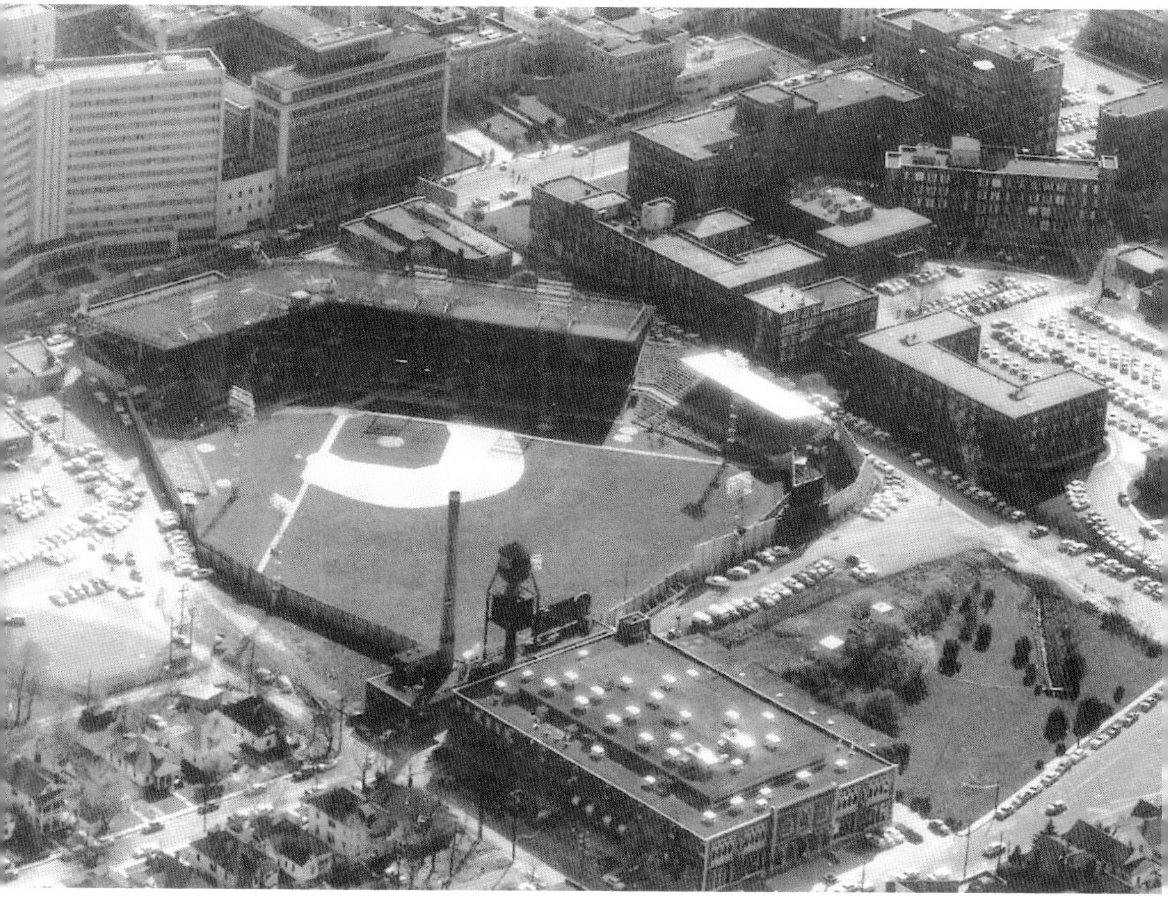

The new wing to Baptist Hospital casts its shadow over Russwood Park. In 1945, the team ownership purchased 33 acres of land 6.5 miles from downtown Memphis on Park Avenue to build a new multipurpose stadium. The new park would accommodate football in the hopes of obtaining a professional team. Since the team owned the stands and lights, they would be moved to the new location. By August 1945, the grading on the new site was complete, but then the Memphis Chicks purchased Russwood Park, and the Chicks would remain at Russwood. Over the years, there had been several small fires reported at Russwood, and it was common practice for the team to hire off-duty policemen or firemen to patrol the park after a game due to the threat of fire. On July 18, 1952, another fire broke out in the grandstands but was confined and extinguished by the prompt action of the Memphis Fire Department. (Courtesy of Memphis and Shelby County Room, Memphis Public Library and Information Room.)

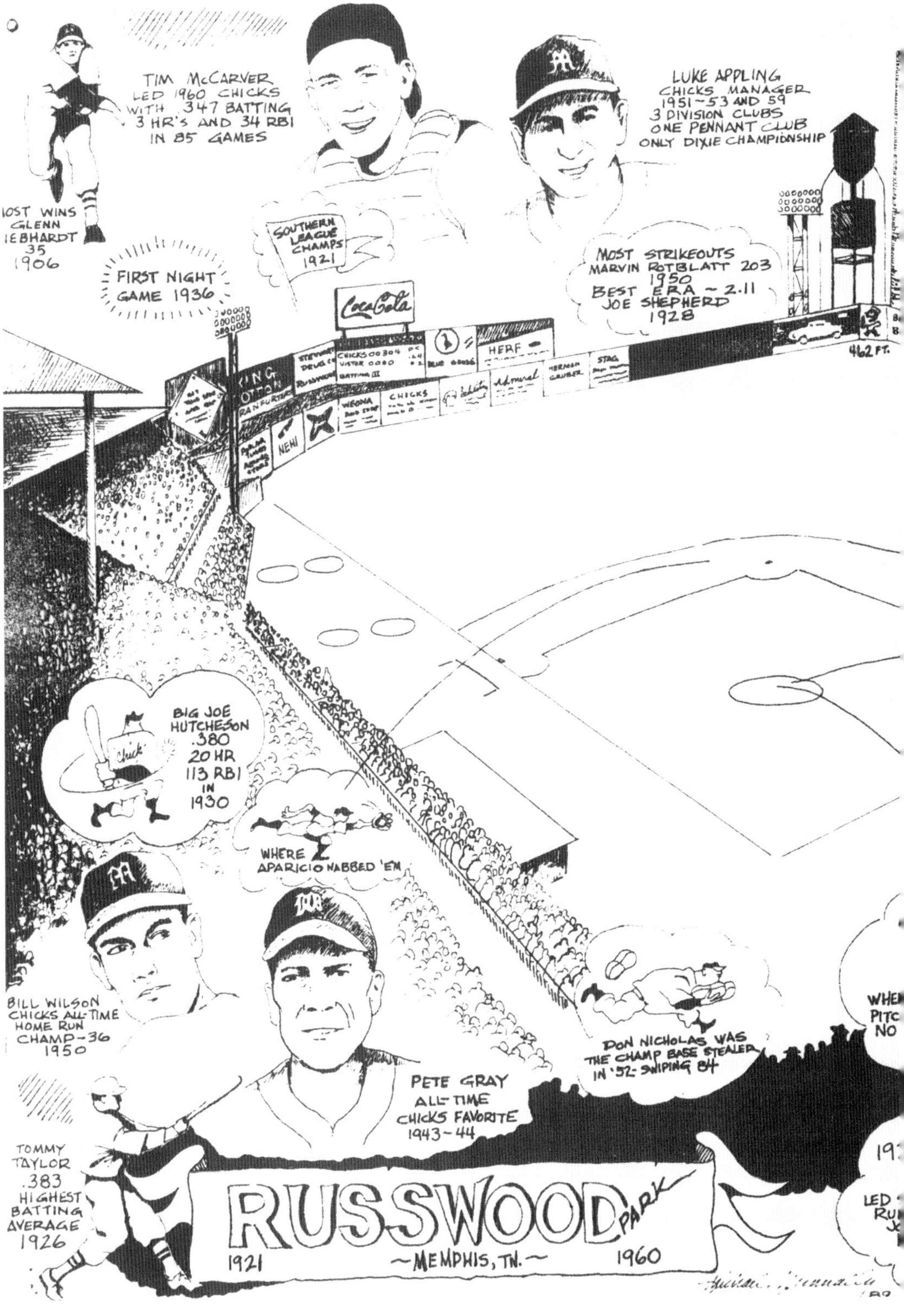
TIM McCARVER
LED 1960 CHICKS
WITH .347 BATTING
3 HR'S AND 34 RBI
IN 85 GAMES
LUKE APPLING
CHICKS MANAGER
1951-53 AND 59
3 DIVISION CLUBS
ONE PENNANT CLUB
ONLY DIXIE CHAMPIONSHIP
GLENN
35
1906
SOUTHERN
LEAGUE
CHAMPS
1921
FIRST NIGHT
GAME 1936
MOST STRIKEOUTS
MARVIN ROTBLATT 203
1950
BEST ERA - 2.11
JOE SHEPHERD
1928
Coca-Cola
HERF
STAG
Admiral
CHICKS
NEHI
462 FT.
BIG JOE
HUTCHESON
.380
20 HR
113 RBI
IN
1930
Chick
WHERE
APARICIO NABBED 'EM
BILL WILSON
CHICKS ALL-TIME
HOME RUN
CHAMP-36
1950
DON NICHOLAS WAS
THE CHAMP BASE STEALER
IN '52- SWIPING 84
PETE GRAY
ALL-TIME
CHICKS FAVORITE
1943-44
TOMMY
TAYLOR
.383
HIGHEST
BATTING
AVERAGE
1926
RUSSWOOD PARK
1921
~MEMPHIS, TN.~
1960

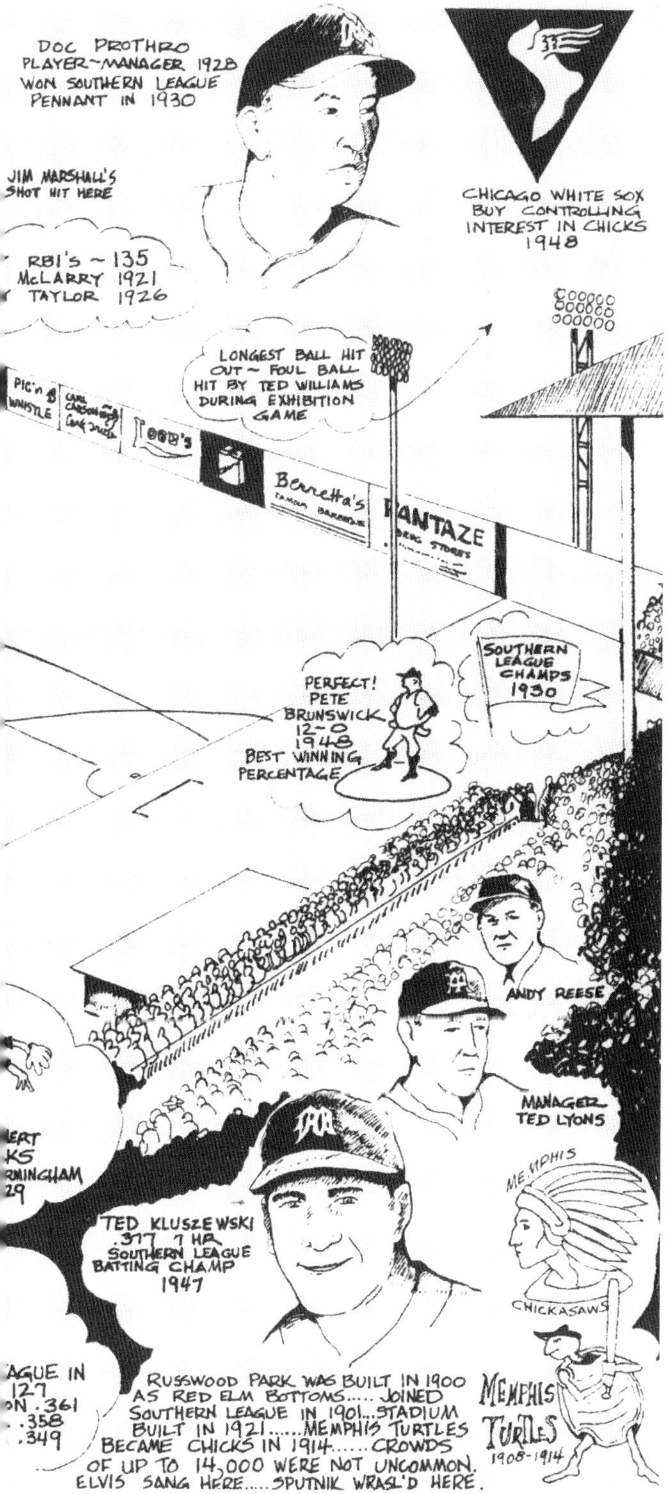

This drawing of Russwood Park was done by artist Michael L. Nunnally and is reminiscent of those that appeared in the *Sporting News* back in the 1950s and 1960s. It reveals the character of the park and depicts the history with sketches of the most memorable players and games. (Author's collection.)

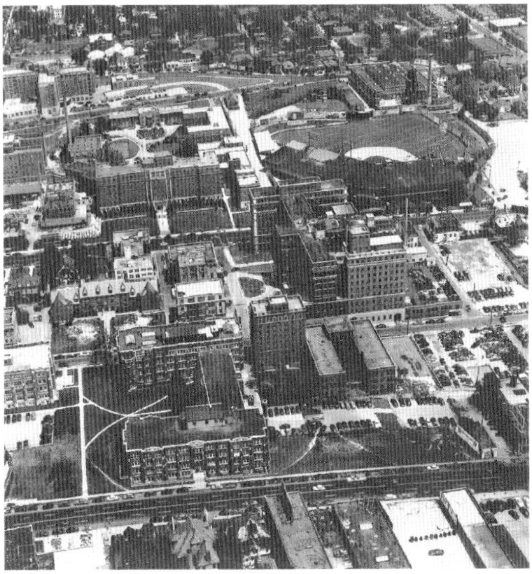

While in their primes, James Dean, Marilyn Monroe, and John F. Kennedy were lost to a generation of fans, and memories keep them frozen in all their youth and glory. So it is with Russwood Park for old Chicks fans. The fact is Russwood Park was doomed from early on, as it was surrounded by hospitals that wanted the land for a parking lot. Only a few months before Russwood burned, the mayor of Memphis asked that plans to build a new baseball stadium at the fairgrounds be accelerated. The fire on April 16, 1960, spared fans the agony of watching the demolition of their beloved park. (Author's collection.)

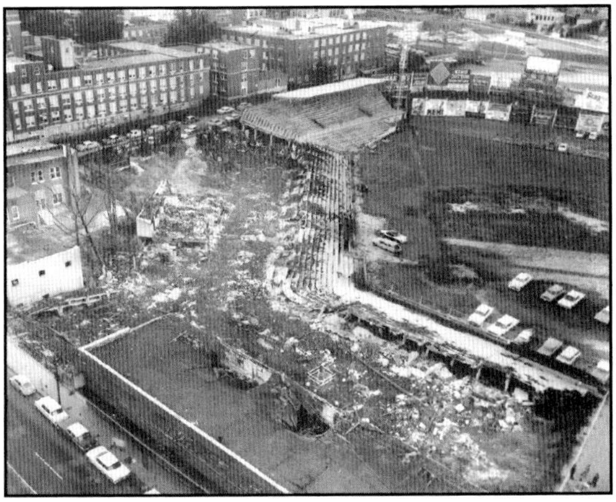

This image of the destruction of Russwood Park on April 17, 1960, hung on the wall at Pappy and Jimmy's Restaurant on Madison Avenue until it closed. (Author's collection.)

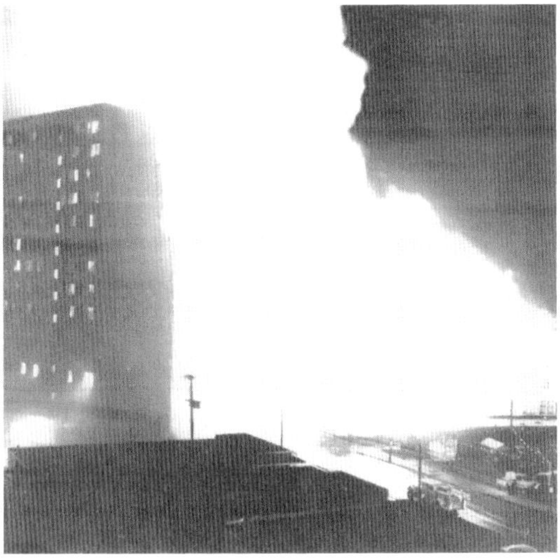

This photograph of the actual fire shows the size of the flames in contrast to the 12-story east wing of Baptist Hospital. Factors that contributed to the fire were a fresh coat of paint on the grandstands and debris still in the park from the game. When Gardner rebuilt the park in 1921, it could have been a completely concrete-and-steel stadium; however, wood was used for the risers of the grandstands. It is possible Gardner used wood due to Memphis being the hardwood capital of the nation at the time, and using wood was seen as a civic duty. (Author's collection.)

In 1959, Rocky Colavito won the home-run crown for the American League. He was extremely popular with Cleveland fans. During the Chicago-Cleveland exhibition game on April 17, 1960, Frank Lane traded Colavito. In the sixth inning, Colavito walked. As he stood on first, manager Joe Gordon summoned him to the dugout and told him he had been traded. The fans in Cleveland rioted, and Lane was hanged in effigy. Cleveland would not be a contender for 40 years. So was born the curse of Rocky Colavito. The curse started the same night when Russwood burned. (Author's collection.)

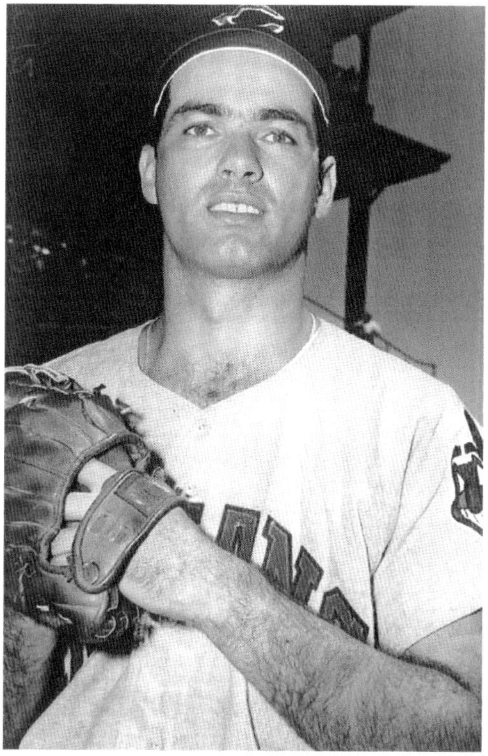

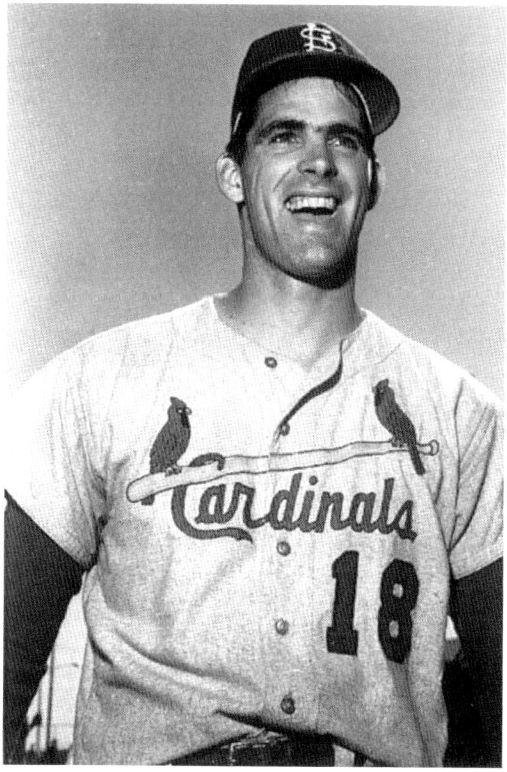

Mike Shannon played for the 1960 Memphis Chicks and soon moved on to play for the St. Louis Cardinals along with teammate Tim McCarver. The retirement of Cardinals great Stan Musial can partly be blamed on Shannon. In 1963, Musial said, "I knew it was time to retire when a teammate had also been on the same high school football team with my son." (Author's collection.)

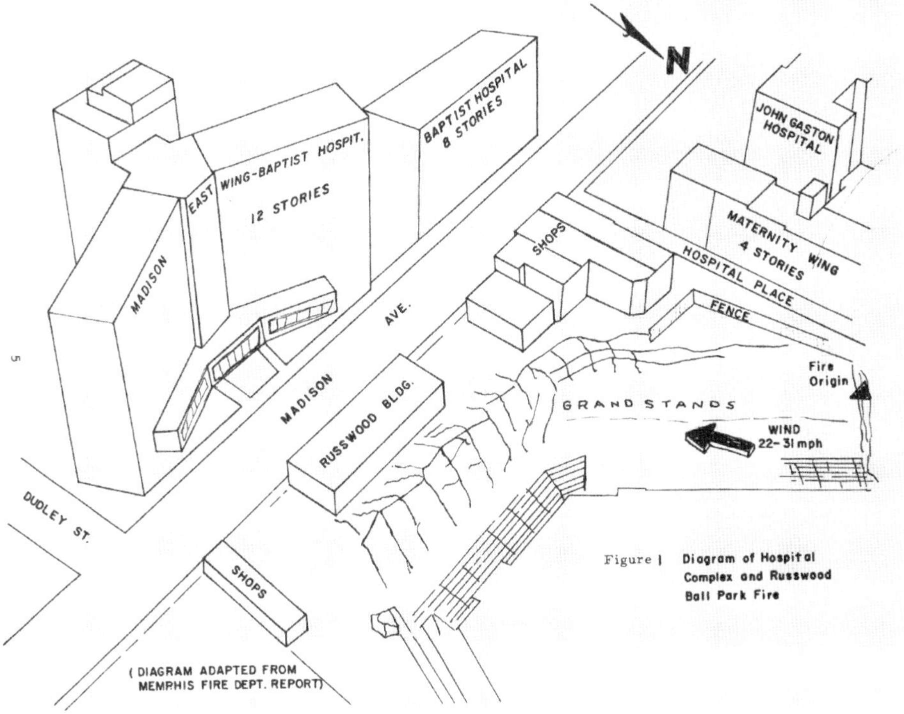

This drawing from the fire report shows the origin of the blaze, the layout of the park in connection to the hospitals, and other buildings surrounding the park. No doubt, the sudden increase in winds that night greatly increased the spread of the fire and the complete destruction of the grandstand area. (Author's collection.)

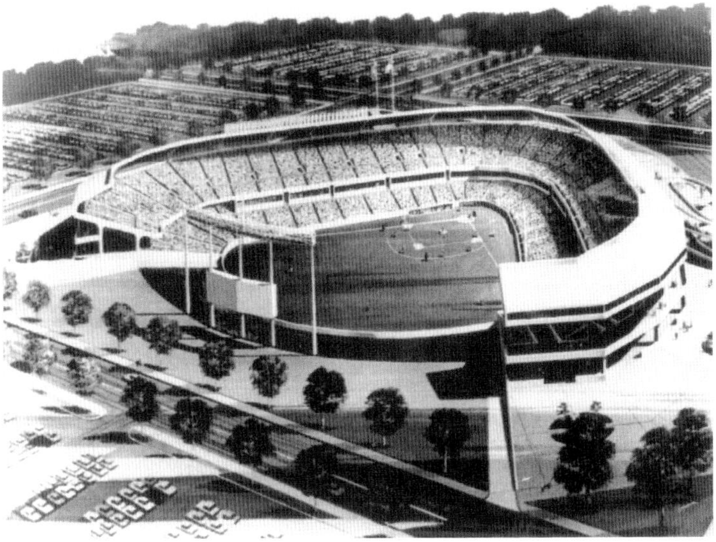

Several different designs were discussed for a new multipurpose stadium to be built at the fairgrounds. This one, a more baseball-oriented stadium, was passed over for a football-only stadium. (Courtesy of Memphis and Shelby County Room, Memphis Public Library and Information Center.)

6

THE MEMPHIS RED SOX

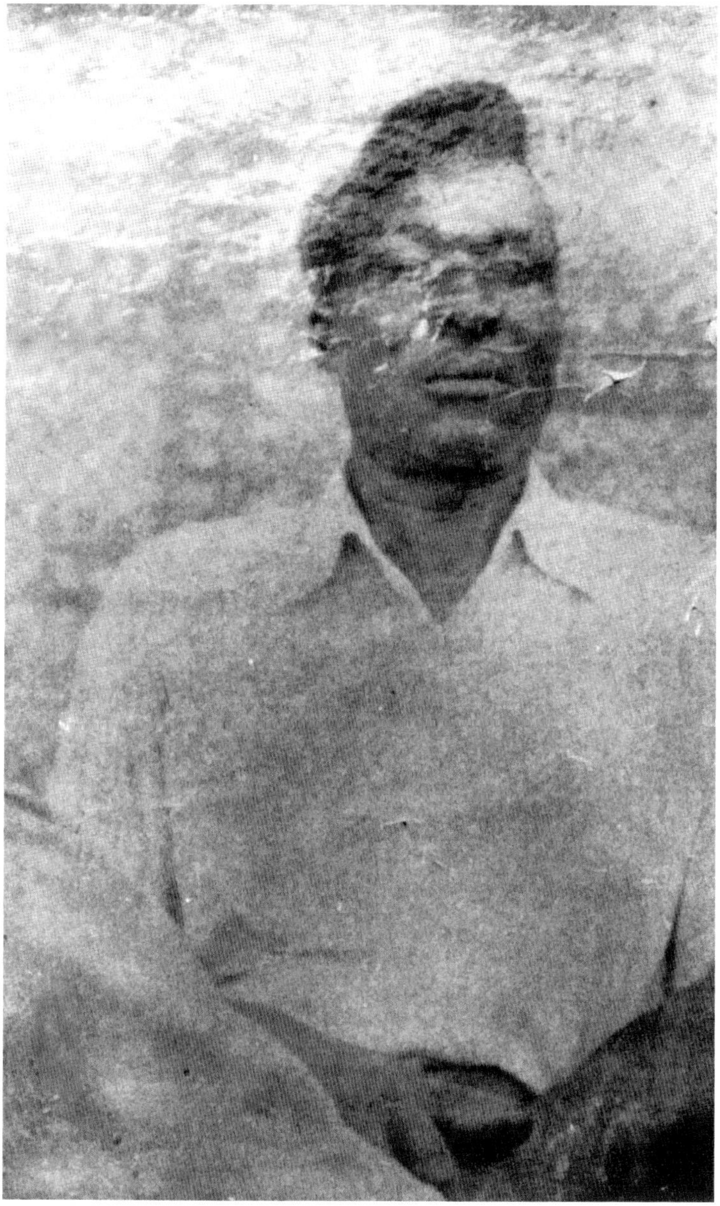

This early-1920s photograph of a Memphis Red Sox player is identified only as Charles. He is holding a baseball in his right hand. As early as the 1880s, several attempts were made to organize a southern African American league of baseball. A Birmingham newspaper advertised in 1904 that the Negro team from Memphis would be in town to play a series of games with the Birmingham Giants. The larger growth and success of baseball going back to after the Civil War was always mirrored in the African American community. (Author's collection.)

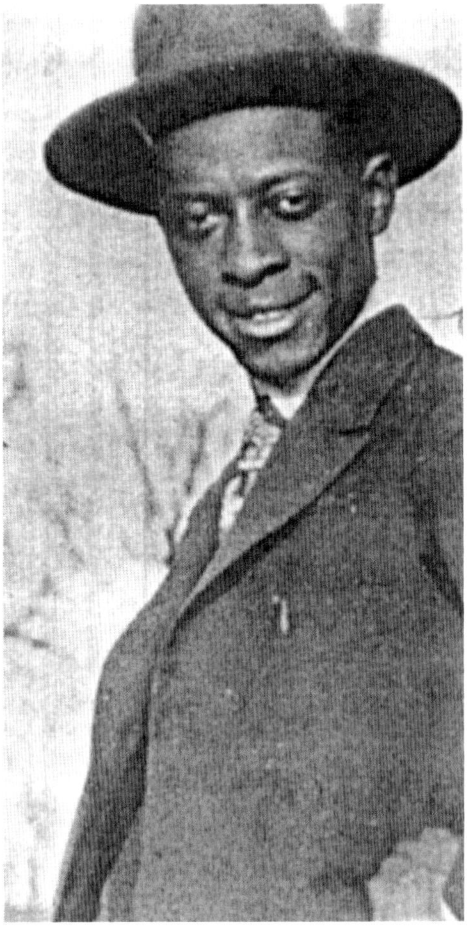

In 1932, the Martin brothers of Memphis purchased the Memphis Red Sox baseball club from C.T. Lewis. In part, the sale to the Martins was due to loans made to Lewis, who could not meet the payments. Running a baseball club that depends on barnstorming games and the weather could be a risky business. (Author's collection.)

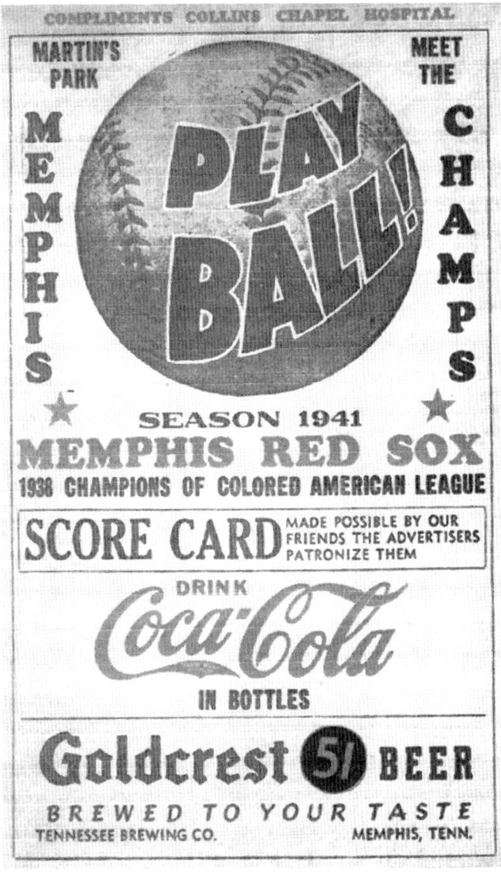

This example of a scorecard from a Negro-league team is a rare find. It provides some facts: the ballpark was already called Martin Stadium in 1941, and it very plainly states that Memphis claims the championship for the 1938 season. (Author's collection.)

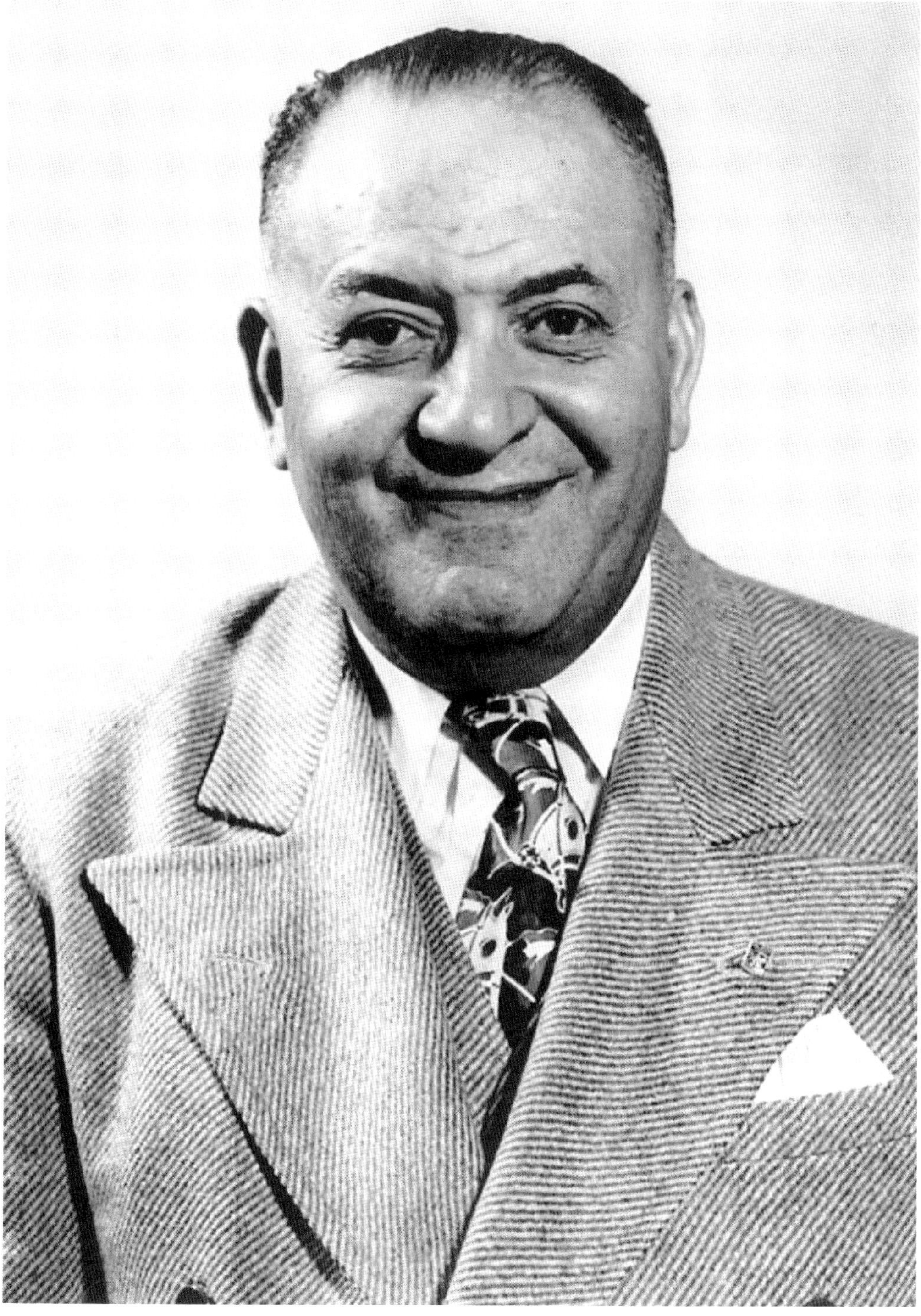

After an unfortunate run-in with the Crump political machine, Dr. J.B. Martin felt it best to move on. Martin went to Chicago and became the president of the Chicago American Giants of the Negro American League in April 1946. (Author's collection.)

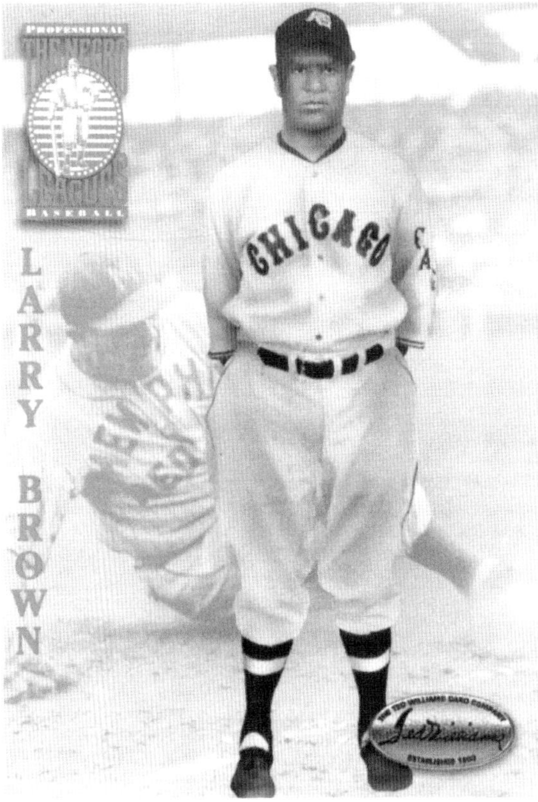

Larry Brown was from Pratt City, Alabama, near Birmingham. His baseball career began with the 1919 Birmingham Black Barons. Then it was on to Chicago and, later, Pittsburgh. For Brown, signing with the Memphis Red Sox in 1923 became a baseball marriage made in heaven. First, he was an outstanding catcher in the early 1940s; then, Brown became the manager of Memphis and excelled in teaching the younger players the essence of the game. Brown was Memphis baseball in the 1940s. (Author's collection.)

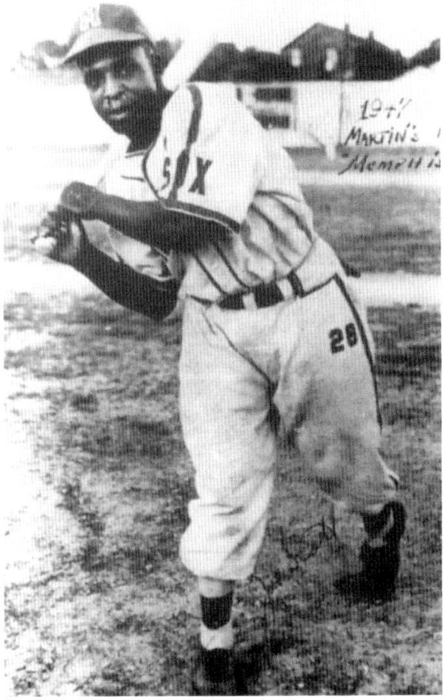

Joe B. Scott was born and raised in Memphis. He would later attend Tilden Tech High School in Chicago. He played in the high school championship game at Wrigley Field. With an offer to attend Marquette University, Scott chose the Air Force. After World War II, he played for the New York Black Yankees but soon returned to Memphis and the Red Sox team. Joe retired after the 1951 season. Like Buck O'Neil before him, Joe has become an ambassador for all of baseball. (Courtesy of Joe B. Scott.)

Marshall Bridges was a first baseman for the Red Sox in the early 1950s. Bridges sometimes pitched if the manager needed him, and it would be his pitching that would take him to the major leagues. Bridges made the team with the St. Louis Cardinals in 1958. His best year was 1962 with the New York Yankees. Somewhere along the line, Bridges acquired the nickname "Sheriff." (Author's collection.)

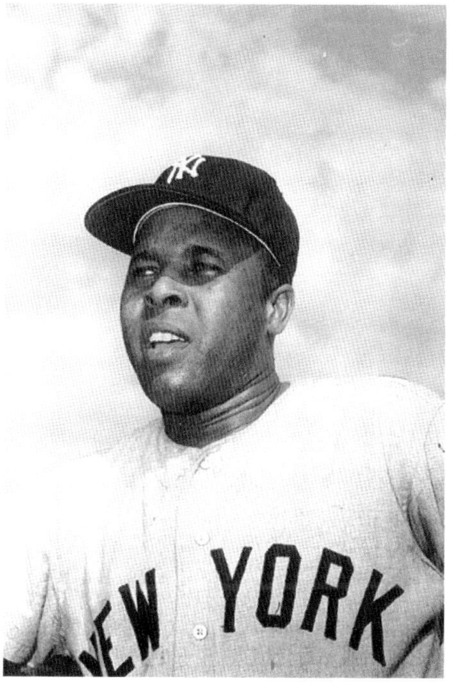

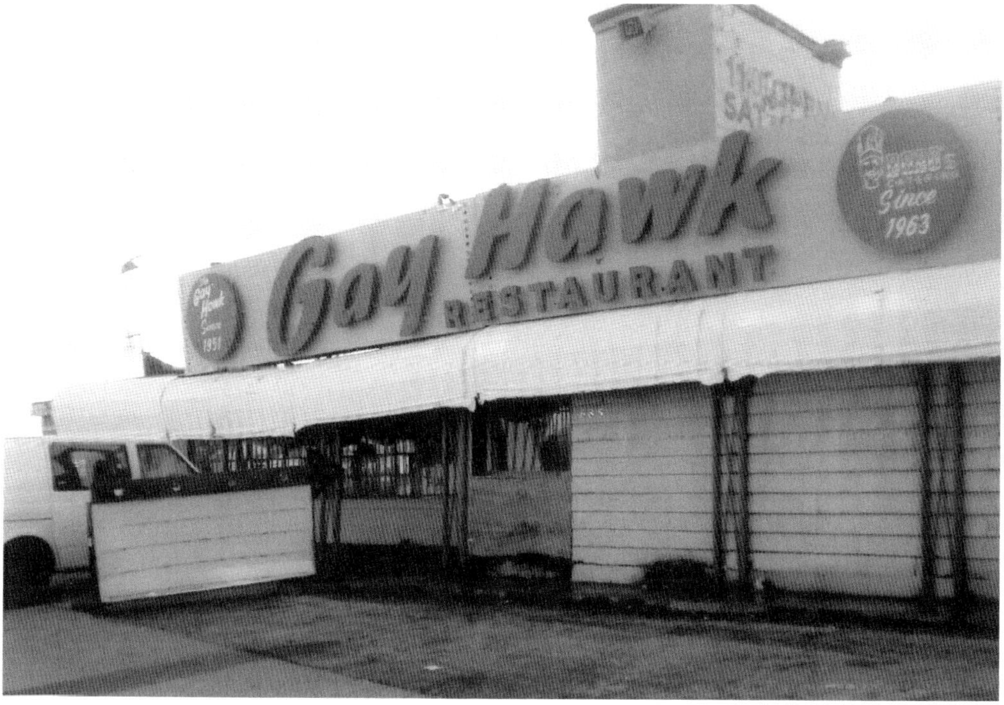

Located at 685 South Danny Thomas Boulevard, the Gay Hawk Restaurant was a favorite stop for the Memphis Red Sox players. As it was located not far from Martin Stadium, players living in the apartments down the left-field line could walk there to eat. The Gay Hawk opened in 1951 and was also a favorite eatery for Memphis musicians at the Stax Studio. (Author's collection.)

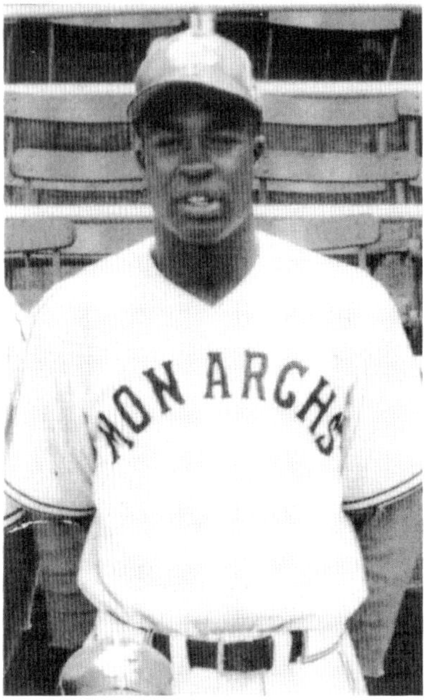

Born in Memphis, Nat Peeples attended Le Moyne College in 1948 but left to play baseball for the Memphis Red Sox. Peeples will always be remembered as the African American player who broke the color barrier in the Southern Association. Peeples had a good spring training with the Crackers and pinch hit in the first game against the Mobile Bears. The next night, he started in left field but did not get a hit in four at bats. When the team got to Atlanta, Peeples was optioned to Jacksonville and never played again in the Southern Association. (Author's collection.)

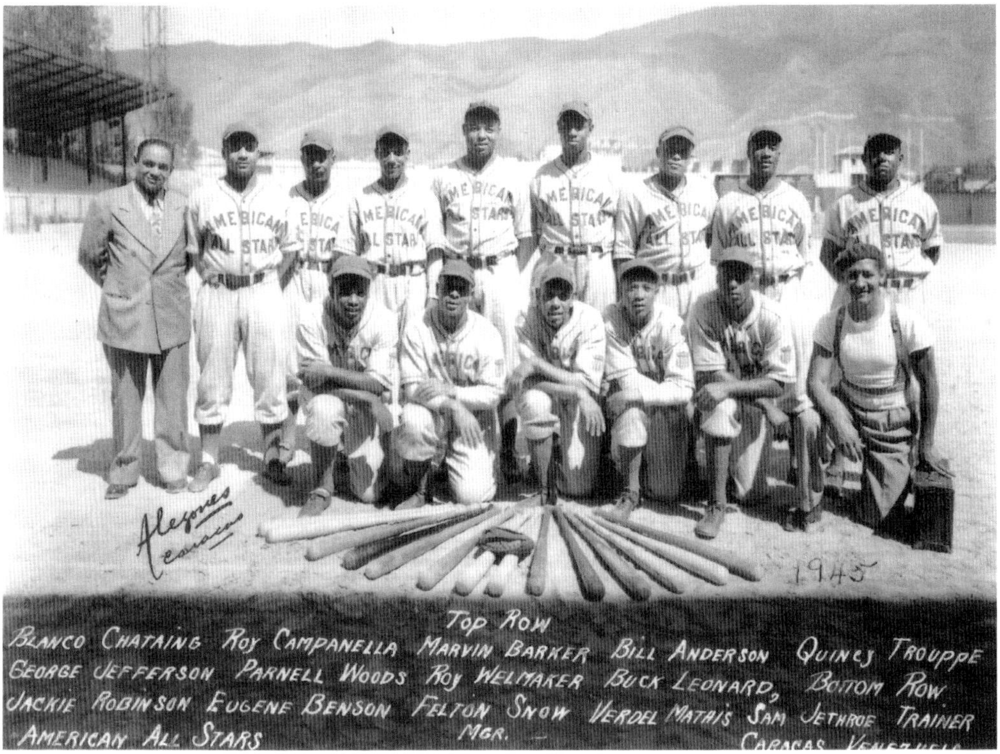

Arguably the best left-handed pitcher in all of Negro League baseball in the 1940s was Verdell Mathis. When he was a small boy, he and his family moved to Memphis from Arkansas. Growing up, he idolized Satchel Paige. As a pitcher for the Memphis Red Sox, Verdell pitched against Paige many times, beating him on several occasions. (Author's collection.)

Cowan "Bubba" Hyde was from Pontotoc, Mississippi. At the age of 14, he tried out for the Memphis Red Sox team. Memphis wanted him, but he was too homesick to stay. After college, Hyde played for the Cincinnati Tigers under Ted Radcliff. Like Brantley, Radcliff brought Hyde along to Memphis. Hyde played in the Memphis outfield from 1938 to 1950 and made the East-West All-Star game in 1943 and 1946. (Author's collection.)

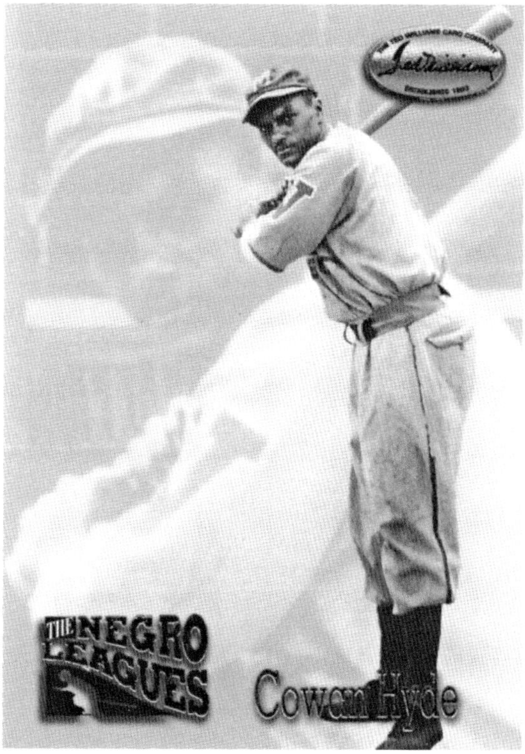

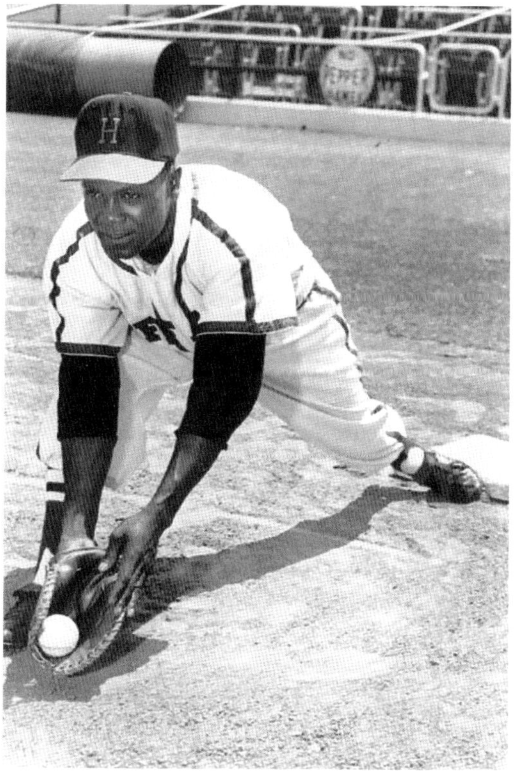

Bob Boyd joined the Memphis Red Sox in 1947. Over the next three years, he never batted under .350; this led to his signing with the Chicago White Sox. Boyd spent eight years in the major leagues. His best season was with the Baltimore Orioles in 1957, when he batted .318. Boyd earned the nickname "the Rope" for the screaming line drives he hit. (Author's collection.)

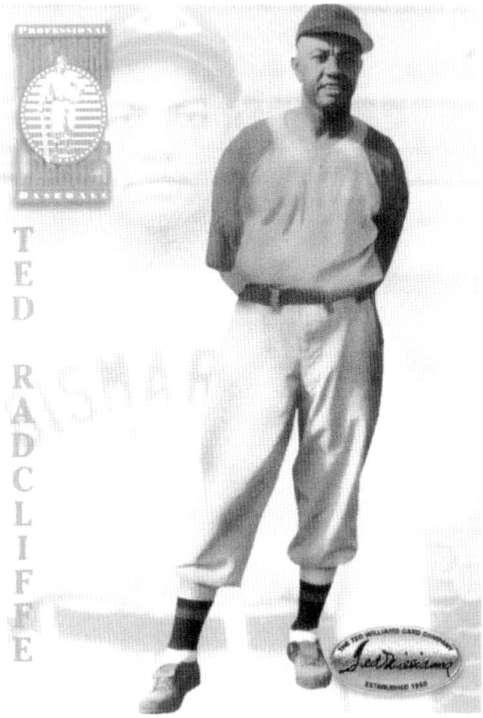

One of the icons of Negro League baseball is Ted "Double Duty" Radcliff. His longevity in the game and his ability to pitch and catch made him a legend. Radcliff led Memphis to its only championship in 1938 during a three-year stint from 1937 through 1939. The Red Sox played the first three games of the championship series with Atlanta, winning all three. Atlanta refused to play another game, and Memphis declared itself the winner. (Author's collection.)

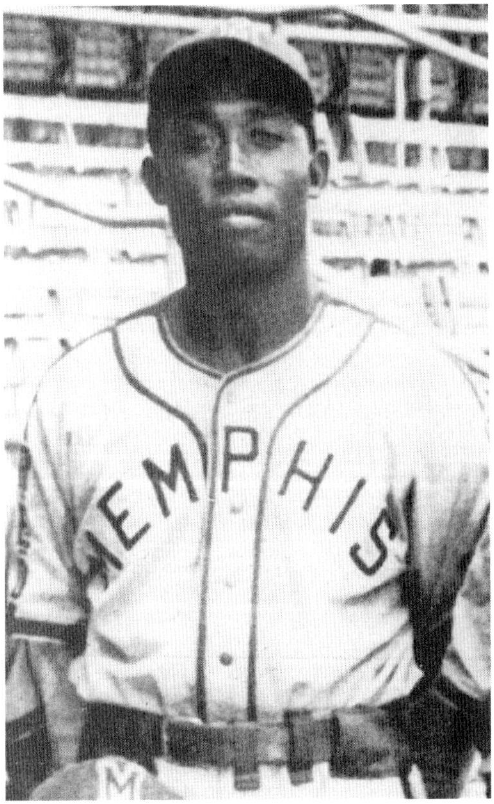

Casey Jones played his entire 16-year career with the Memphis Red Sox. He learned how to catch and served as backup for Larry Brown in the 1940s. Jones made the all-star squad in 1950 and 1951. (Author's collection.)

Felix "Chin" Evans pitched several seasons for the Memphis Red Sox. His 1946 record of 15-1 gained him the starting job in the all-star game. Evans was also known as a good hitter, able to play the outfield in between pitching turns if needed. (Author's collection.)

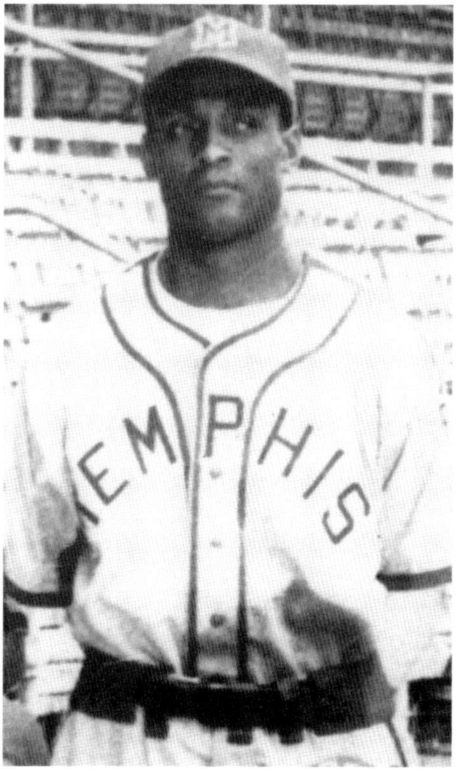

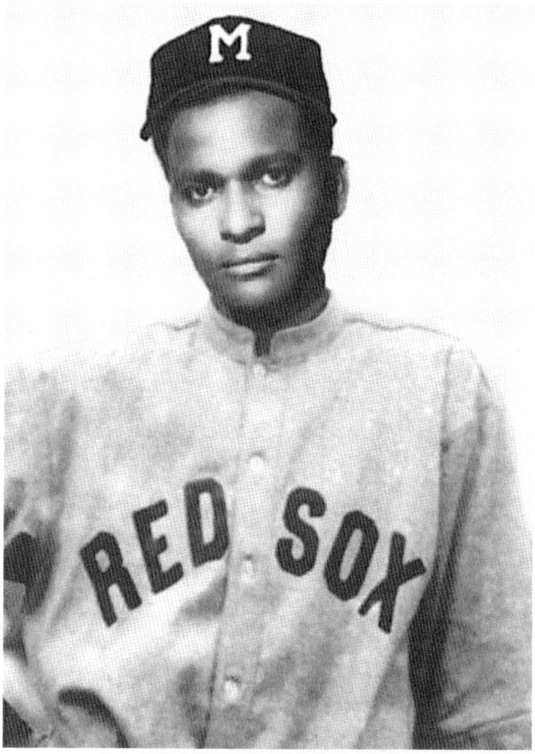

At the age of 17, Charley Pride began his baseball career with the 1953 Memphis Red Sox. In 1954, he played for the Louisville Clippers. The Louisville club needed a dependable bus, so Pride was traded to Birmingham, basically for a bus. After Army duty, Pride returned to the Memphis Red Sox in 1958. After several years in low-level minor-league baseball, Pride made an unlikely career change to country music. He was a pioneer in baseball, and he would change country music as well. (Author's collection.)

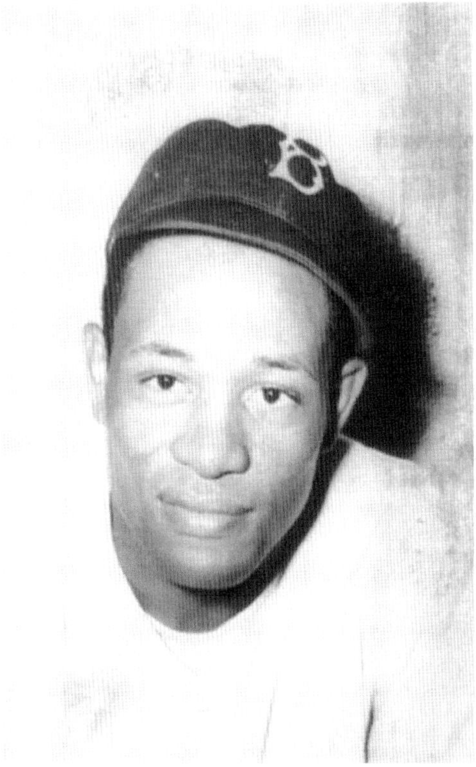

Dan Bankhead started out as a third baseman but switched to pitching in 1941. He was drafted in World War II but returned to baseball in 1946. During the 1946 off-season, Dan played baseball in Puerto Rico. His pitching in winter ball got the attention of the Brooklyn Dodgers. Later in August, Branch Rickey, general manager of the Brooklyn Dodgers, flew to Memphis to see Bankhead pitch. Rickey paid the Red Sox $15,000 for Bankhead. On August 27, 1947, Dan became the first African American to pitch in the major leagues. (Author's collection.)

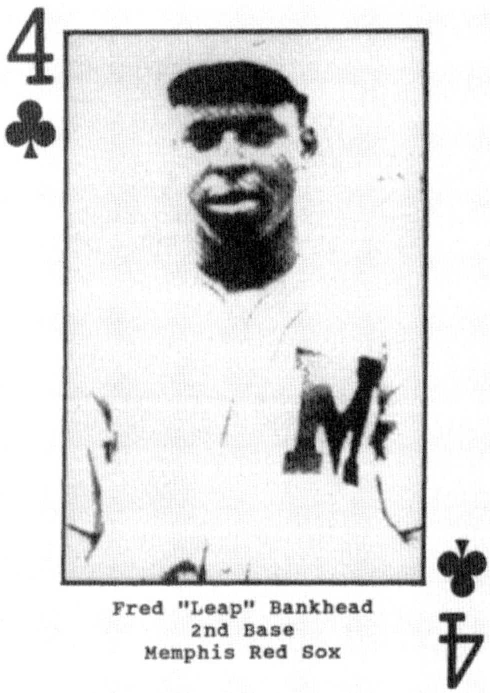

Fred Bankhead was one of five brothers from Empire, Alabama, who played Negro-league baseball. He played nine straight seasons for the Red Sox. In 1942, Bankhead was selected to the East-West All-Star Team. (Author's collection.)

St. Louis native Russell Mosley signed out of high school with the St. Louis Cardinals in 1955 and was sent to Albany, Georgia. Unfortunately, Mosley was cut before the season and planned to return home. Another player told Russell about the Memphis Red Sox. On the trip back to Missouri, they stopped in Memphis, and Russell tried out for the team. He made the squad and played infield for the Red Sox for three seasons, from 1955 to 1957. His manager was "Goose" Curry. (Author's collection.)

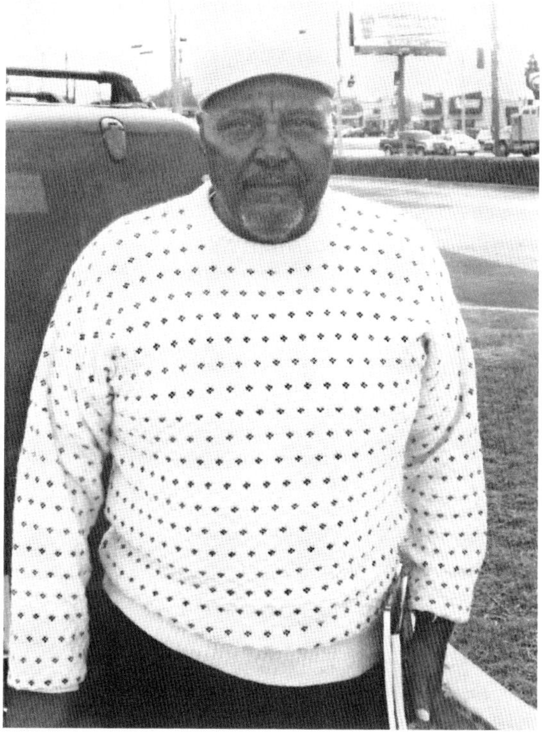

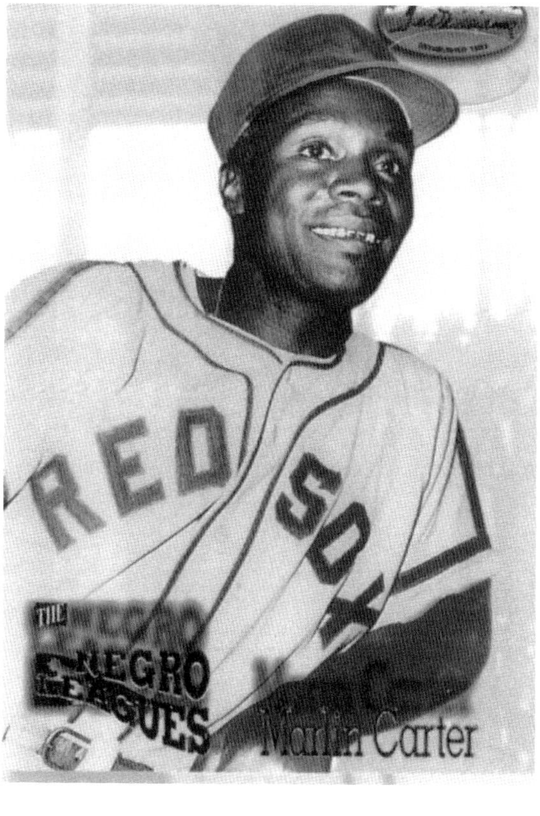

Marlin "Pee Wee" Carter was a fixture for the Memphis Red Sox in the 1930s and 1940s. He was a versatile infielder who consistently hit .300. Carter was named to the 1942 East-West All-Star Team as a Memphis Red Sox. He played for Memphis 8 out of his 19 years in Negro-league baseball. After his baseball career ended, Carter chose to stay in Memphis. (Author's collection.)

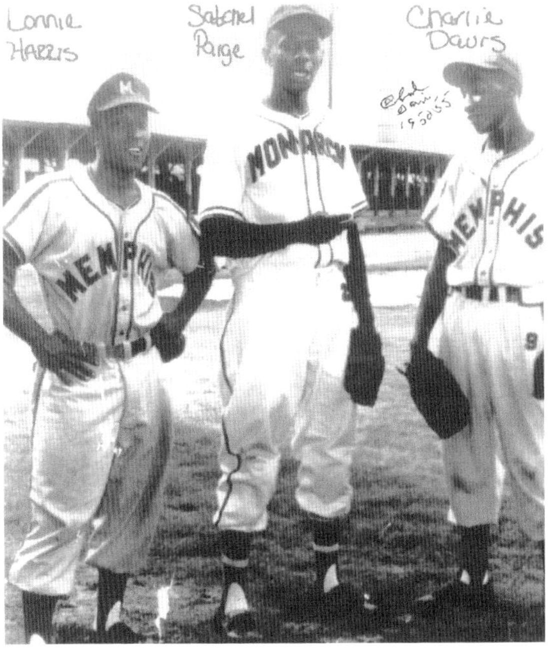

Charlie Davis (right) was from Fort Valley, Georgia. From 1950 to 1955, he pitched for the Memphis Red Sox, earning a place in the 1953 East-West All-Star Game. His pitching performances earned him the nickname "the Whip." Davis is shown here with teammate Lonnie Harris (left) and the great Satchel Paige of the Kansas City Monarchs. (Courtesy of Charlie Davis.)

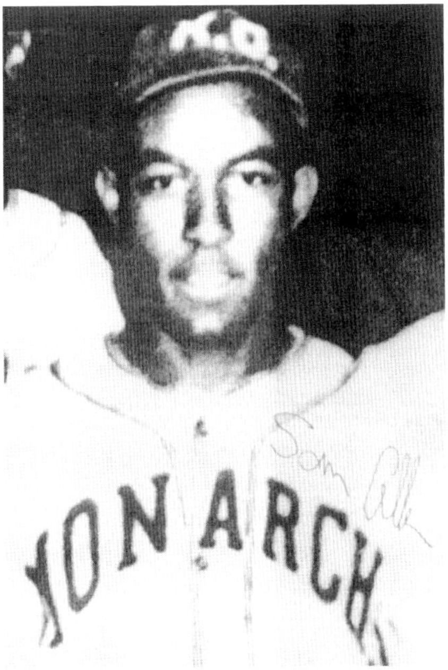

Sam Allen played for the Kansas City Monarchs, the Raleigh Tigers, and the 1959 Memphis Red Sox. Allen was an outfielder for Memphis along with Frank Williams, older brother of Hall of Fame player Billy Williams of the Chicago Cubs. (Courtesy of Sam Allen.)

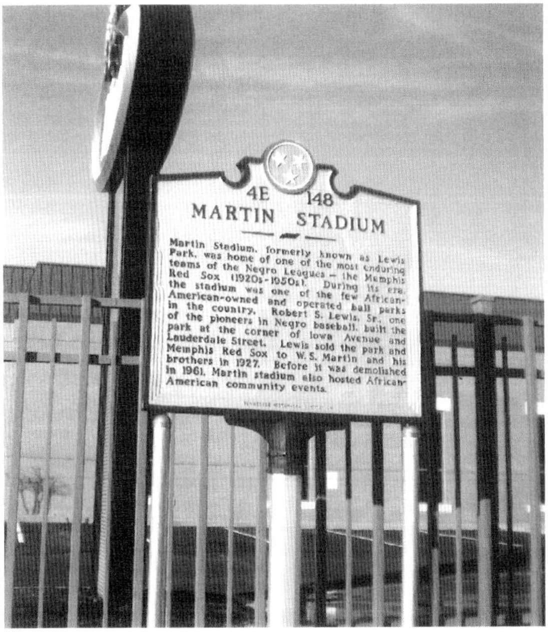

All that remains as a reminder of Martin Stadium is a plaque on Crump Boulevard. The concrete ballpark featured rooms behind the left-field bleachers that were used by players. The park was originally built and owned by C.T. Lewis and also called Red Sox Park. (Author's collection.)

7

The Memphis Blues

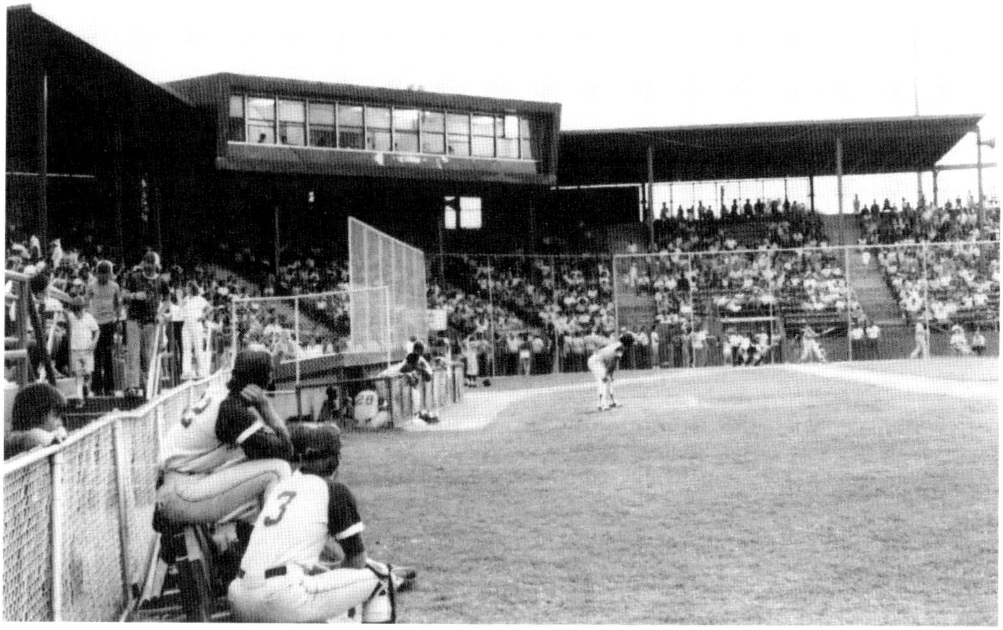

From 1961 to the spring of 1968, Memphis baseball fans sang the blues with no professional baseball team. Then, in 1968, professional baseball returned to Memphis; not as a member of the new Southern League but as part of the Texas League. There would be no connections to the past. The team's name, "Blues," was chosen for its association with the musical heritage of the city. Games were played at the Fairgrounds No. 3 newly enlarged baseball field, once used for high school games. The ballpark was given the official name of Blues Stadium. (Author's collection.)

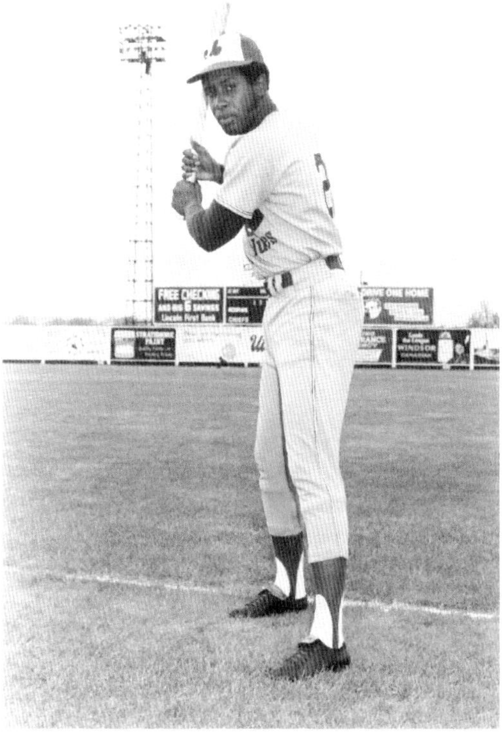

Jerry White played for the Memphis Blues in 1974 and 1975. He posted a very solid season in 1975, with a .297 batting average. His major-league career lasted 12 seasons. (Author's collection.)

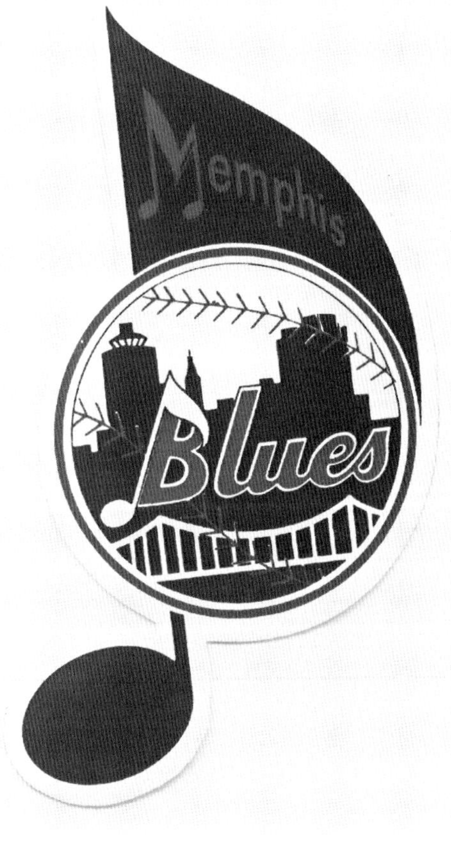

Professional baseball had been absent from Memphis for seven years, when a group headed by Jerry Foley of the Early Maxwell Associates returned the sport to Memphis. The New York Mets offered a working agreement for a team in the Texas League. The 1968 Memphis Blues would play in the Texas League with two other former rivals, Little Rock and Shreveport. (Author's collection.)

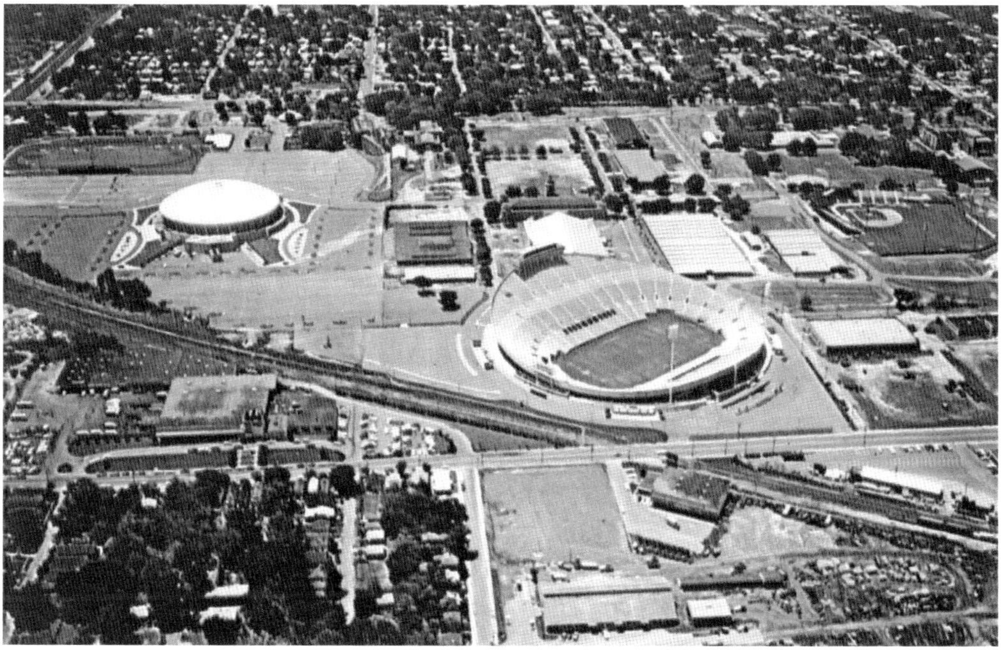

This early-1970s postcard shows an aerial view of the Memphis Sports Complex, the Coliseum, the Liberty Bowl, and Blues Stadium at the far right. Blues Stadium would go through many renovations as it evolved into Tim McCarver Stadium with the return of the Chicks. The stadium was adequate and functional, but many felt that aesthetically it left a lot to be desired. (Author's collection.)

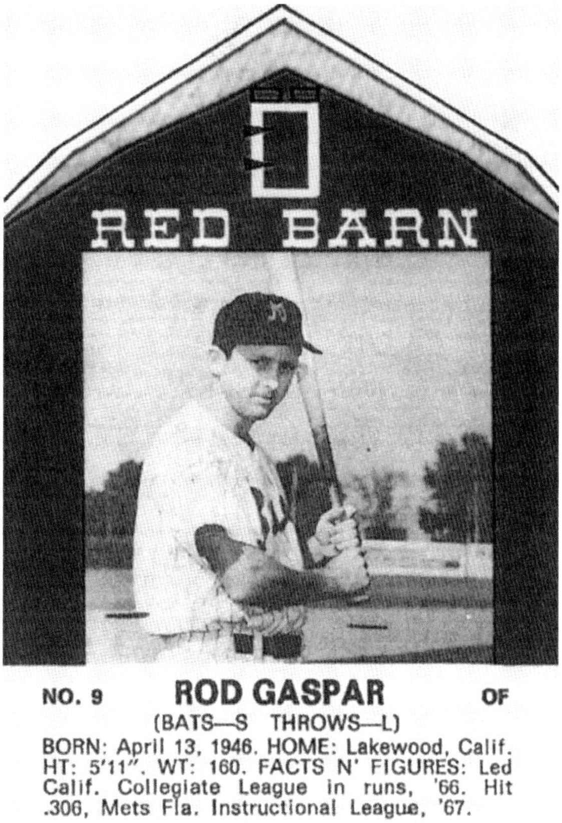

Red Barn, an early entry in the fast-food burger business, supported the 1968 Memphis Blues by issuing Memphis Blues baseball cards. Only eight cards are known to exist, with this Ron Gaspar being one of the 1968 Blues who played in the majors. There were a couple of Red Barn restaurants in Memphis; the most notable was on Lamar Avenue across the street from the Atlantic Mills discount department store. (Courtesy of Chris Drago.)

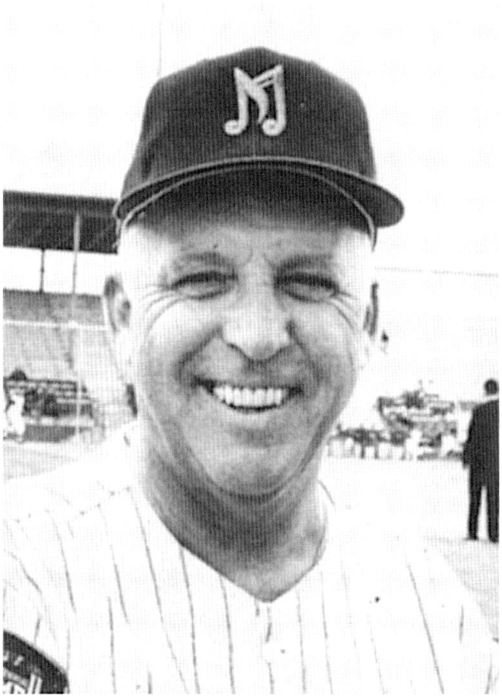

John Antonelli, a Memphis boy, was an outstanding pitcher for Catholic High School who signed and played for the Memphis Chicks. By 1951, John was out of baseball, but in 1969 he was asked to help coach the Blues just for home games, but he went on as interim and finally full-time manager in 1970. Baseball was in John's blood. After his tenure in Memphis, he continued to manage and coach in the Mets organization. (Author's collection.)

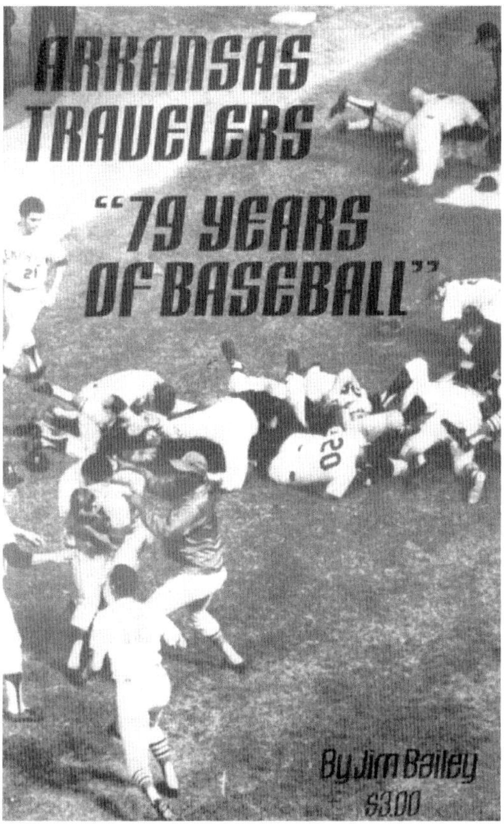

One of the most famous baseball brawls happened on August 29, 1968, in Little Rock. The Travelers had a commanding 12-game lead over Memphis when a Travelers pitcher hit Blues hitter Greg Goosen. Then all hell broke out. This was not a typical baseball bench-clearing brawl, where everyone huddles around the fighting players trying to pull them apart. The fight even caught the attention of the *New York Times*. Jim Bailey used this photograph of the incident on the cover of his *Arkansas Travelers: 79 Years of Baseball*. (Author's collection.)

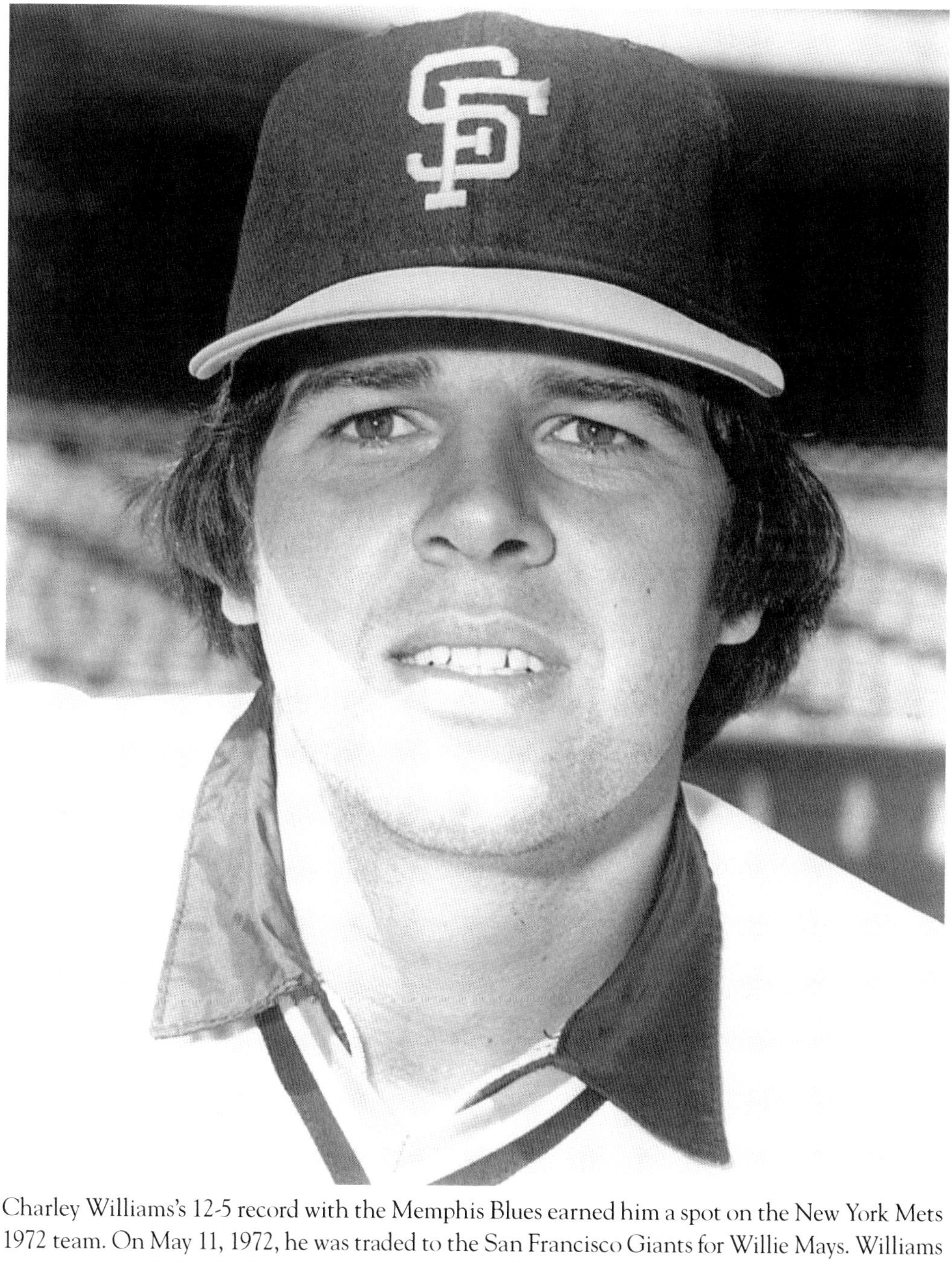

Charley Williams's 12-5 record with the Memphis Blues earned him a spot on the New York Mets 1972 team. On May 11, 1972, he was traded to the San Francisco Giants for Willie Mays. Williams went on to pitch for the Giants for seven years, but his place in baseball trivia will always be as the only player ever to be traded for Willie Mays. (Author's collection.)

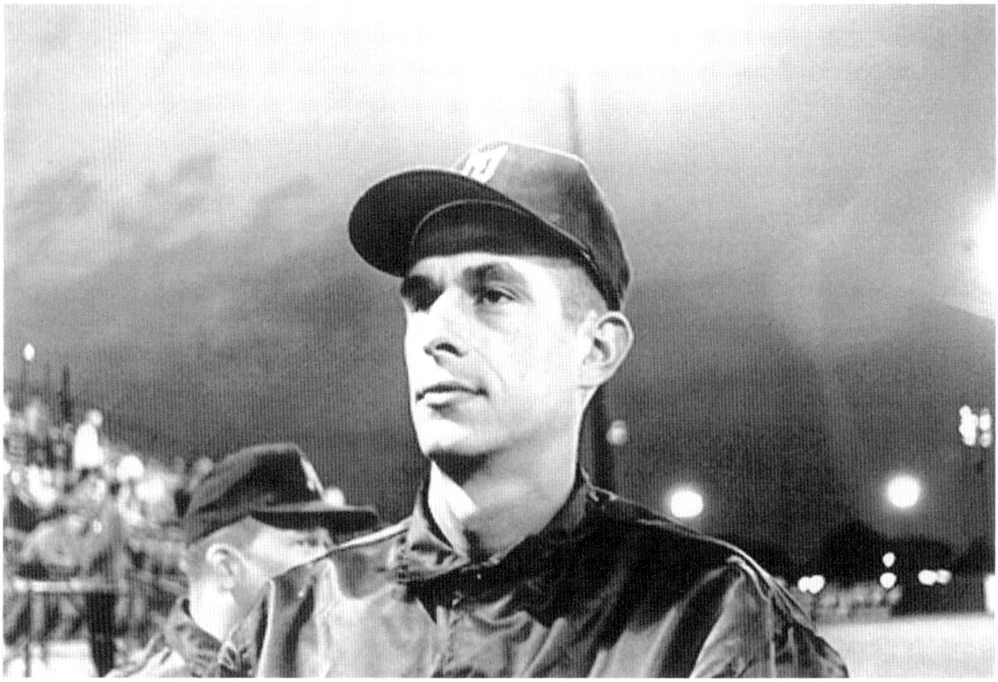

Dennis Musgraves was a member of the 1968 Memphis Blues. Musgraves had pitched in five games for the 1965 New York Mets, and in the fifth game he was the starting pitcher. He allowed only one run in seven innings but hurt his arm in the process. The injury would require two surgeries, and Dennis would spend the next six years trying to work his way back to the Mets. (Author's collection.)

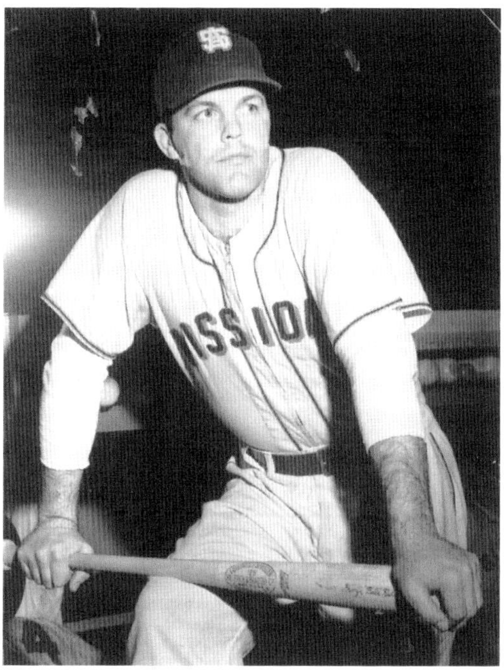

When Joe Frazier was announced as the new manager for the Memphis Blues for the 1973 season, it was not his first time in Memphis. Old Chicks fans would remember Frazier as an outfielder for the 1951 squad. Joe hit 13 home runs and batted in 86 runs. The Blues finished second under Frazier's leadership and then won the championship. Frazier's success with the Blues helped land him the Mets managerial job in 1975. Frazier replaced former Blues manager Ray McMillan. (Author's collection.)

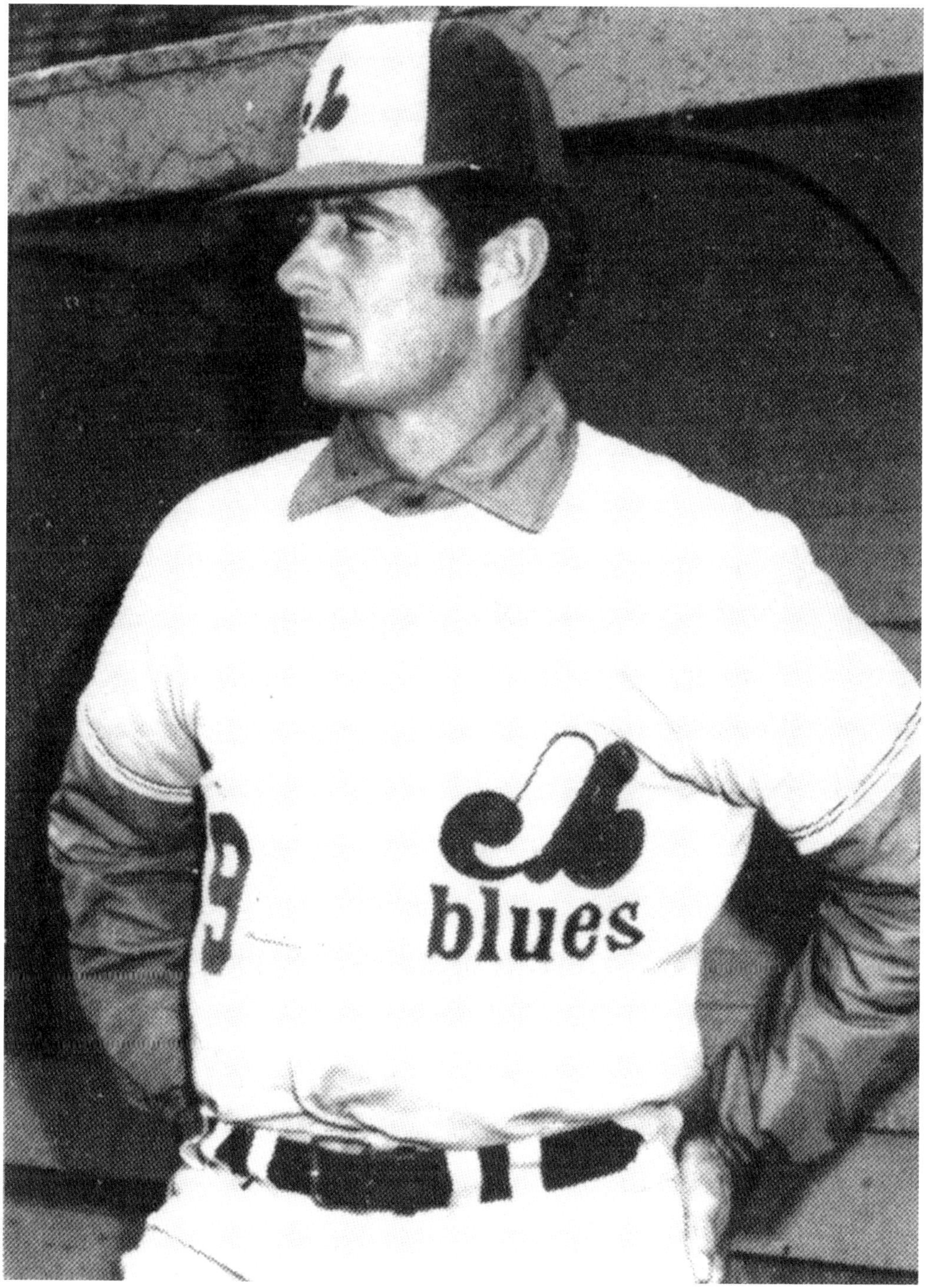

Karl Kuehl managed the Memphis Blues for two seasons. In 1974, the Blues finished first in the league, only to lose in the playoffs. Kuehl's successful seasons in Memphis factored into his being named manager of the Montreal Expos in 1976. That season for Montreal was a disaster, and Kuehl was fired before the end of the season. (Author's collection.)

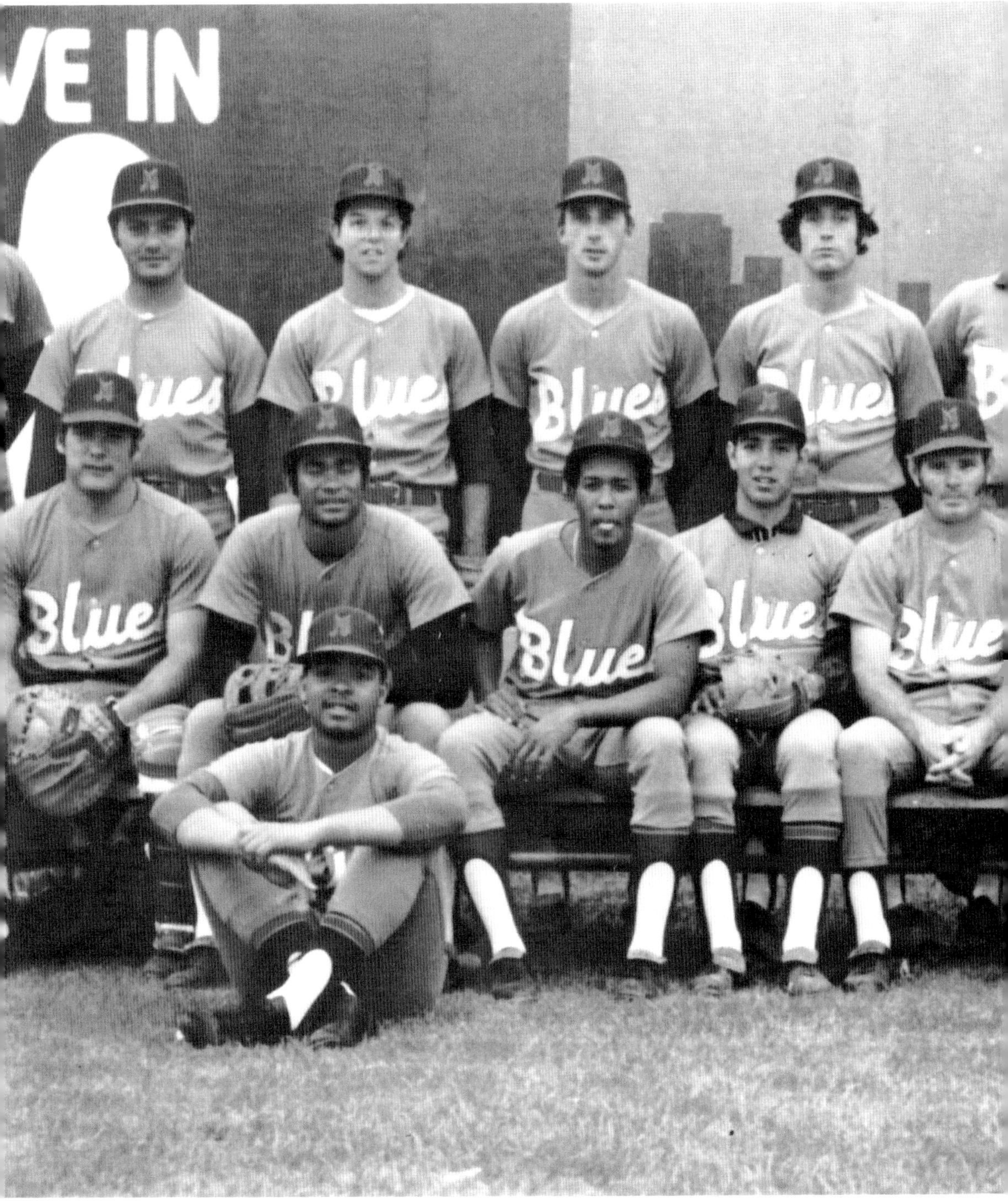

The 1974 Memphis Blues won the league championship. Led by manager Joe Frazier, the Blues finished second and then beat the San Antonio Brewers in a best-of-five playoff series. The Blues offensive was anchored by Gary Carter, Pepe Mangual, and Pat Scanlon. Starting pitchers Craig Caskey and Bob Gebhard were the leaders in wins, and reliever Dale Murray finished out

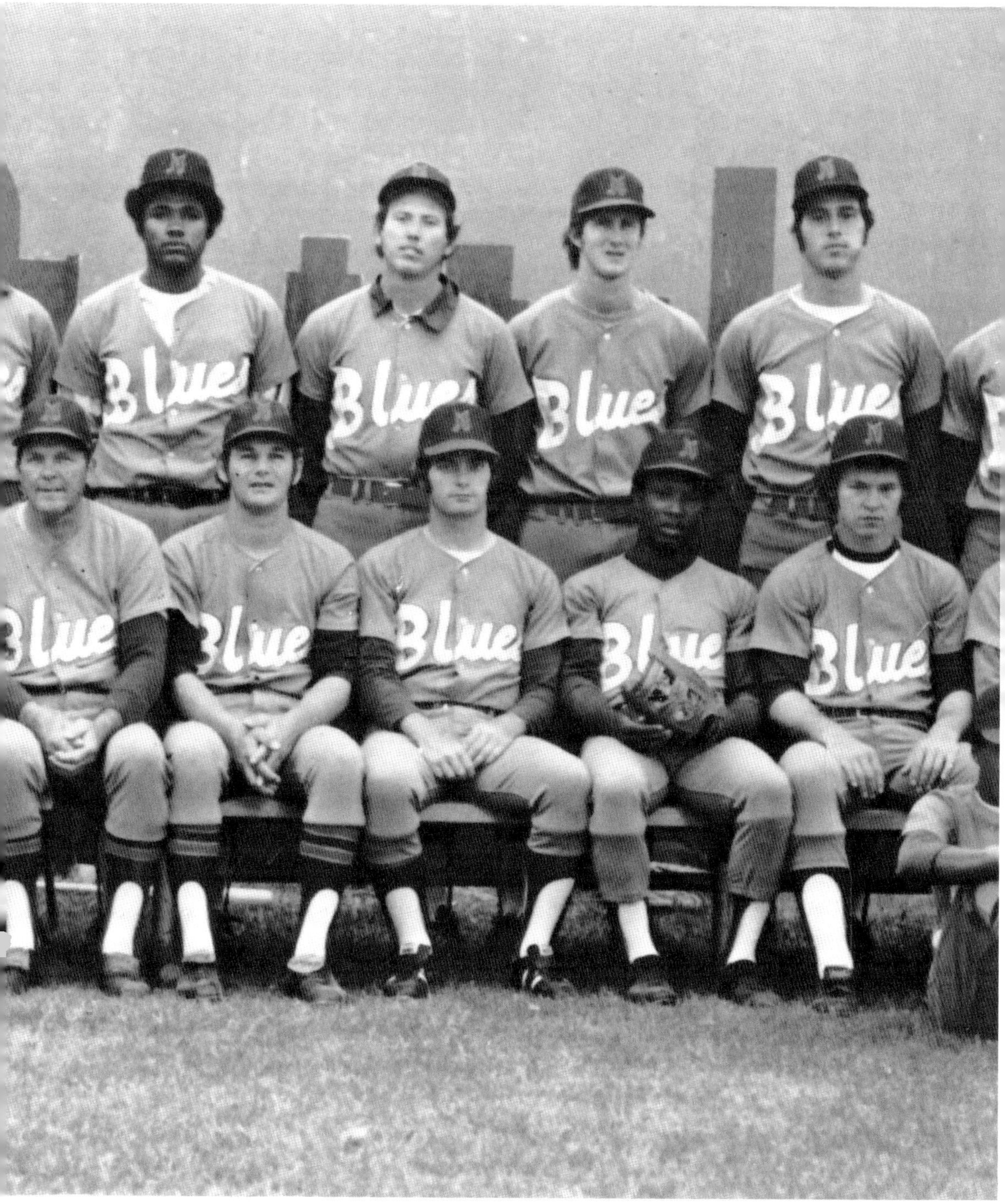

the close ones. Carter can be seen to the far left in the first row in his catcher's gear. Frazier is fifth from the right of Carter. (Courtesy of Memphis and Shelby County Room, Memphis Public Library and Information Center.)

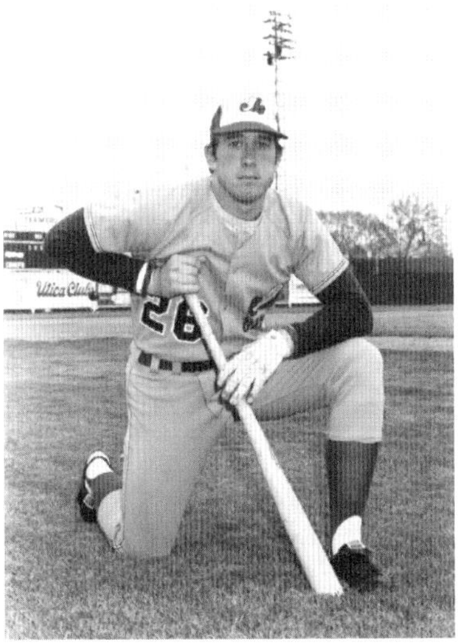

Gary Carter, a hall-of-fame catcher, came up through the Montreal Expos minor-league system. By 1974, Carter was with the Triple-A Memphis Blues and had an outstanding season with 23 home runs and 83 RBI, which led to a call-up to the Expos in September. Carter was in the majors to stay. In his book *The Gamer: An 11-Time All-Star's Inside Story of the Pain, Grit, Guts, and Glory of Life in the Majors*, Carter's only reference to his season in Memphis is "the Expos Triple A team." (Author's collection.)

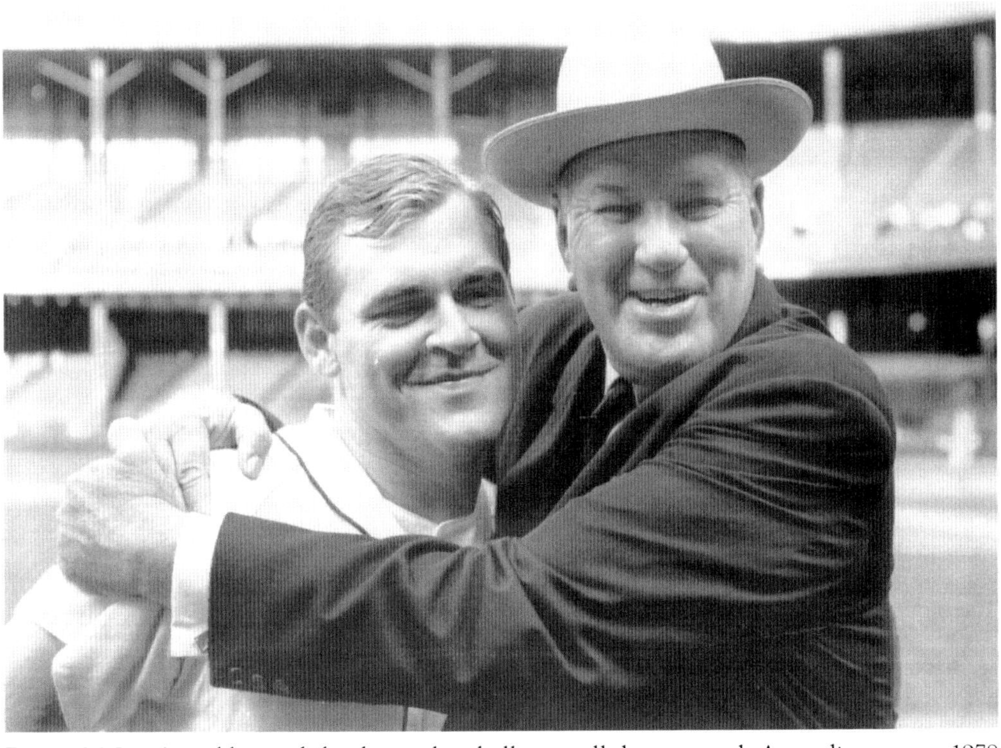

Denny McLain's problems while playing baseball are well documented. According to a c. 1978 article in *Memphis Magazine*, McLain and friend Jerry Bilton supposedly purchased the Blues. According to *Sports Illustrated*, McLain worked miracles, selling a record number of season tickets and upgrading concessions. Twenty games into the 1976 season, the Blues had made more money than in 1975. By season's end, though, the Blues were $335,000 in the red. Total debts of $460,000 led to the franchise being returned to the league. McLain is shown here during better days with Dizzy Dean. (Author's collection.)

In 1976, the Blues became the Triple-A franchise for the Houston Astros through the connections of Denny McLain. This picture shows Floyd Bannister wearing the Astros-influenced jersey—the Memphis Blues wore uniforms in shades of orange. (Author's collection.)

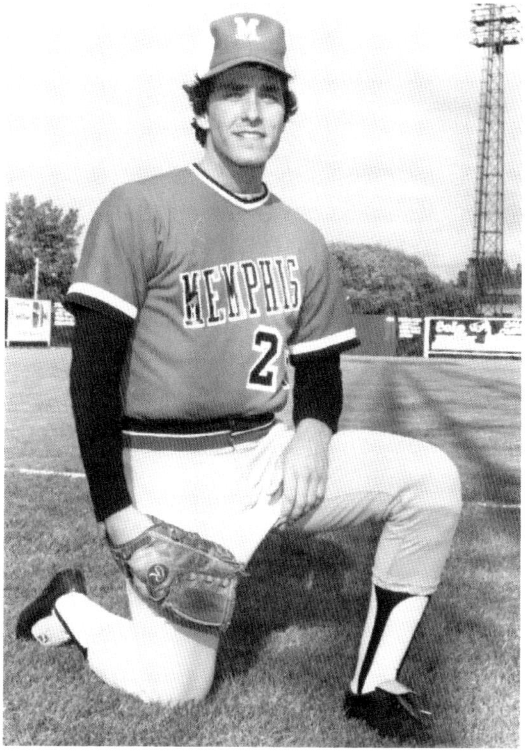

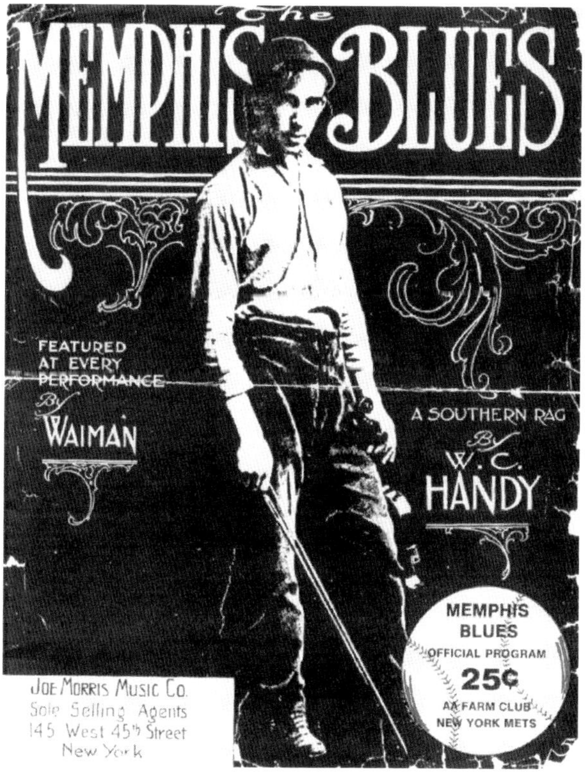

In 1968, when professional baseball returned to Memphis, the name Memphis Blues was chosen. No doubt it was the song "Memphis Blues" by W.C. Handy that inspired the name for the new team. Handy, a nationally recognized blues musician, had written a campaign jingle for Boss Crump. The tune was later changed with new lyrics to become "Memphis Blues." The cover for the 1912 sheet music was an inspiration for the 1973 Memphis Blues program. (Author's collection.)

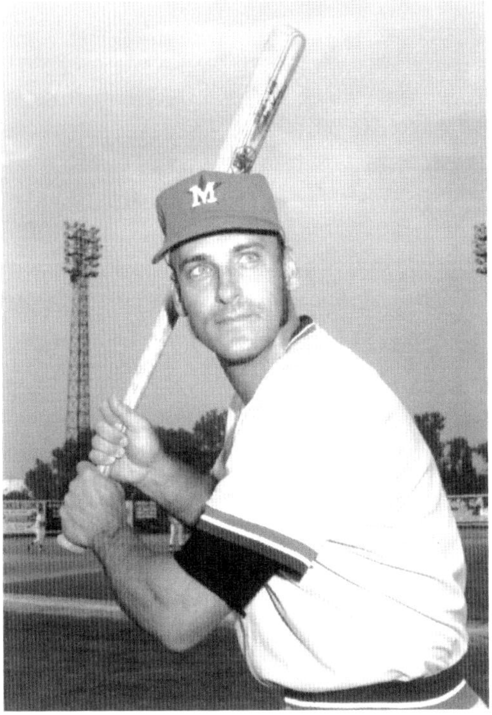

Art Howe (left) and Terry Puhl (below) were key members of the 1976 Blues team. Both men would go on to be mainstays of the Houston Astros for years. The black-and-white photographs do not do justice to the Astros-orange uniforms the Blues wore that year. (Both, author's collection.)

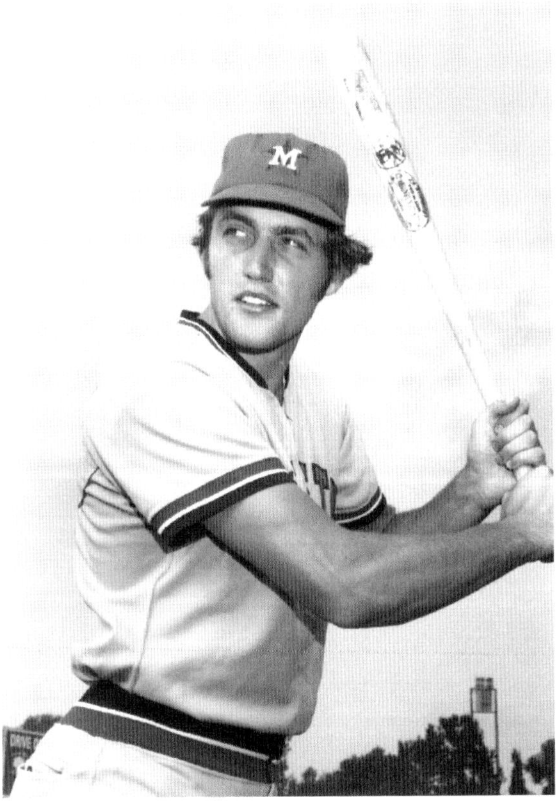

8

The Chicks Return

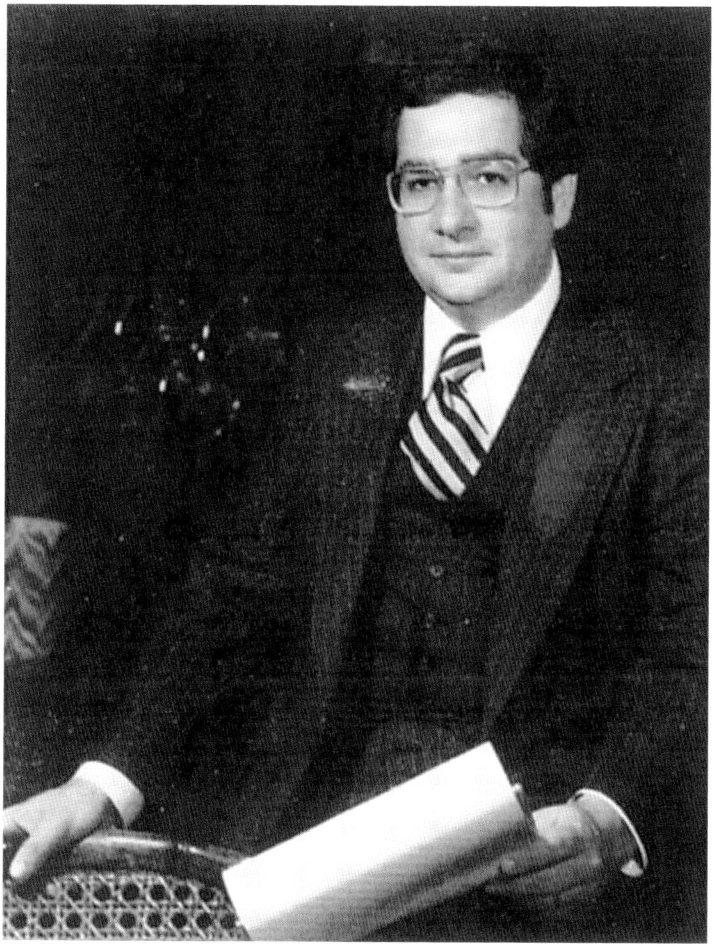

After a one-year absence from baseball, Avron Fogelman brought minor-league baseball back to Memphis. Instead of rejecting the past, the new team would embrace it. The Memphis Chicks would be reborn as part of the Southern League. Pete Gray was brought back to relive the past, and the history of the Chickasaws filled the program. Blues Stadium was renamed Tim McCarver Stadium. McCarver was a Memphis boy and a member of the 1960 Chicks. Some new twists were added to the Chicks team: Blooper and Sam the Medicine Man. (Author's collection.)

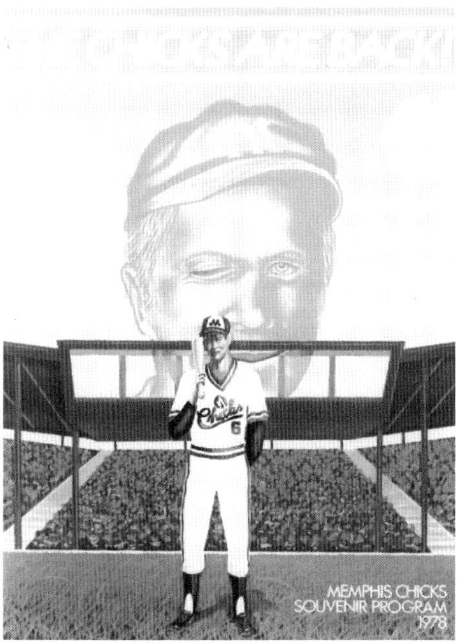

With the demise of the Memphis Blues after the 1976 season, Memphis became the largest city in the nation without a professional sports team. Avron Fogelman and his business associate Dean Jernigan together acquired a team in the Southern League and a major-league affiliation with the Montreal Expos. A contest was held for fans to select the new team's name. The majority selected Chicks—to no one's surprise—and Memphis was back where it belonged. (Author's collection.)

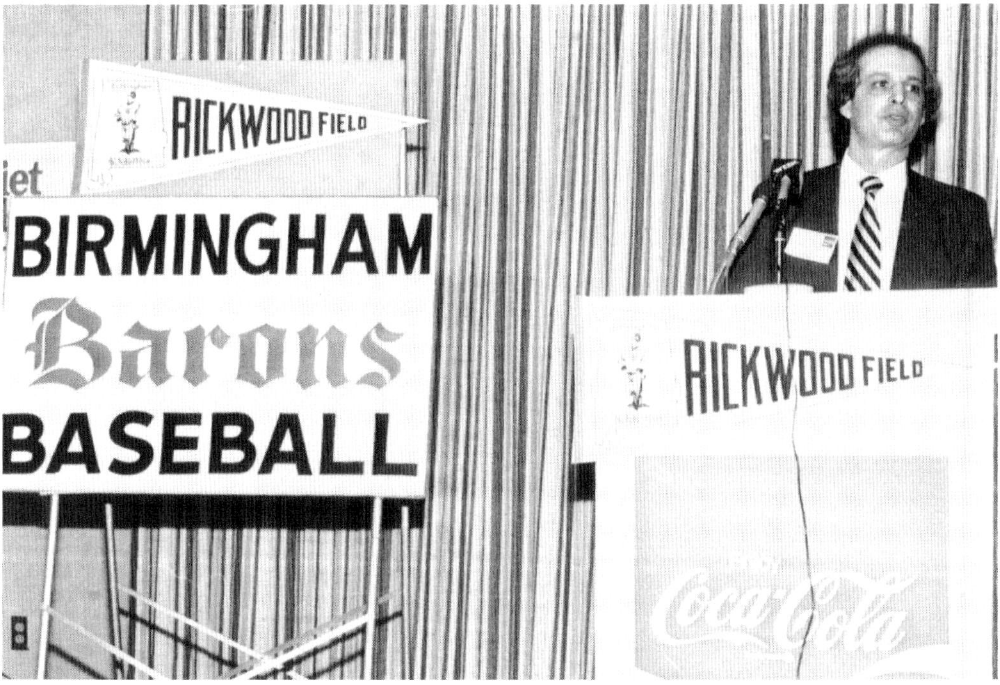

Art Clarkson served as assistant general manager for the 1976 Memphis Blues. Clarkson left Memphis after the demise of the Blues, but Avron Fogelman brought the master of promotions back to Memphis as the general manager of the 1978 Chicks. Clarkson did a wonderful job promoting the team and bringing fans out to the game; so good, in fact, that a group from Birmingham, Alabama, gave him the opportunity to bring baseball back to that city. (Courtesy of the Friends of Rickwood.)

Aaron Fogelman rightly receives much of the credit for bringing baseball back to Memphis in 1978. But the behind-the-scenes story is one of Dean Jernigan. It was Jernigan's talks with the Southern League that led to a franchise being offered. Then, Jernigan seized the moment, convincing Montreal to move a Double-A team to Memphis in the Southern League, which was no small accomplishment. (Author's collection.)

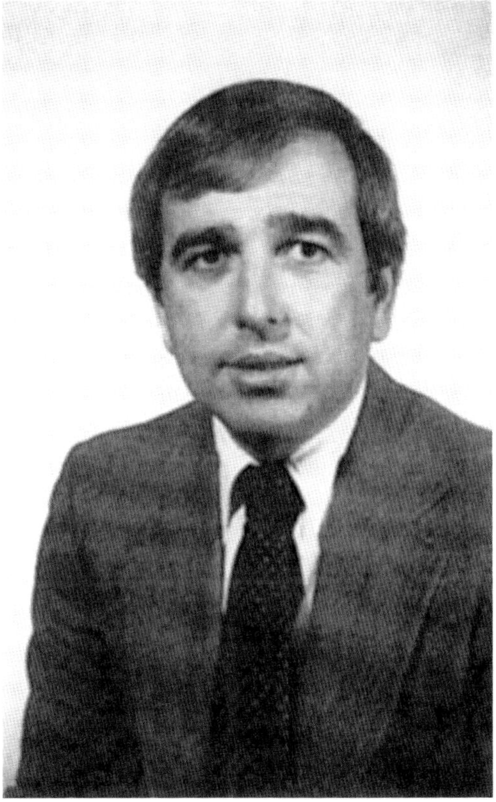

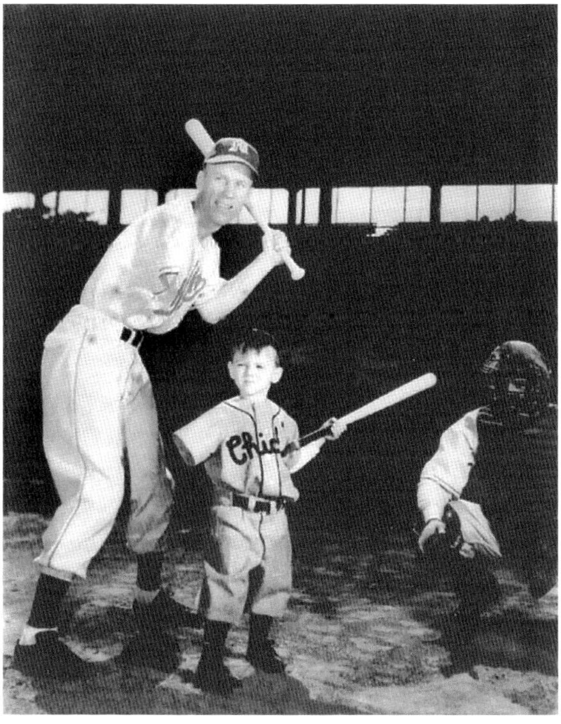

Pete Gray's return to Memphis was special—over 9,000 fans thought so. Gray last played for the Chicks in 1944, when he was league MVP. Gray and his remarkable career would be introduced to a new group of fans with the 1986 made-for-television movie, *A Winner Never Quits*. Memphis's warm welcome of him on April 15, 1978, said a lot about the fans. Gray is shown here encouraging a young boy, who also lost an arm in an accident. (Author's collection.)

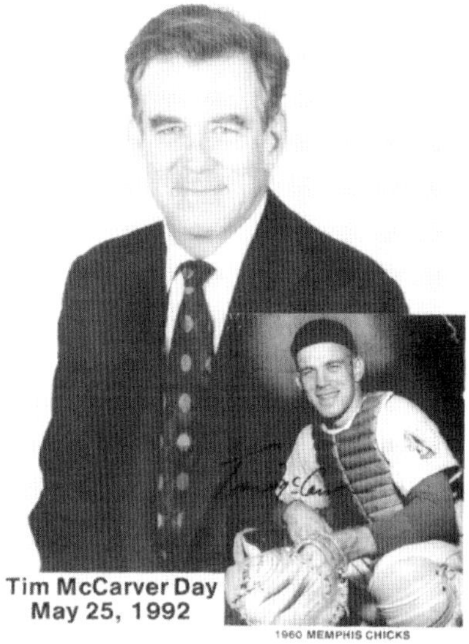

There was no doubt that a new name would have to be decided for Blues Stadium. The most popular choice was Tim McCarver Stadium, as Tim was arguably the most popular major-league player to come from Memphis. He was part of the 1960 Chicks and was still active as a player at the time. This photograph was the giveaway on Tim McCarver Night. (Author's collection.)

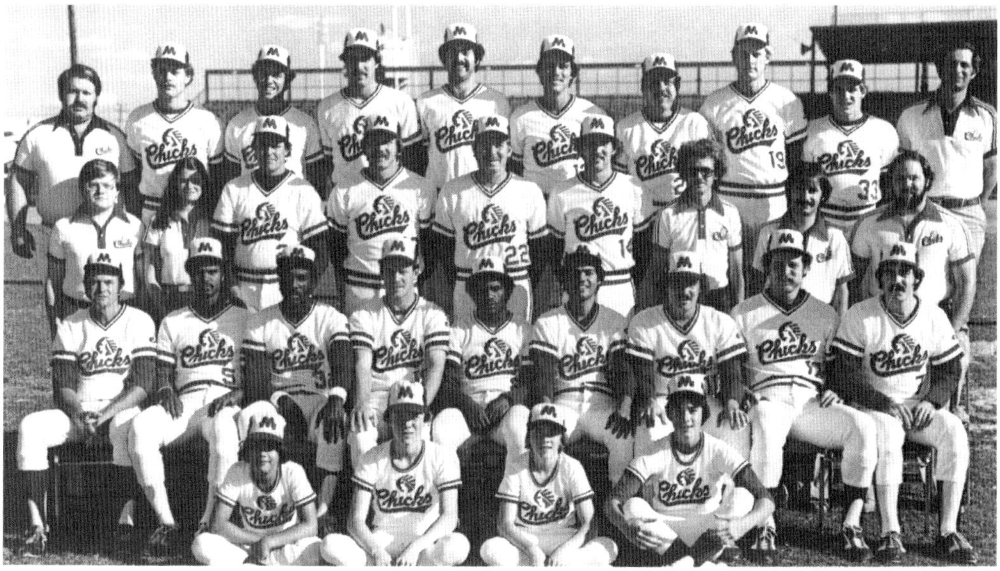

MEMPHIS "CHICKS" - AA SOUTHERN LEAGUE · 1979

(L to R) Bat Boys: Fred Sala, Donn Birmingham, Marc Riseling, Scott Ritchie, NOT PICTURED: Jarvis Wilson, Sean Doyle. FIRST ROW: Billy Gardner, Mgr., Godfrey Evans, Anthony Johnson, Steve Lovins, Tim Raines, Julio Perez, Rick Williams, Ray Crowley, Jeff Gingrich. SECOND ROW: Dave Chase, Office Mgr., Randye Ringler, Promotions Dir., Warren Hemm, Randy Schafer, Bryn Smith, Mike Finlayson, Jim McManus, Stadium Mgr., Rick Rizzs, Broadcaster, Emmo Hein, Assistant GM. THIRD ROW: Bill Armstrong, Trainer, Steve Michael, Pat Rooney, Dave Hostetler, Bob Tenenini, John Scoras, Doug Simunic, Charlie Lea, Rick Engle, Art Clarkson, Gen. Mgr.

Photograph by ROD PHILLIPS -Memphis

Undoubtedly, one of the best Chicks teams between 1978 and 1997 was the 1979 squad. Ten of the 1979 players would go on to play in the majors, and seven of them would have significant careers. The 1979 team easily won the first half of the season. The Chicks then played the Nashville Sounds for the Western Division Championship; the Sounds won two out of three games. (Author's collection.)

The 1979 Memphis Chicks were good, but they got much better when Tim Wallach arrived in June. Wallach had finished his college career leading Cal State Fullerton to the NCAA Championship. With no time in the lower minors to adjust to using wooden bats, Wallach had no trouble putting up big offensive numbers. His 18 home runs and 51 RBI in less than a half season were impressive. Wallach was that special player who lived up to being a first-round draft selection. (Author's collection.)

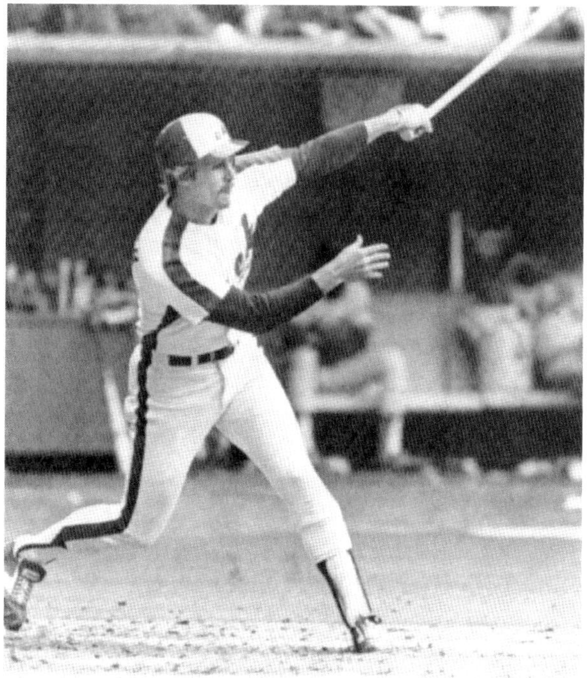

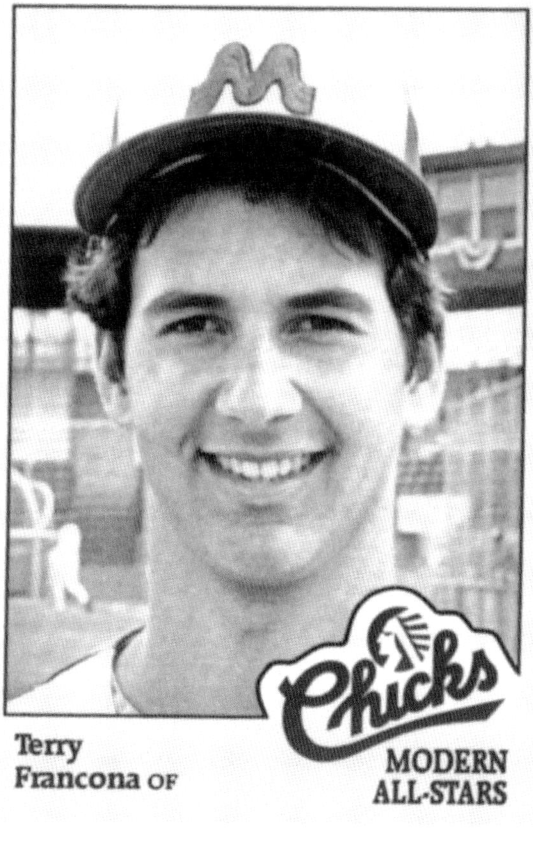

Terry Francona played left field for the Chicks in 1981 and 1982. He batted .300 in 1981 and a very impressive .348 in 1982. Most fans will remember his rifle arm throwing out runners at home plate from left field. Until the Boston Red Sox won the 2004 World Series, Francona was probably best remembered as Michael Jordan's manager with the Birmingham Barons. (Author's collection.)

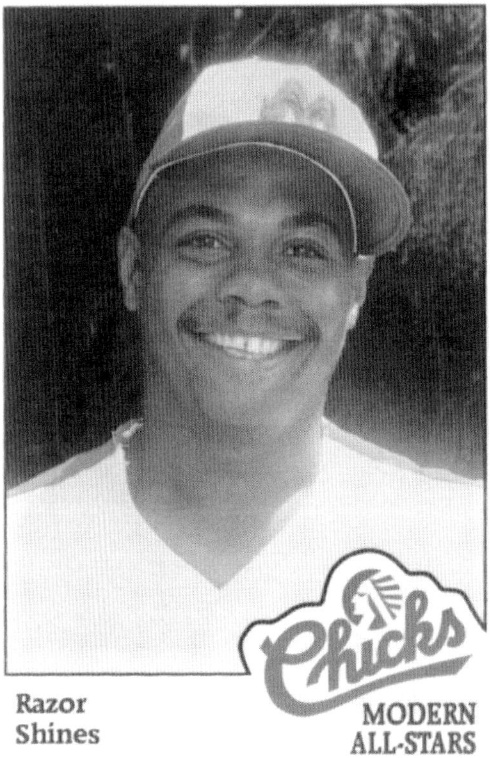

One of the all-time most popular Chicks was Razor Shines. He was the 1983 Chicks MVP even though he did not play with Memphis the entire season. His name, his personality, and his hustle made him a fan favorite everywhere he played. Who can forget, as Razor came up to bat, the playing of the Gillette Razor jingle by the Chicks organist? (Author's collection.)

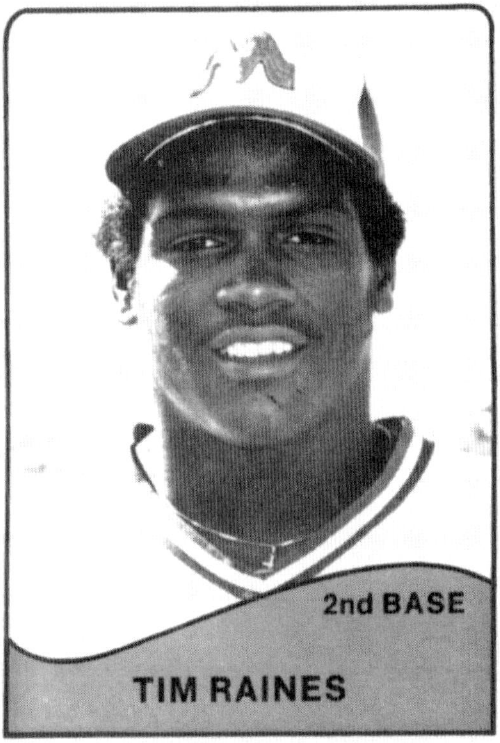

Tim Raines, one of the all-time best leadoff hitters in major-league baseball history, played for the Memphis Chicks in 1979. His season in Memphis included 104 runs scored, 59 stolen bases, and a .294 batting average. Raines went on to have a 23-year major-league career. (Author's collection.)

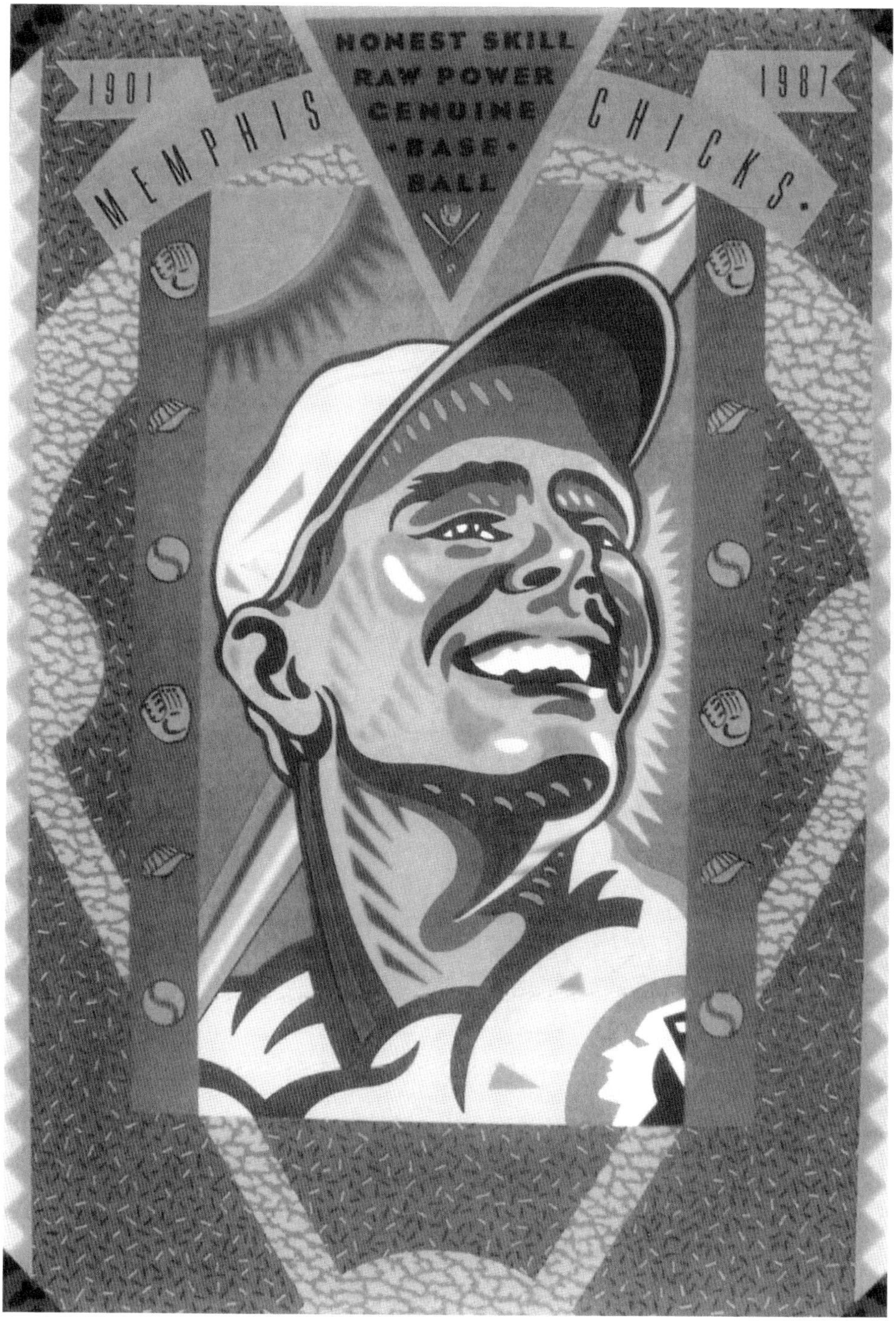

In 1982, one of the Memphis Chicks giveaway promotional items was this stylish Art Deco poster. It was just another free item for the local fans, but then the poster appeared on television, on the wall of Jerry Seinfeld's apartment above his computer. The story of how it got in Seinfeld's apartment would be worth hearing. (Author's collection.)

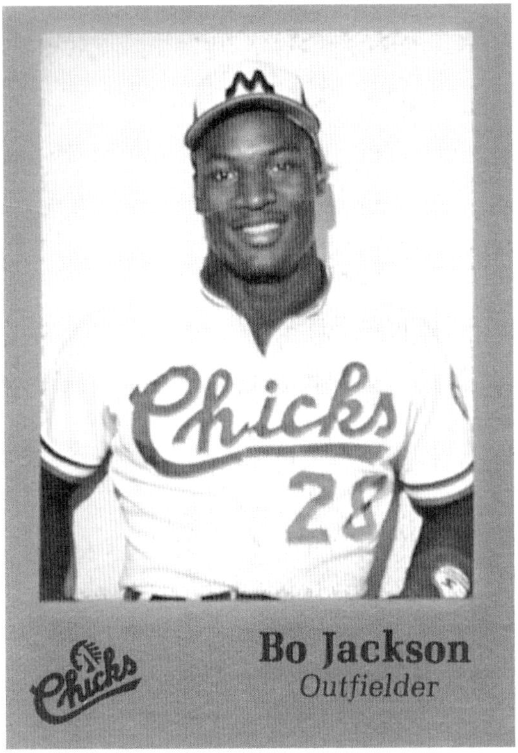

Memphis had not seen a new player create so much excitement with the fans since the arrival of Pete Gray in 1943 when Bo Jackson came to town. Jackson, the Heisman Trophy winner at Auburn and the no. 1 draft pick of the NFL's Tampa Bay Buccaneers, attracted more than just the die-hard baseball fans—everyone went to see what he could accomplish. Attendance not only increased in Memphis, but fans around the Southern League got caught up in "Bo Fever." (Author's collection.)

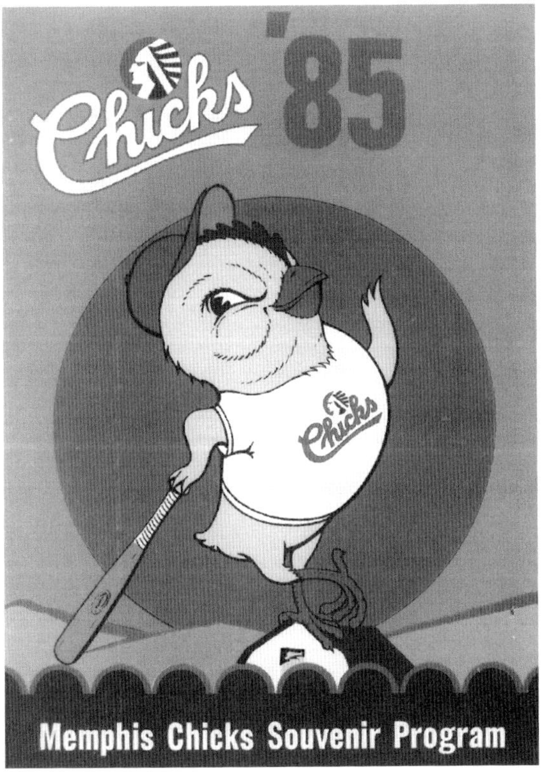

With the return of the Chicks to Memphis, many fans did not understand the meaning of the name. By 1978, the use of Chickasaws had been lost. It was not uncommon to explain to newcomers that Chicks was a nickname for Chickasaws, the Native Americans who had inhabited the Memphis area. New fans had to understand that the Chicks had nothing to do with chickens. When the 1985 program with a picture of a cute baby chick appeared, it was hard to make the argument that the name was not referring to the bird, and the name Chickasaws became a lost cause. (Author's collection.)

Only a true die-hard Chicks fan will remember the night in 1980 when a real baseball brawl broke out between the Chicks and the Charlotte Orioles. Charlotte's John Shelby had just hit a two-run home run to give the Orioles a 4-2 lead. Chicks pitcher Greg Bargar then threw the next pitch behind Cal Ripken Jr.'s head. Ripken charged the mound after being tripped up by Chicks catcher Tom Wieghaus. Six players were ejected, including Ripken—certainly not the Cal Ripken most remember. (Author's collection.)

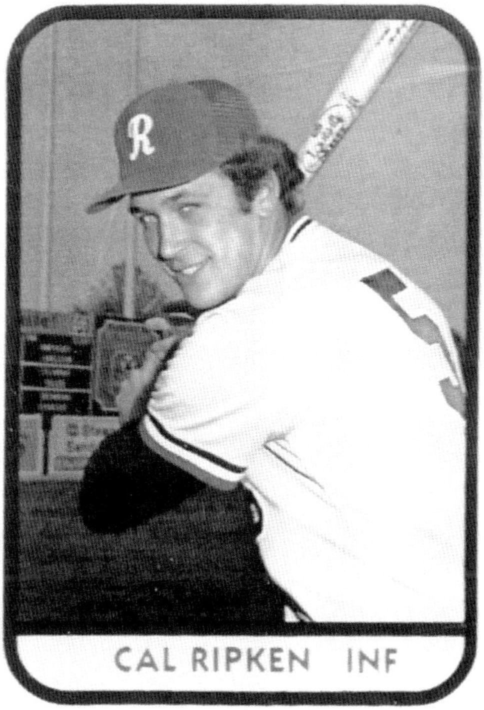

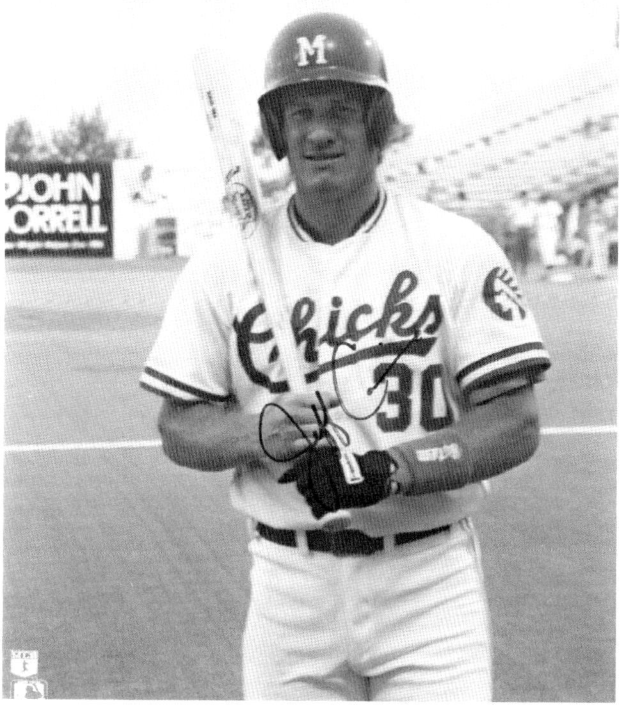

The high point of the era of Chicks baseball that was affiliated with the Kansas City Royals was the 1990 championship team. Not since 1978 had the Chicks produced a league champion. The 1990 team was led by MVP Jeff Conine. Several other future major leaguers also contributed to the success of the team: players like Sean Barry, Brent Mayne, and Brian McRae made the championship possible. A pitching staff anchored by Scott Centala, Richard LeBlanc, and Dennis Moeller kept Memphis in the hunt. (Author's collection.)

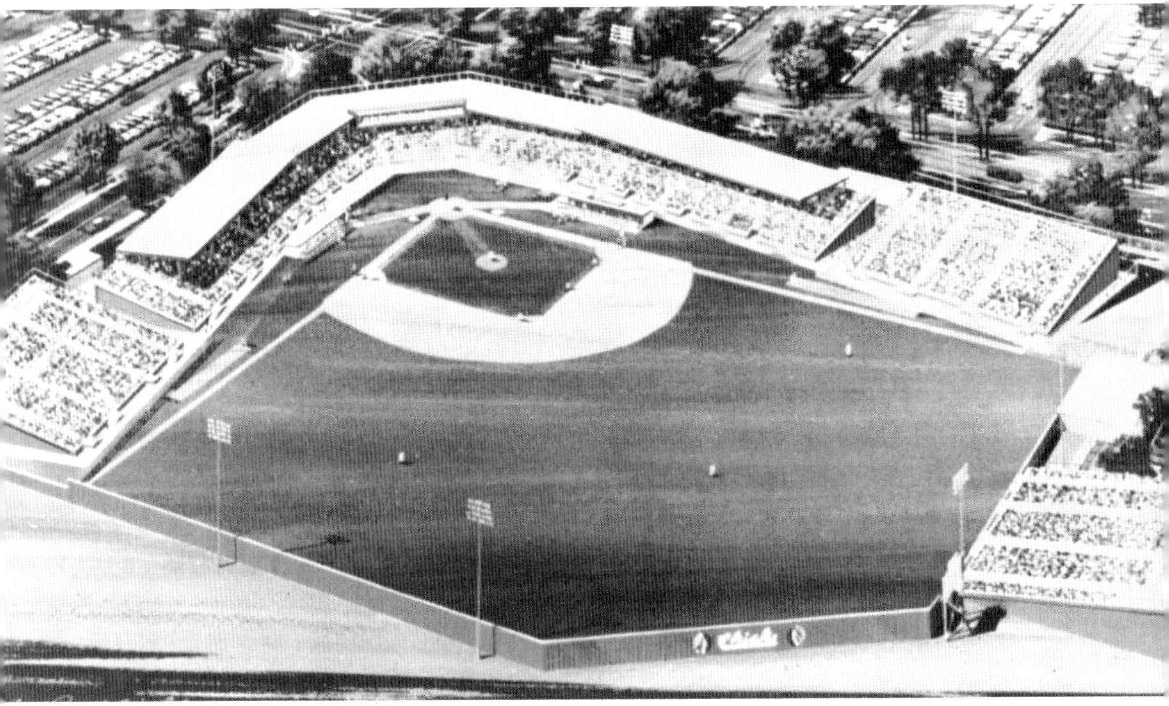

What started out as Fairgrounds No. 3 evolved into Blues Stadium and in 1978 became Tim McCarver Stadium, a product of countless additions and remodels. There was no overall architectural theme that brought the remodels together; increased seating capacity seemed to be the only priority. The artificial grass infield was an oddity no one else seemed to copy. After the Redbirds left, the days of Tim McCarver Stadium were numbered. In spite of its lack of classic ballpark appeal, it still was the site of countless baseball memories for Memphis fans. As time goes by, fans only remember the good times enjoyed there with friends and the special players they saw. Tim McCarver Stadium will not be forgotten by true Memphis baseball fans. (Author's collection.)

9

The Redbirds and AutoZone Park

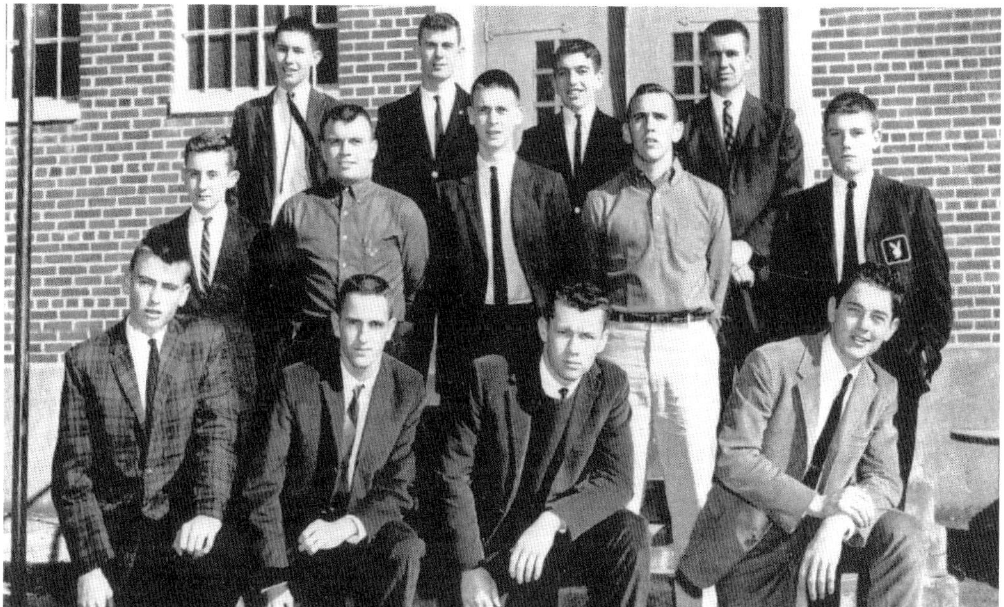

Dean Jernigan is located in the center of the back row in this 1962 Messick Panthers baseball team picture. Jernigan played shortstop on the 1962 team that played Science Hill High School of Johnson City for the Tennessee High School State Championship. Messick lost the game when Steve Spurrier singled in the winning run. Science Hill defeated Christian Brothers in 1963 for a second straight championship. (Courtesy of the Memphis Redbirds.)

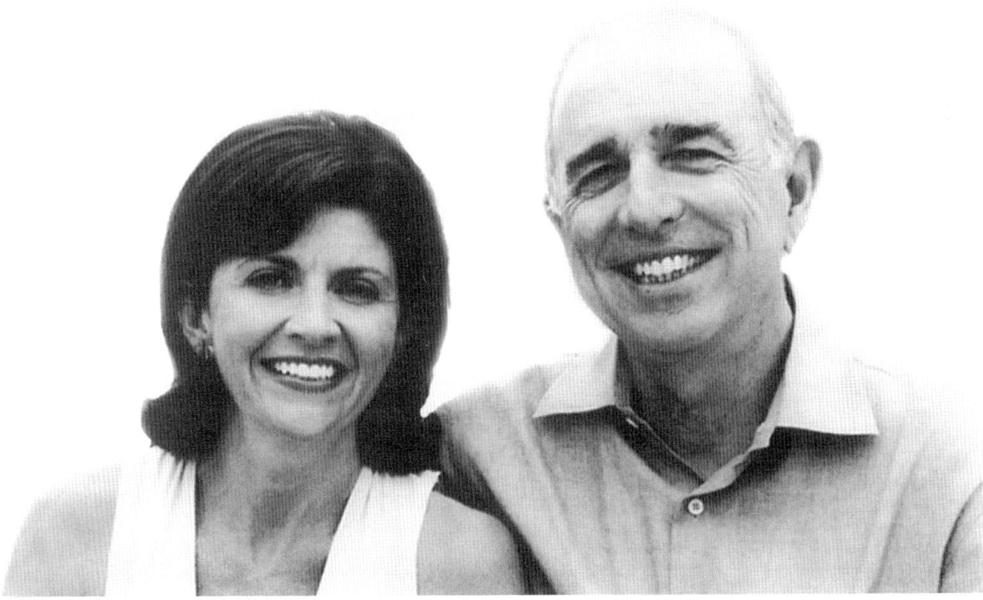

After negotiations to purchase the Memphis Chicks fell apart, Dean and Kristi Jernigan turned their energies toward getting baseball back to Memphis in a new and different way. First, another franchise would have to be obtained; and second, a new stadium would need to be built. To achieve all of this, the Jernigans came up with a not-for-profit plan: profits would fund two youth baseball charities. It was time to think outside the box. (Courtesy of the Memphis Redbirds.)

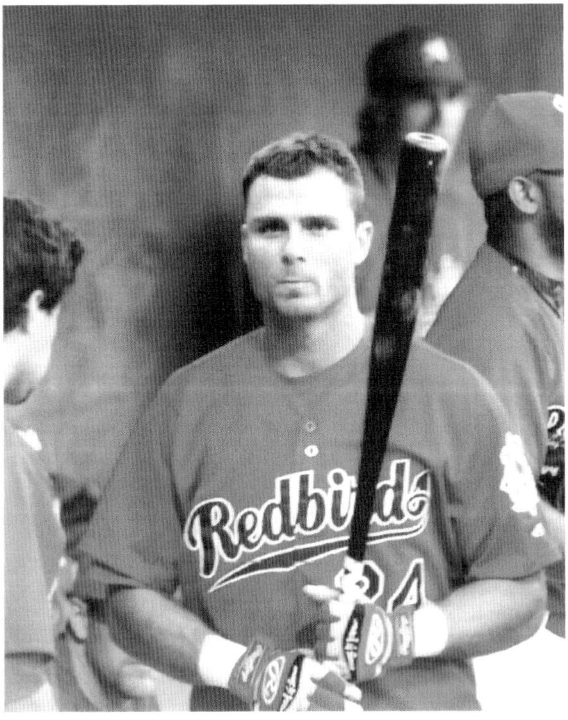

Not many people can reinvent themselves as Rick Ankiel did in baseball. In 1999, he came to the Redbirds as a pitching phenom. While starting game one of the National League Division Series in 2000 for the St. Louis Cardinals, he completely lost his control on the mound, ruining his pitching career. Ankiel spent time with Memphis in 2001 trying to fix his pitching problems. He then made the decision to become a position player in 2005. He even went down to the minors, working his way back to Memphis in 2007 and posting a remarkable season with 32 home runs. (Courtesy of Allison Rhoades/Memphis Redbirds.)

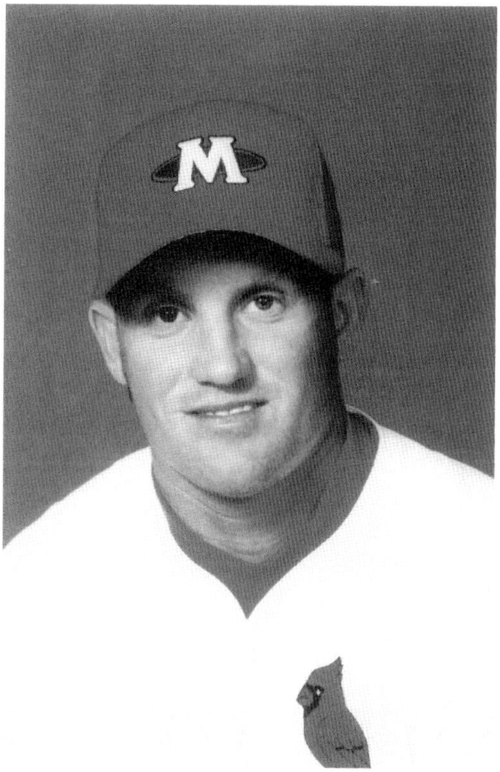

Any fan-favorite player of the Memphis Redbirds will have to live up to the example set by Richard "Stubby" Clapp. From 1999 to 2002, Clapp kept fans in the game with his hustling style of play exemplified by his constantly dirty uniform. On April 21, 2007, Memphis honored that hustle by retiring Clapp's number—the first player so recognized by the Memphis Redbirds. Below, Clapp performs his customary flip to begin each home game. He spent four years with Memphis playing infield for the Redbirds. His flip at the beginning of each home game became a tradition fans did not want to miss. In 2009, Clapp was named one of Memphis's "Athletes of the Decade." (Both, courtesy of the Memphis Redbirds.)

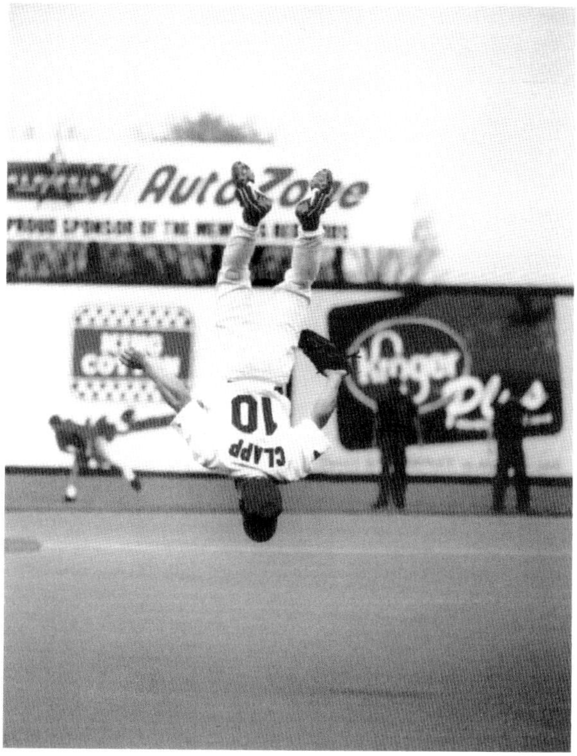

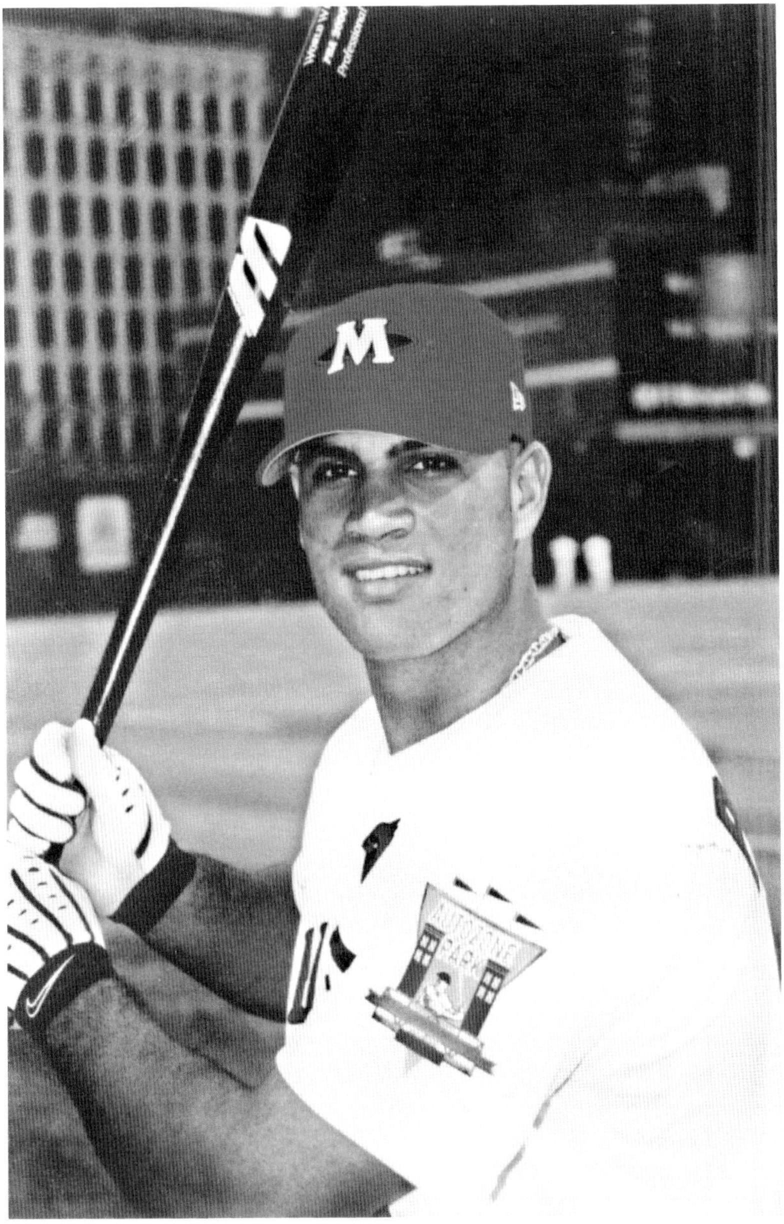

The term "a cup of coffee" is used in baseball to describe a player's brief time with a team. In 2000, Albert Pujols had a cup of coffee with the Memphis Redbirds, having spent most of the 2000 season in low- and high-A minor leagues. Pujols played three games for the Redbirds, hitting no home runs. Then, in the championship series as a pinch hitter, Pujols hit a home run to win the league championship for Memphis. The seat out past the right-field wall is marked for this feat. The next year, Albert was scheduled to begin the year at Memphis, but early Cardinal injuries sent him to the big club, where he went on to become National League Rookie of the year in 2001. A player like "Prince Albert" only comes around once in a lifetime. (Courtesy of the Memphis Redbirds.)

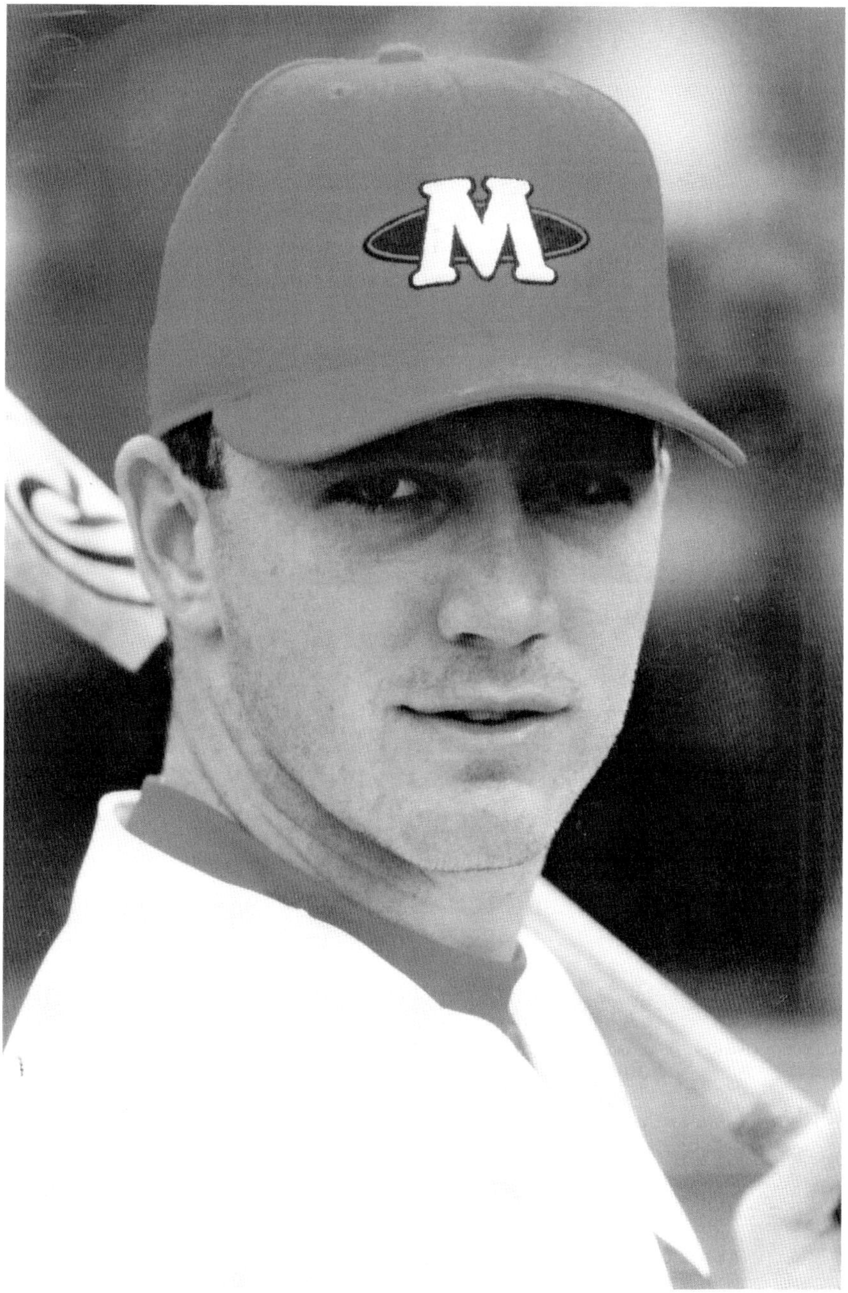

In 1997, J.D. Drew had won just about every major college baseball award possible while at Florida State University. He also became the first college player to hit 30 home runs and steal 30 bases in the same season. Then, he was drafted by the Philadelphia Phillies, but they refused to pay the amount demanded by Drew's agent. After playing in an independent league in 1997, Drew signed with the St. Louis Cardinals in 1998. Drew spent little time running through the Cardinals farm system. Part of that whirlwind tour included 26 games with the Memphis Redbirds. (Courtesy of the Memphis Redbirds.)

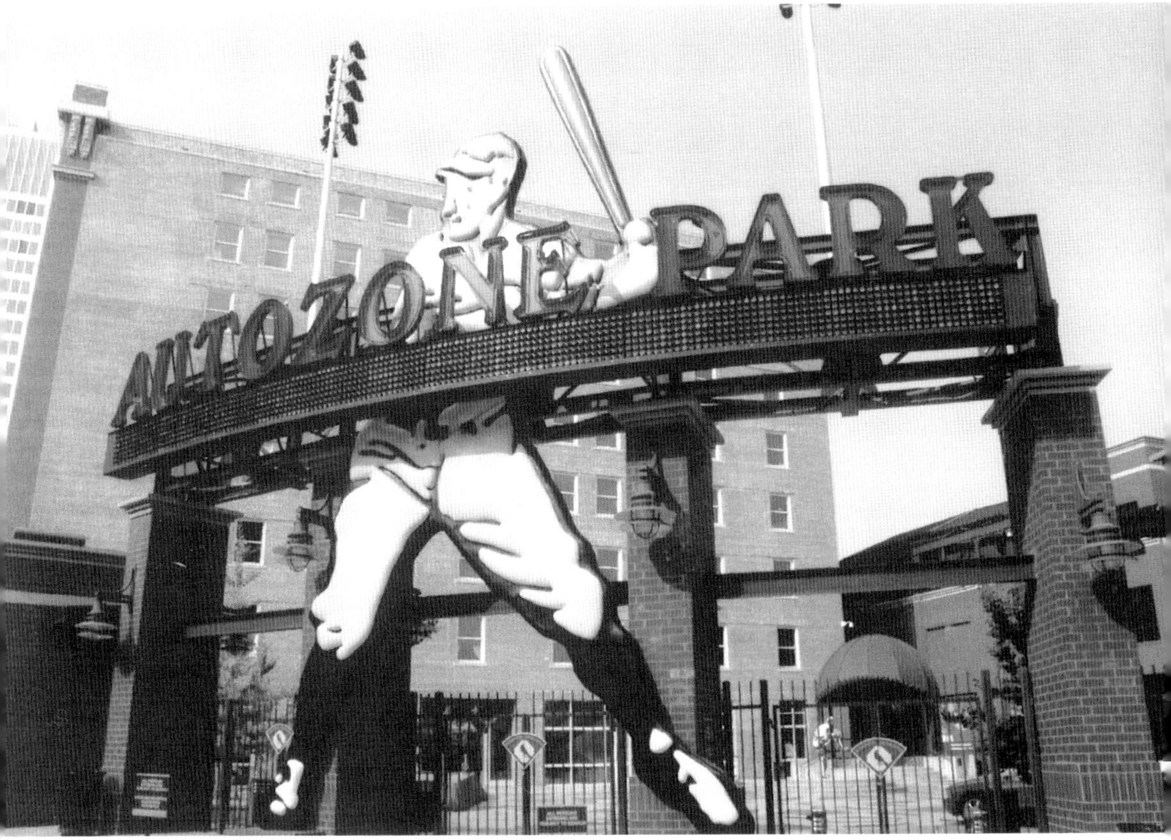

At the corner of Union Avenue and Third Street stands the entrance to AutoZone Park. The standard for all minor-league parks to come, AutoZone Park opened to rave reviews in 2000. Guarding the front gates is Nostalgia Man, the iconic new symbol of baseball in Memphis who has an uncanny resemblance to Lou Gehrig. (Courtesy of Ben Powell.)

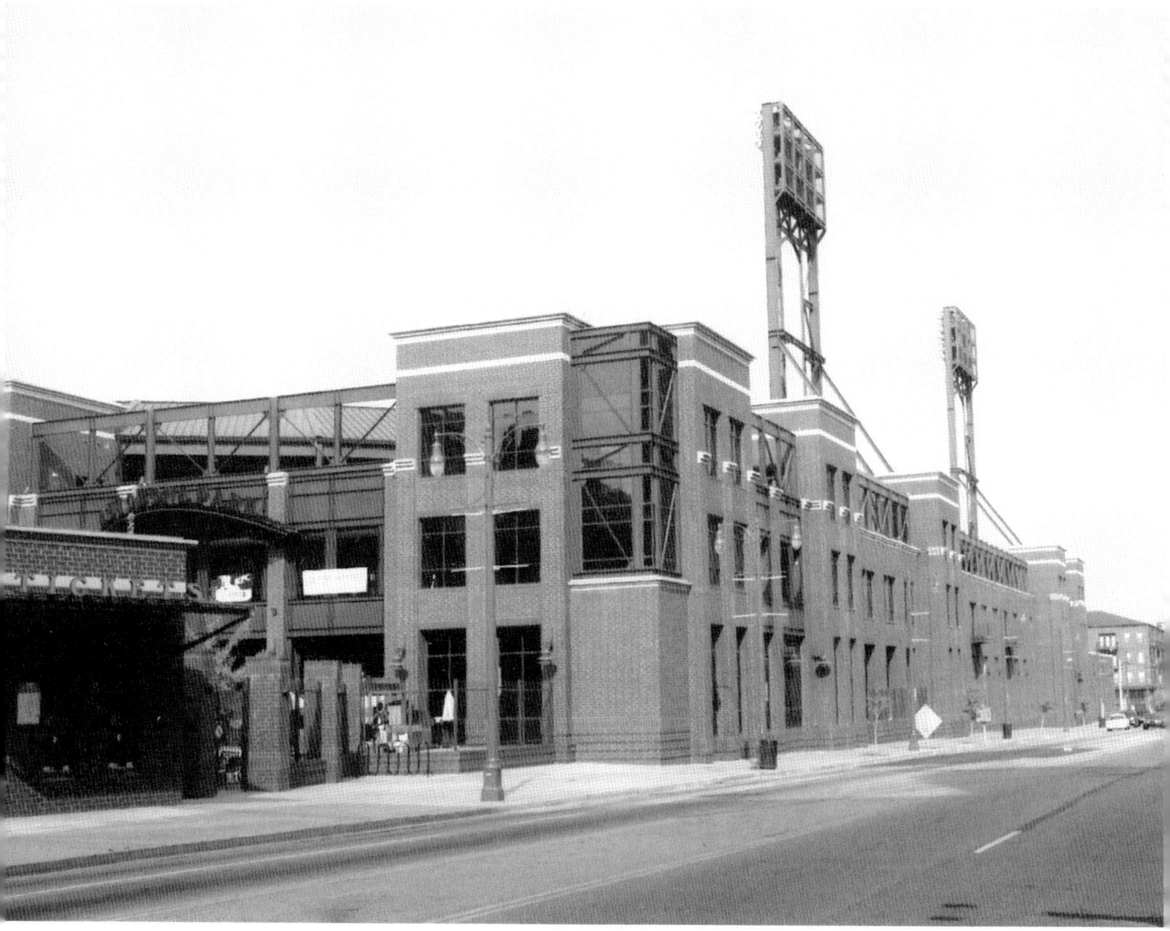

The beautiful exterior of AutoZone Park enhances the downtown area. Looking down Union Avenue from the front entrance, visitors will notice the brickwork combined with structural steel to form a look similar to Camden Yards, the first of the retro classic–styled major-league baseball parks. (Courtesy of Ben Powell.)

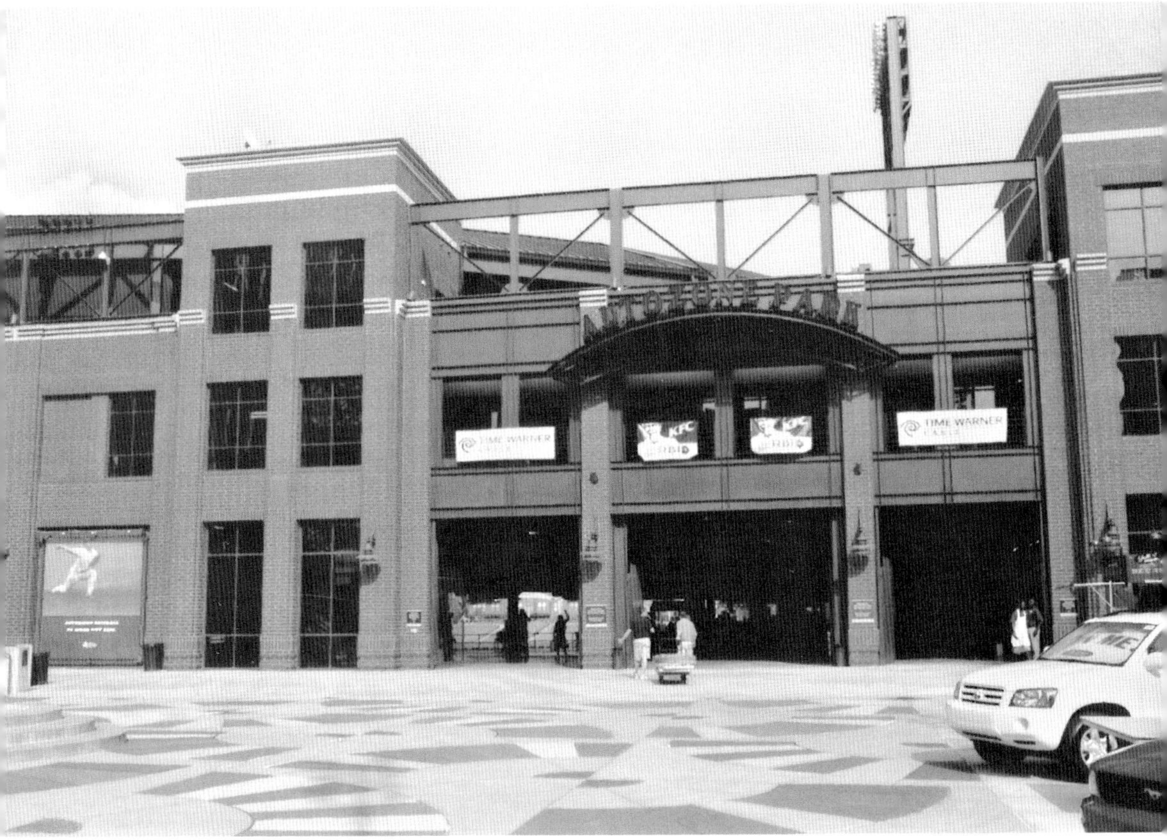

Upon entering the front gate of AutoZone Park, visitors are in the Plaza, a busy area for pregame events, which include live music and the Redbird Dancers and Cheerleaders. The gift shop is to the left and is full of merchandise for every fan's needs. The Plaza is the perfect place for fans to meet friends before going to their seats. (Courtesy of Ben Powell.)

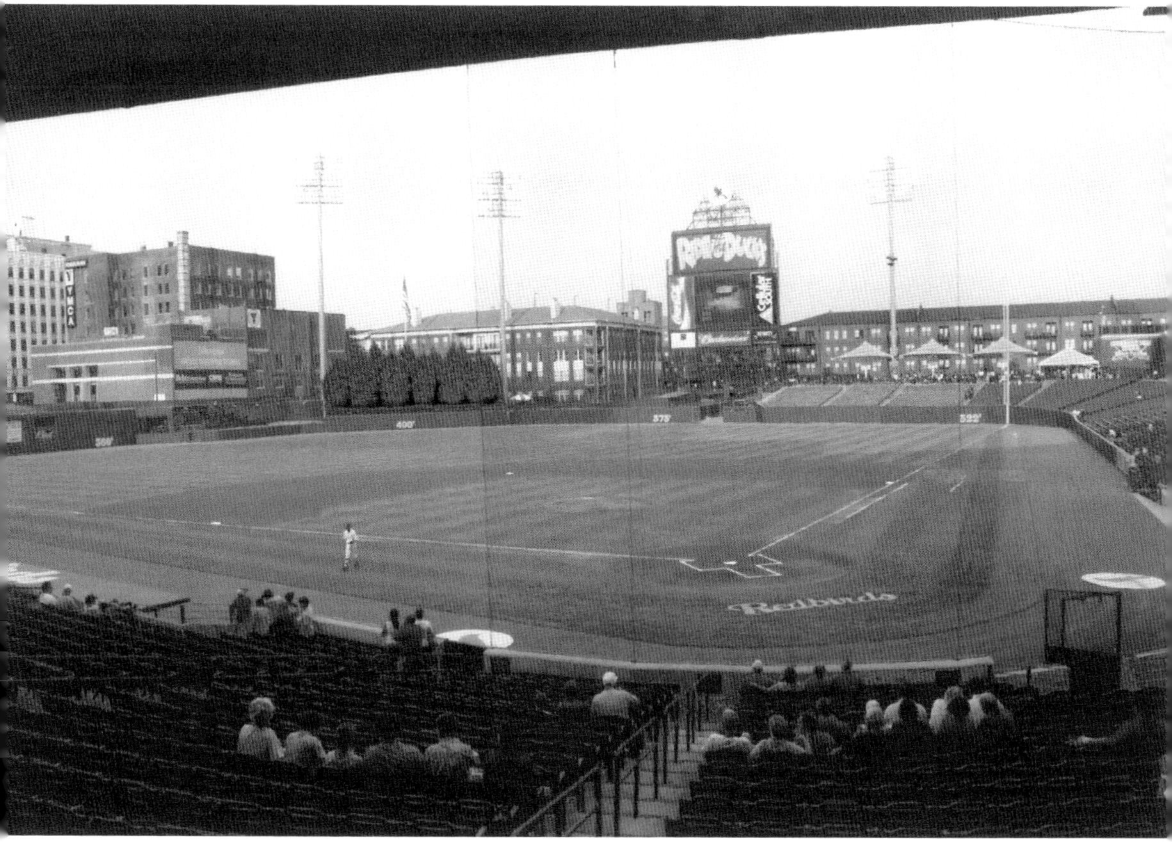

A few steps after entering the concourse, attendees are drawn to the panoramic view of the playing field. There is so much to take in: the berm in left field, the YMCA building past center field, and the new condominiums past the right-field fence. The combination of the rich green grass, the hitter's background of evergreen trees, and the brick facades of the buildings beyond the ballpark create a classic view. (Courtesy of Ben Powell.)

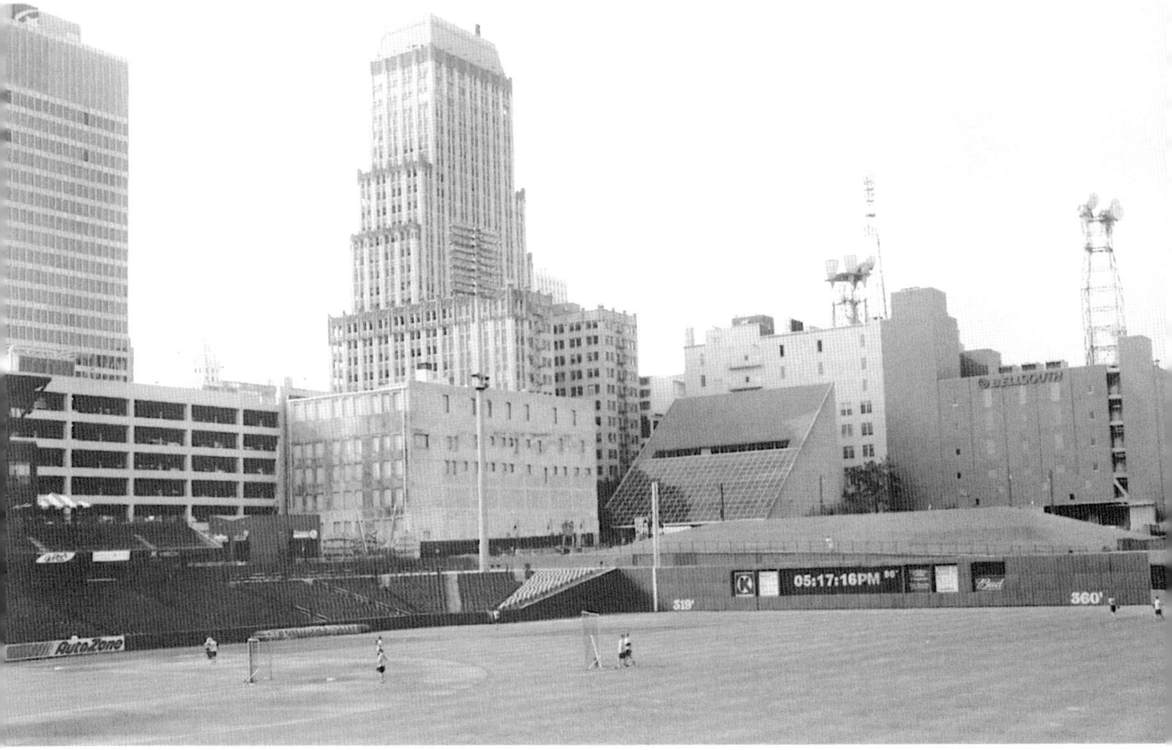

A unique architectural feature of AutoZone Park beyond the left-field fence is the berm. It is the ideal place for a family to take a blanket, relax, and watch the game, but it also speaks to the past. On page 9 is a photograph the fans at the Red Elm Bottom sitting on the slope watching the game, just as families do today. The early inhabitants of the Memphis area, the Chickasaw Indians, built berms now known as Indian mounds. (Courtesy of Ben Powell.)

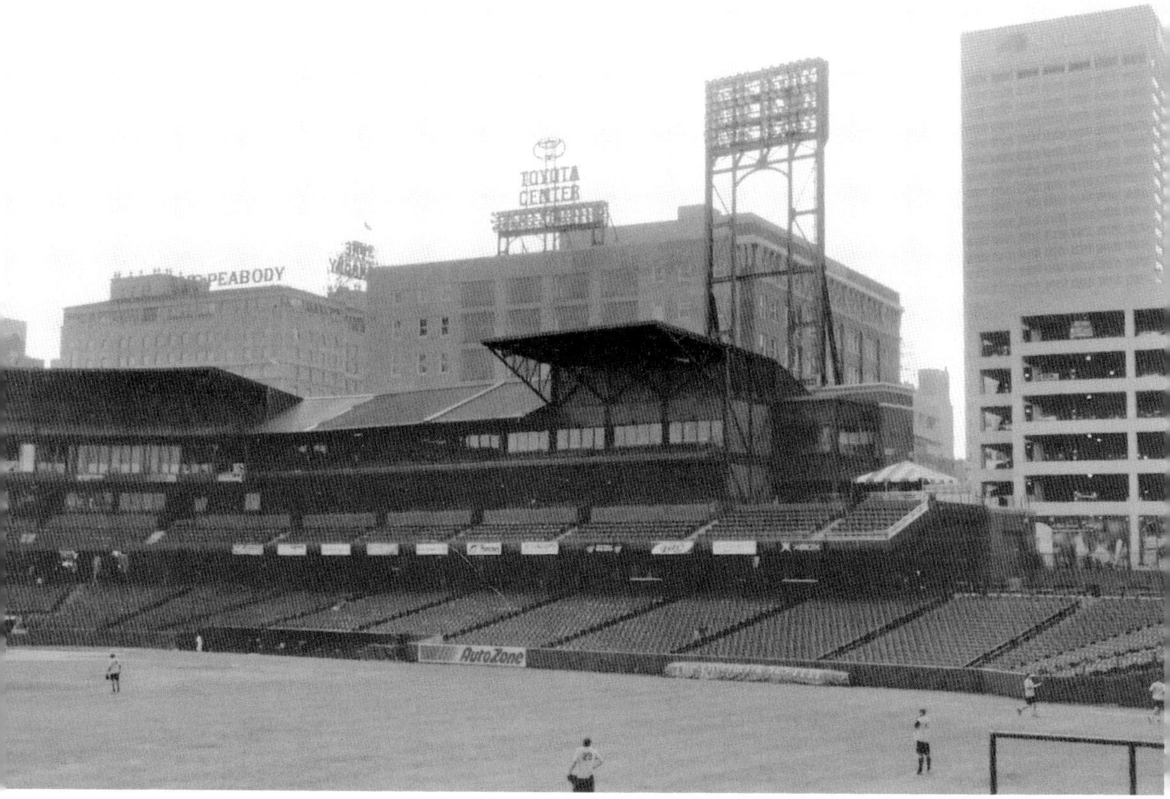

Seen from center field over the stands is the downtown area that complements the park. Across the street is the famous Peabody Hotel, and next to the park is the Toyota Center, hopefully the home of a baseball museum one day. The SunTrust Building just beyond the park adds to the picturesque Memphis skyline. (Courtesy of Ben Powell.)

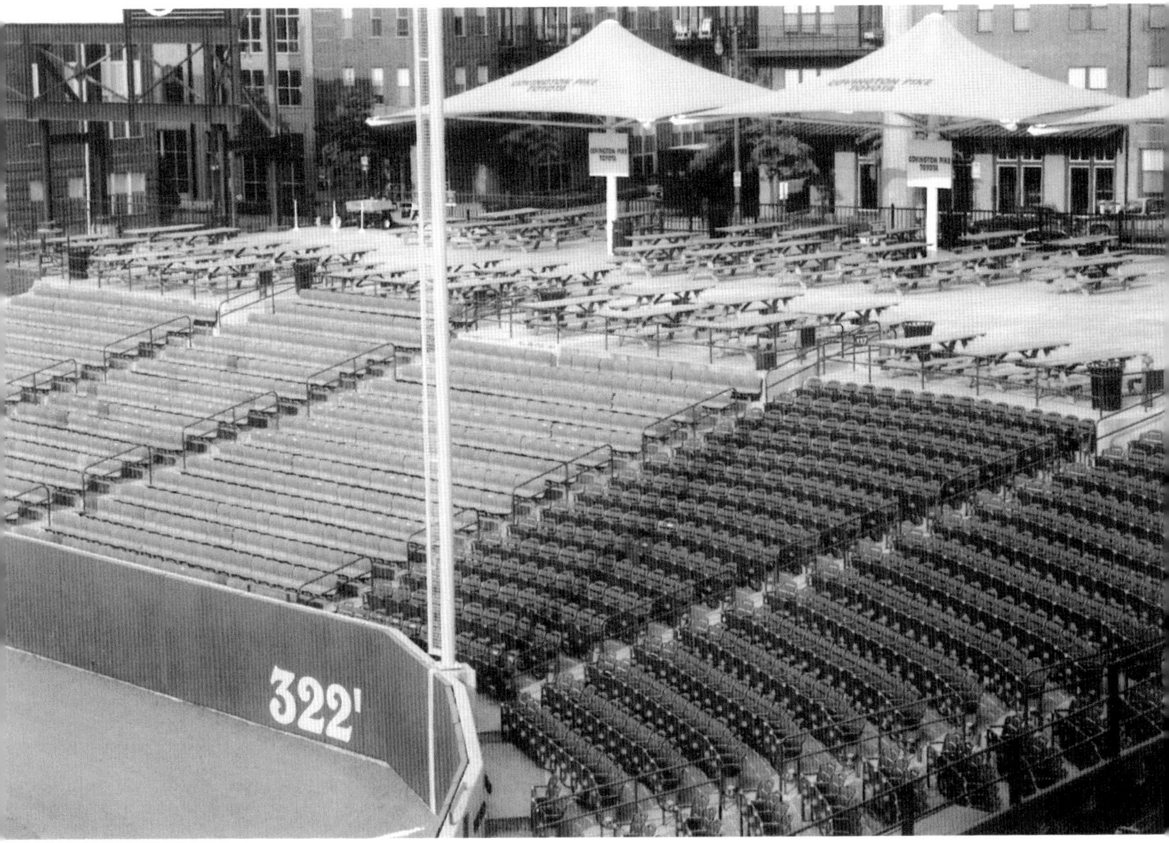

The right-field seating area is something few minor-league ballparks have. The picnic area beyond the seats provides a unique view of the game as well as shade. The odd-shaded seat in the right-field section above the 322-foot sign is the seat that Pujol's dramatic home run hit in 2000. Such a young ballpark is already making history and new memories for the fans. (Courtesy of Ben Powell.)

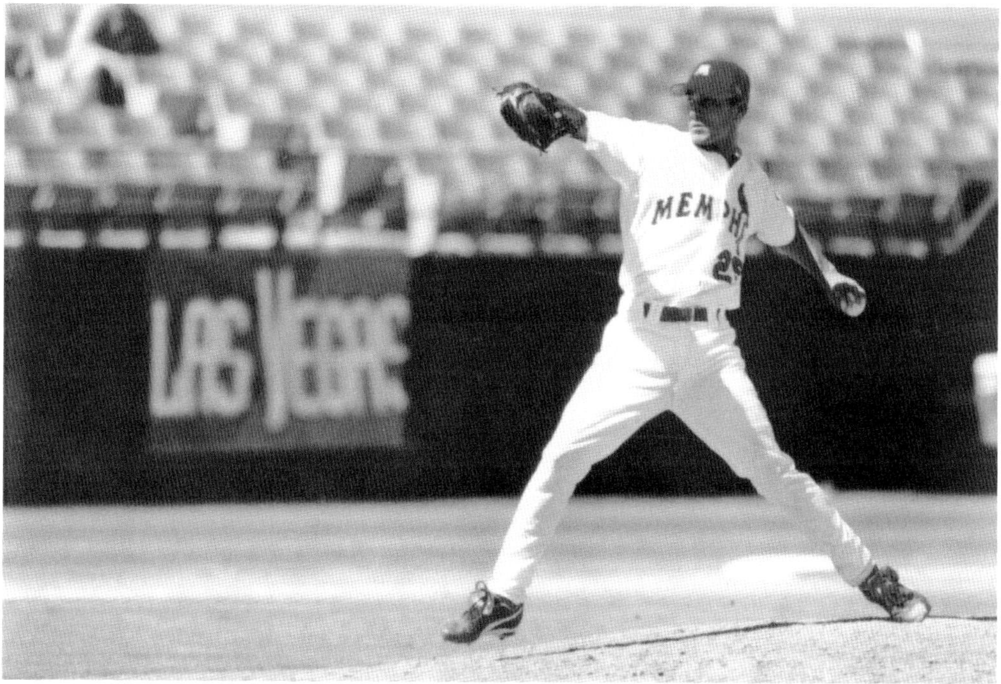

Bud Smith pitched three years for the Memphis Redbirds, from 2000 to 2002. During a call-up to the St. Louis Cardinals, Smith made history when he threw a no-hitter against the San Diego Padres on September 3, 2001, during his rookie season. He became only the 18th pitcher to throw a no-hitter in his rookie season. On July 29, 2002, Smith was traded to the Philadelphia Phillies, but he never made it back to the major leagues. (Courtesy of the Memphis Redbirds.)

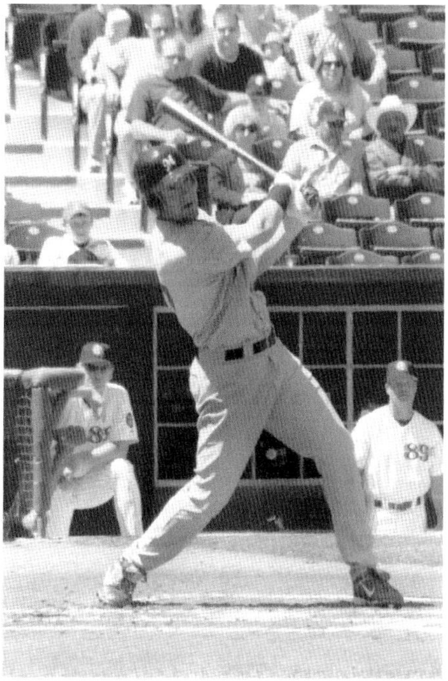

After spending time with four different major-league teams, Ryan Ludwick signed as a free agent after 2006 with the St. Louis Cardinals. Ludwick started the season with the Redbirds, playing in 29 games, slamming eight home runs, and batting .340. Called up to St. Louis, Ludwick posted four good years with the Cardinals before being traded to San Diego in 2009. (Author's collection.)

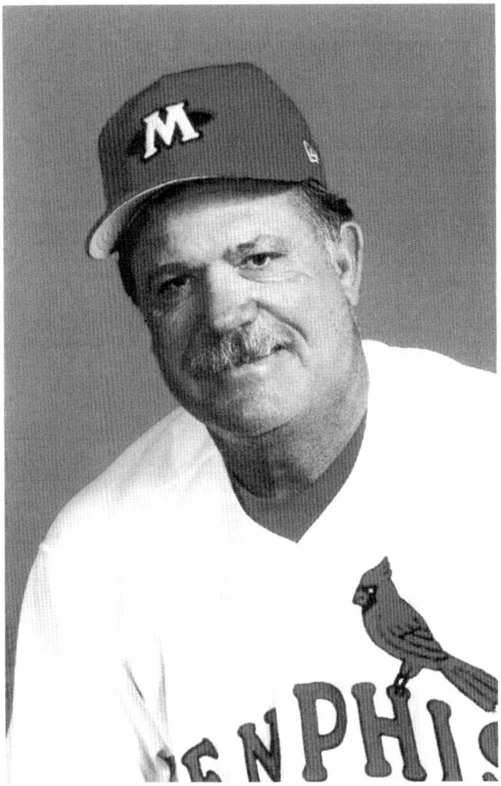

For the first five years of Memphis Redbirds baseball, Gaylen Pitts was the manager of the team. The highlight of his tenure was the championship won in 2000, when Albert Pujols hit the game-ending home run. Pitts resigned in 2002. He had double hip-replacement surgeries in 2004 and in 2009 returned to baseball as a special assistant for player development. (Courtesy of Larry Inman/Memphis Redbirds.)

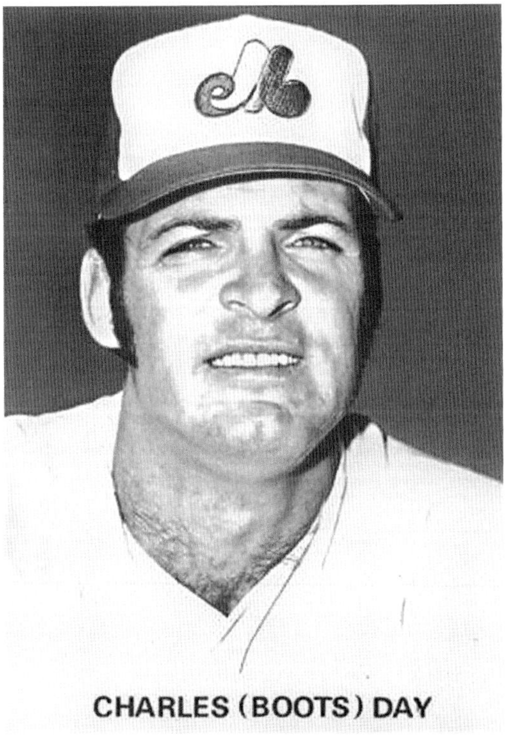

"Boots" Day spent three years as a coach for the Memphis Redbirds, but he has more history with Memphis than many fans may remember. As a member of the 1968 Arkansas Travelers, Day hit the home run that clinched the Eastern Division for Arkansas—a game remembered more for the 10-minute brawl than Day's home run. Also, in 1974, Boots played 21 games for the Triple-A Memphis Blues while in the Montreal farm system. (Author's collection.)

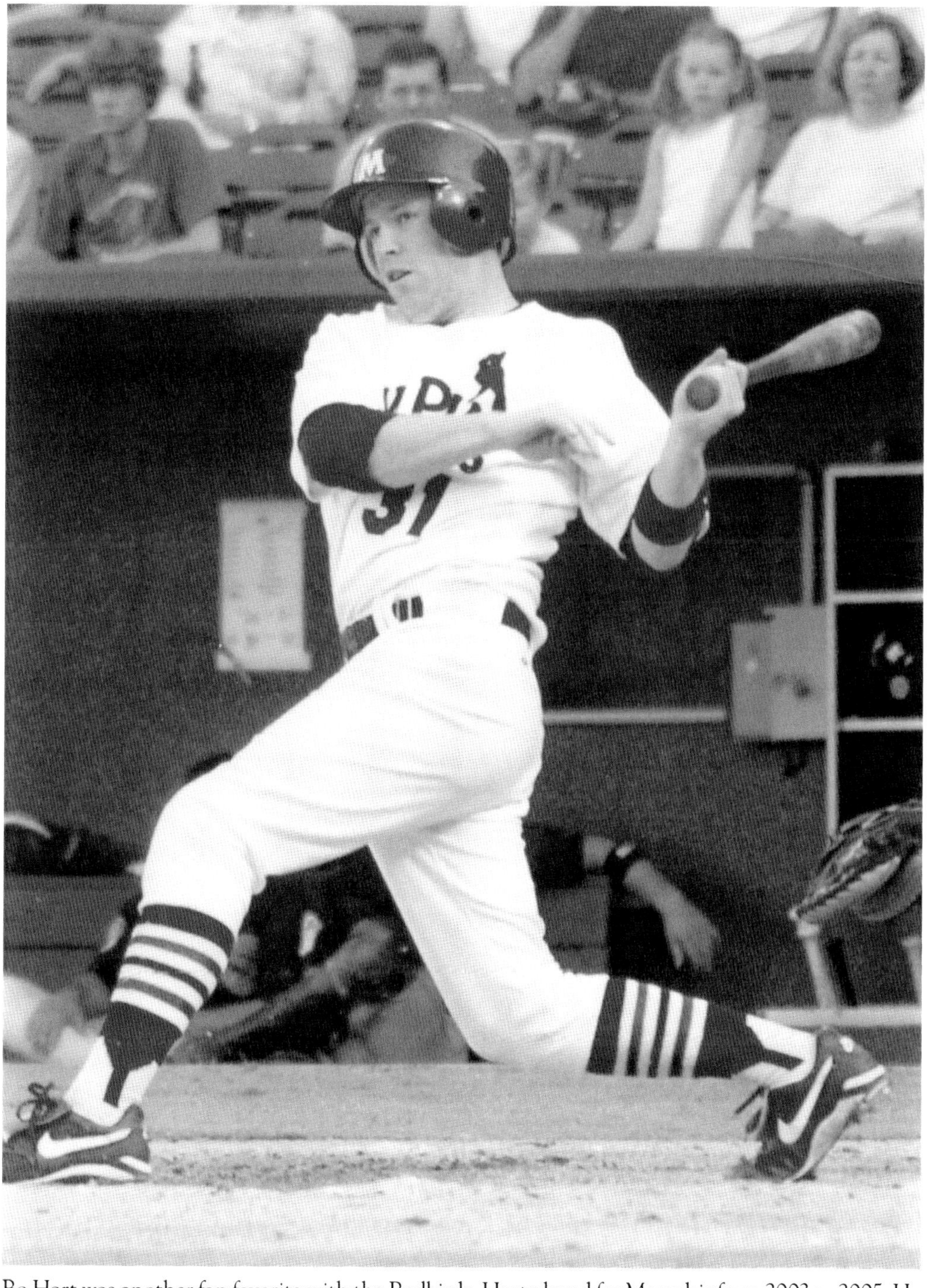

Bo Hart was another fan favorite with the Redbirds. Hart played for Memphis from 2003 to 2005. He set a new major-league record by batting .460 in his first 10 games for the St. Louis Cardinals. Hart retired from playing after the 2008 season. (Courtesy of Allison Rhoades/Memphis Redbirds.)

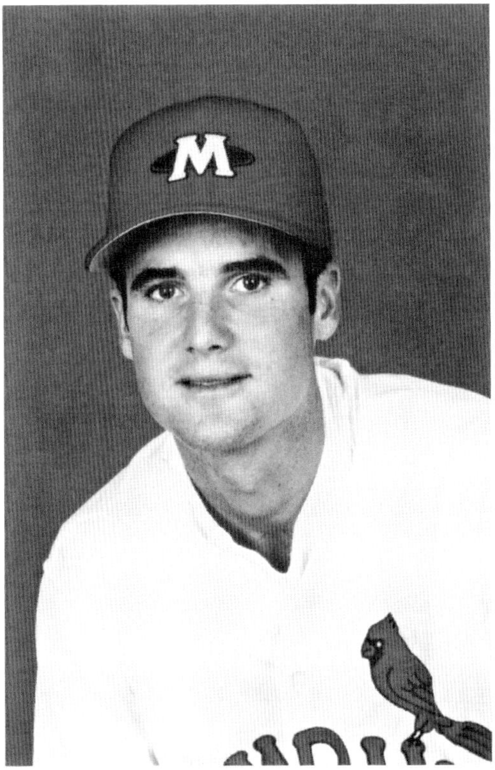

Adam Kennedy played two years for the Redbirds (1998 and 1999) after being drafted by St. Louis in the first round of the 1997 amateur draft. Kennedy was part of the trade that brought Jim Edmonds to St. Louis from Anaheim. (Courtesy of the Memphis Redbirds.)

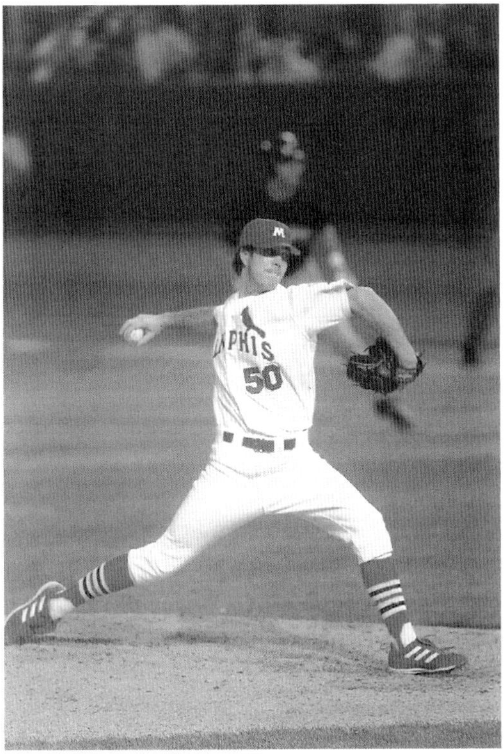

Adam Wainwright signed with the Atlanta Braves right out of high school. After several years in the Braves farm system, he was traded to St. Louis in a deal that sent J.D. Drew to Atlanta. By 2009, Wainwright was the ace of a very good pitching rotation that included Chris Carpenter. (Courtesy of the Memphis Redbirds.)

10

MEMPHIS'S FAVORITE SONS

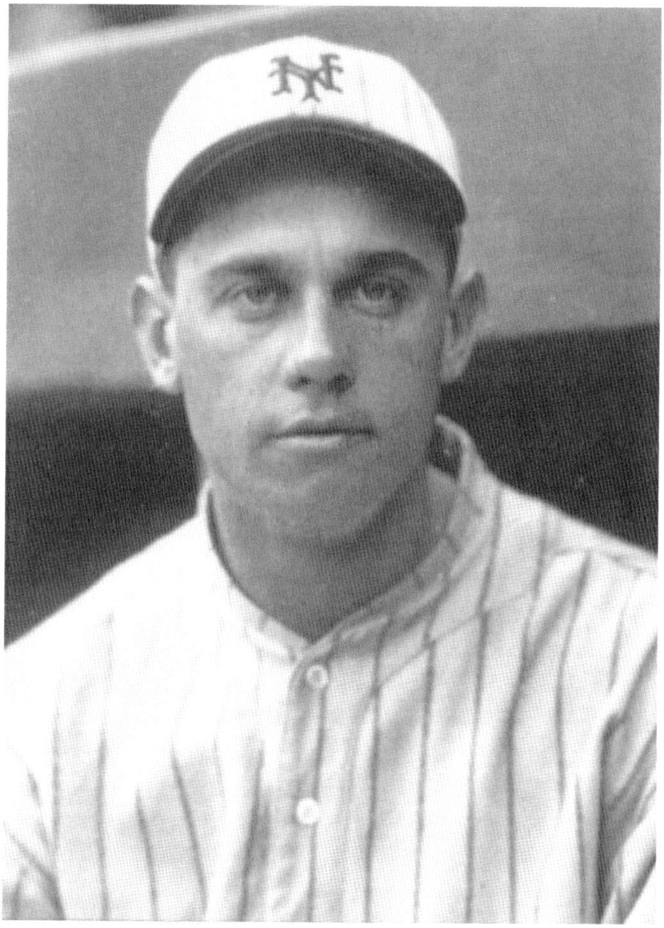

Bill Terry, the last National League player to bat over .400, was not originally from Memphis; Terry was from Atlanta, Georgia. His professional baseball career was placed on hold, as he married and started a family. Terry and his wife moved to Memphis to be near her family. He took a job with an oil company and played semipro baseball. John McGraw came to Memphis to sign Terry at the Peabody Hotel. Terry's nickname became "Memphis Bill." For many years after starring with the New York Giants, Terry lived in Memphis during the off-season. (Author's collection.)

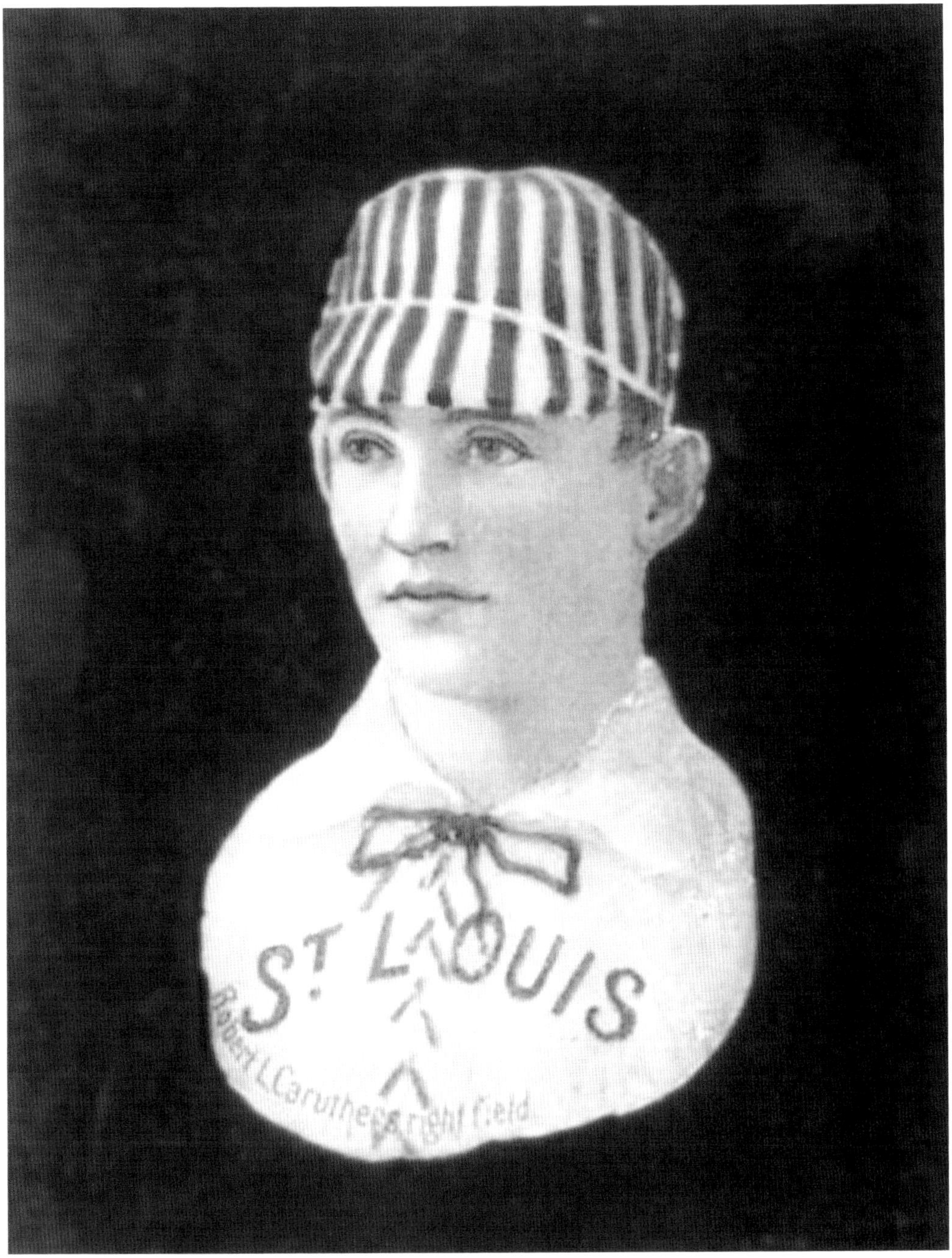

Bob Caruthers was the first player born in Memphis to play in the major leagues. He won an amazing 218 games in a nine-year career playing for St. Louis and Brooklyn, including two seasons of 40 wins—unheard of in the modern era of baseball. Hopefully, the veterans committee will seriously consider him for the Baseball Hall of Fame in the future. Another early Memphian to make it to the major leagues was Jake Wells. He played for five different Southern League teams. (Author's collection.)

Jimmy Moore was not born in Memphis, but he did make Memphis his home after a 13-year professional career. Moore played two years in the majors (1930 and 1931) and was lucky to play in the World Series both years. After leaving baseball, Moore was a successful businessman and was elected to the city commission in 1959. One of his major achievements was getting the Liberty Bowl and Coliseum built. (Author's collection.)

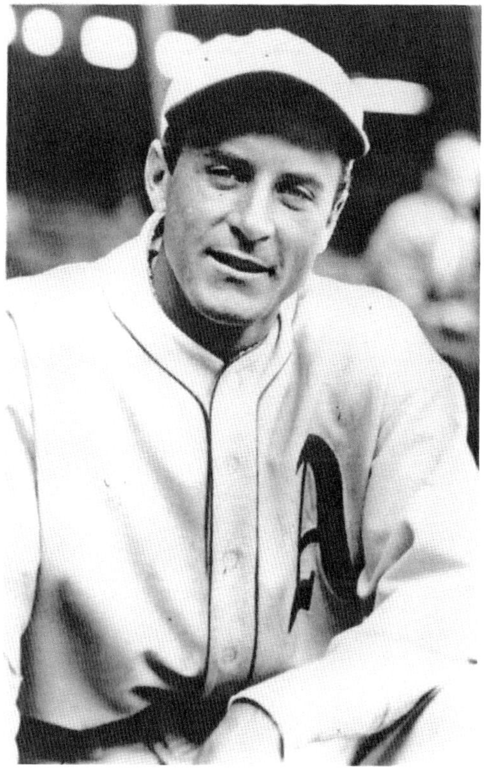

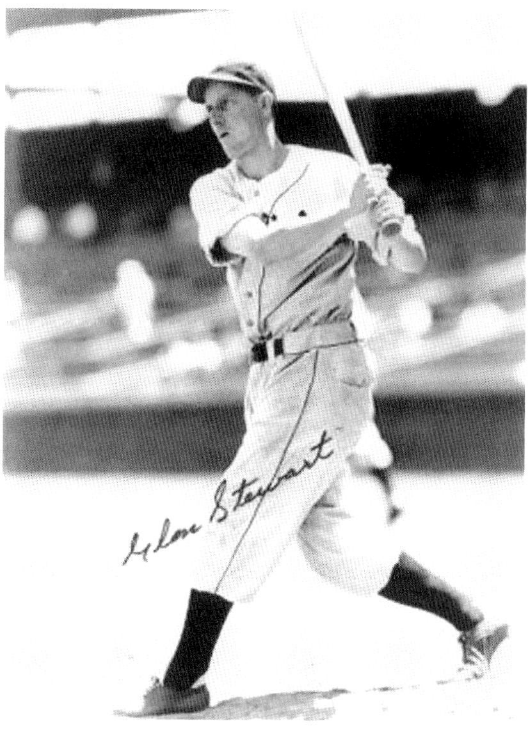

Glen "Gabby" Stewart was all-city in baseball at Central High School. He later played for the New York Giants in 1940. During the war years, he was a member of the Philadelphia Phillies (1943 and 1944). On August 7, 1943, Stewart hit his first home run in the third inning—four innings later, he hit his last major-league home run. Toward the end of his career, Stewart played with the Memphis Chicks in 1948. (Author's collection.)

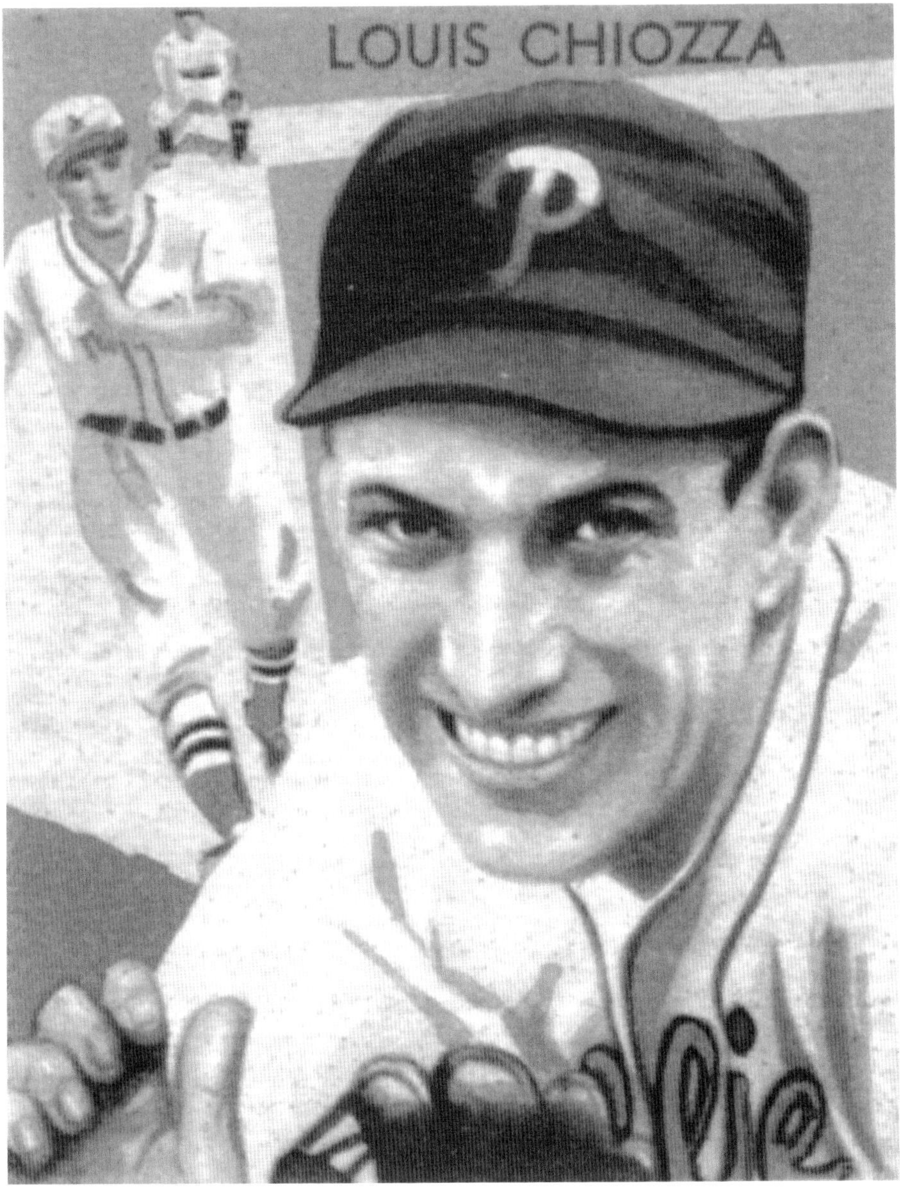

Lou Chiozza was an all-round athlete in high school in Memphis. His two older brothers were also professional baseball players. Lou spent four years in the majors with Philadelphia and the New York Giants. He has the distinction of being the first batter in the first-ever night baseball game in Cincinnati. In 1937, as the New York Giants came to Russwood Park to play an exhibition game against the Chicks, a special Lou Chiozza Day was declared honoring the hometown boy. Lou then celebrated the day by hitting a home run; it was a very special day for "Memphis Lou," as fans called him. In 1942, Doc Prothro added Lou as a third-base coach for all Chicks home games. Lou played for the Memphis Chicks in 1931 and 1933 and then closed out his playing days with the Chicks in 1941. He and his brothers ran a very popular liquor store in Memphis, and Lou was a regular at Chicks and Red Sox games. (Author's collection.)

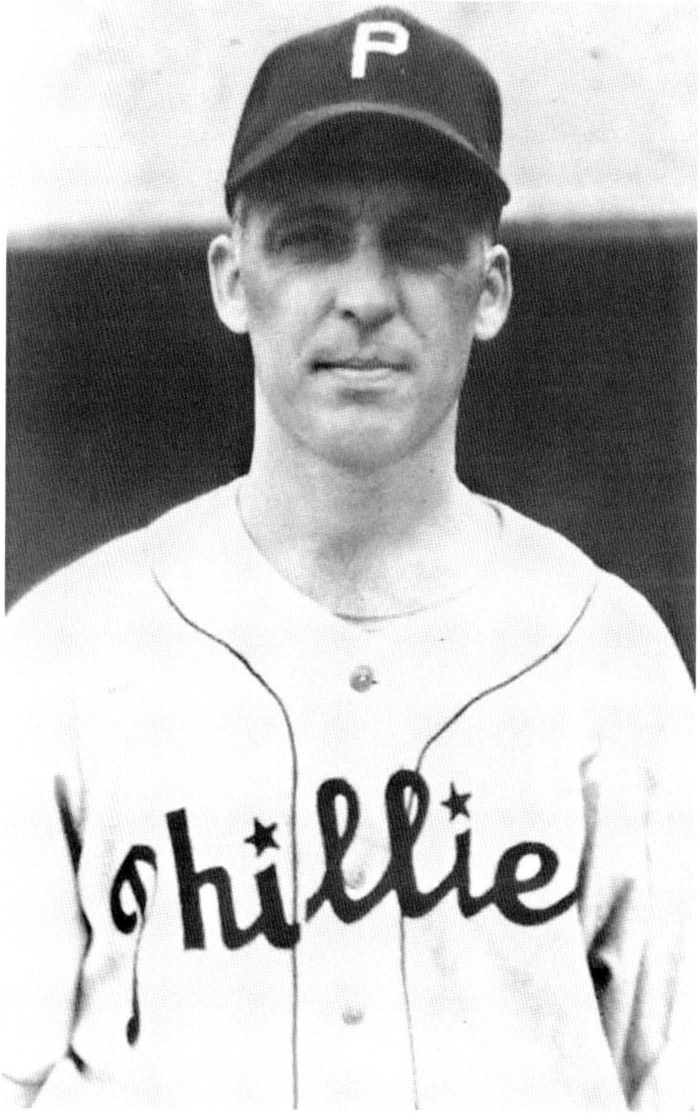

John Antonelli signed with his hometown Memphis Chicks in 1935 at the age of 19. After a few games with Memphis, he was assigned to Lexington in the Kitty League. At Lexington, he was the player/manager—one of the youngest players every to manage a professional team. After 1937, he stopped managing to concentrate on just playing the infield. During the war years, Antonelli played parts of two seasons with St. Louis and Philadelphia in the National League. By 1950, his playing career was over, and he scouted part time for the Chicago White Sox but for the most part was out of baseball until 1968. That is the year the New York Mets brought their Double-A Texas League team to be the Memphis Blues. Antonelli became a coach for the Blues, succeeded Pete Pavlick as manager in 1969, and led the team to the Texas League Playoff Championship. He continued to manage Memphis through the 1972 season. Afterward, he managed in the Mets farms system through the 1976 season. From 1976 until 1985, Antonelli was a roving infield instructor. He died in 1990 at age of 94. (Author's collection.)

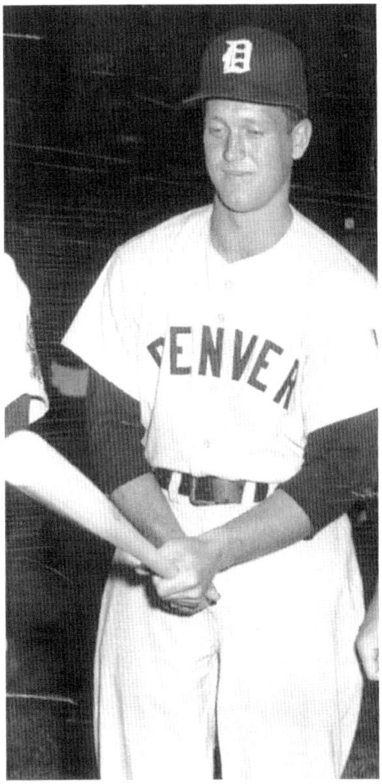

Marv Thornberry was a great baseball and football star at Southside High School in Memphis. He signed with the New York Yankees in 1952. His career with New York did not go well, and he became part of the trade that brought Roger Maris to the Yankees. As a member of the 1962 New York Mets team, he was nicknamed "Marvelous Marv." His last year in professional baseball was 1964. Thornberry would later do radio broadcasts for the Memphis Blues. (Author's collection.)

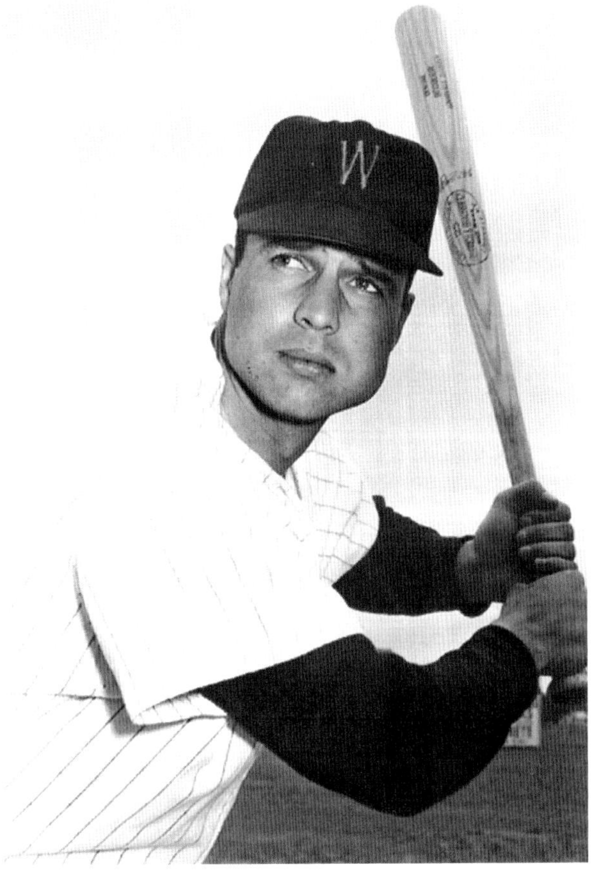

Faye Thornberry, Marv's older brother, also played major-league baseball for several teams, including Boston, Washington, and Los Angeles in the American League. After eight seasons in the majors, he returned to his hometown of Fisherville, Tennessee, to become a very successful trainer of bird dogs. (Author's collection.)

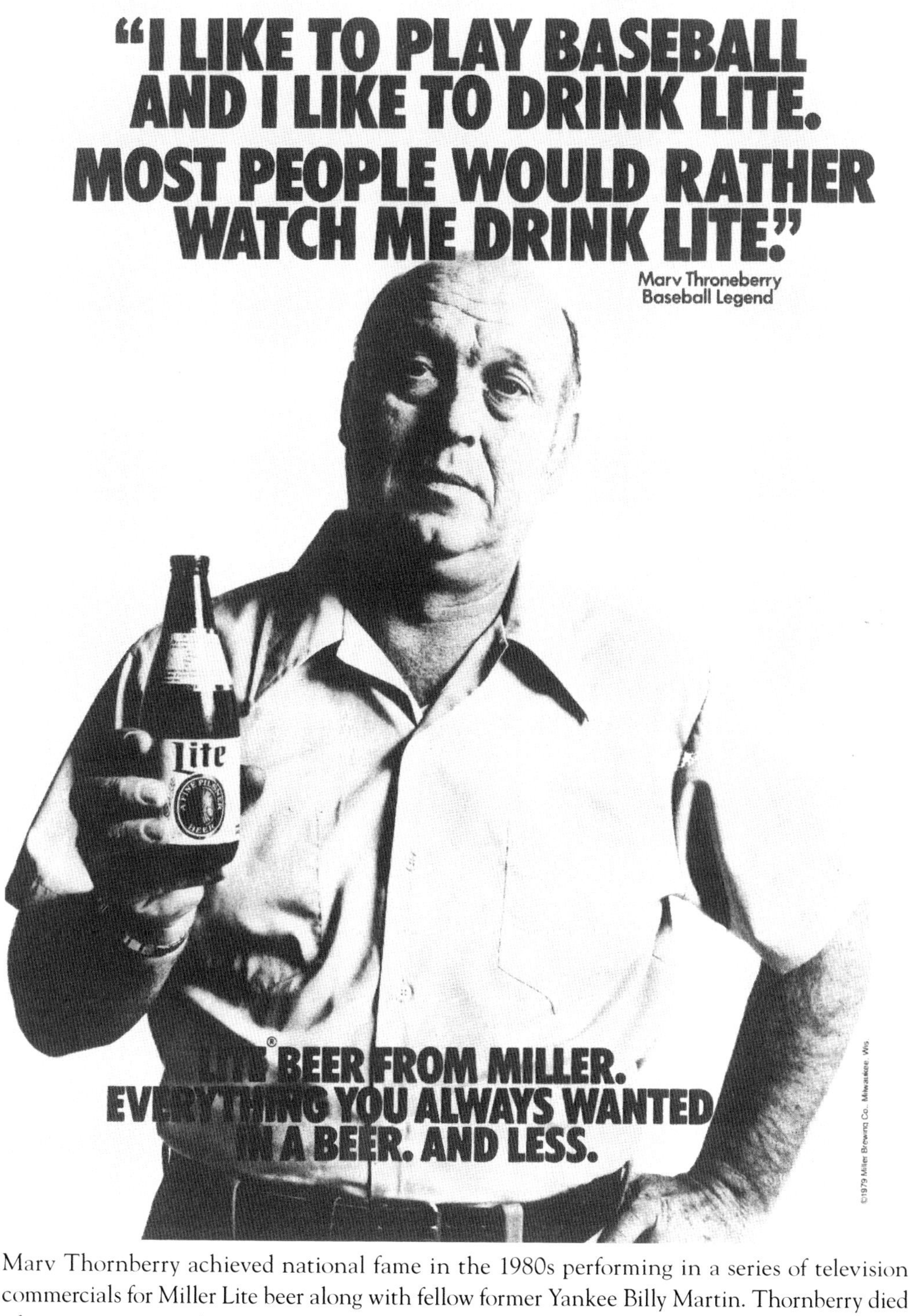

Marv Thornberry achieved national fame in the 1980s performing in a series of television commercials for Miller Lite beer along with fellow former Yankee Billy Martin. Thornberry died of cancer in 1994 in his hometown of Fisherville, Tennessee. (Author's collection.)

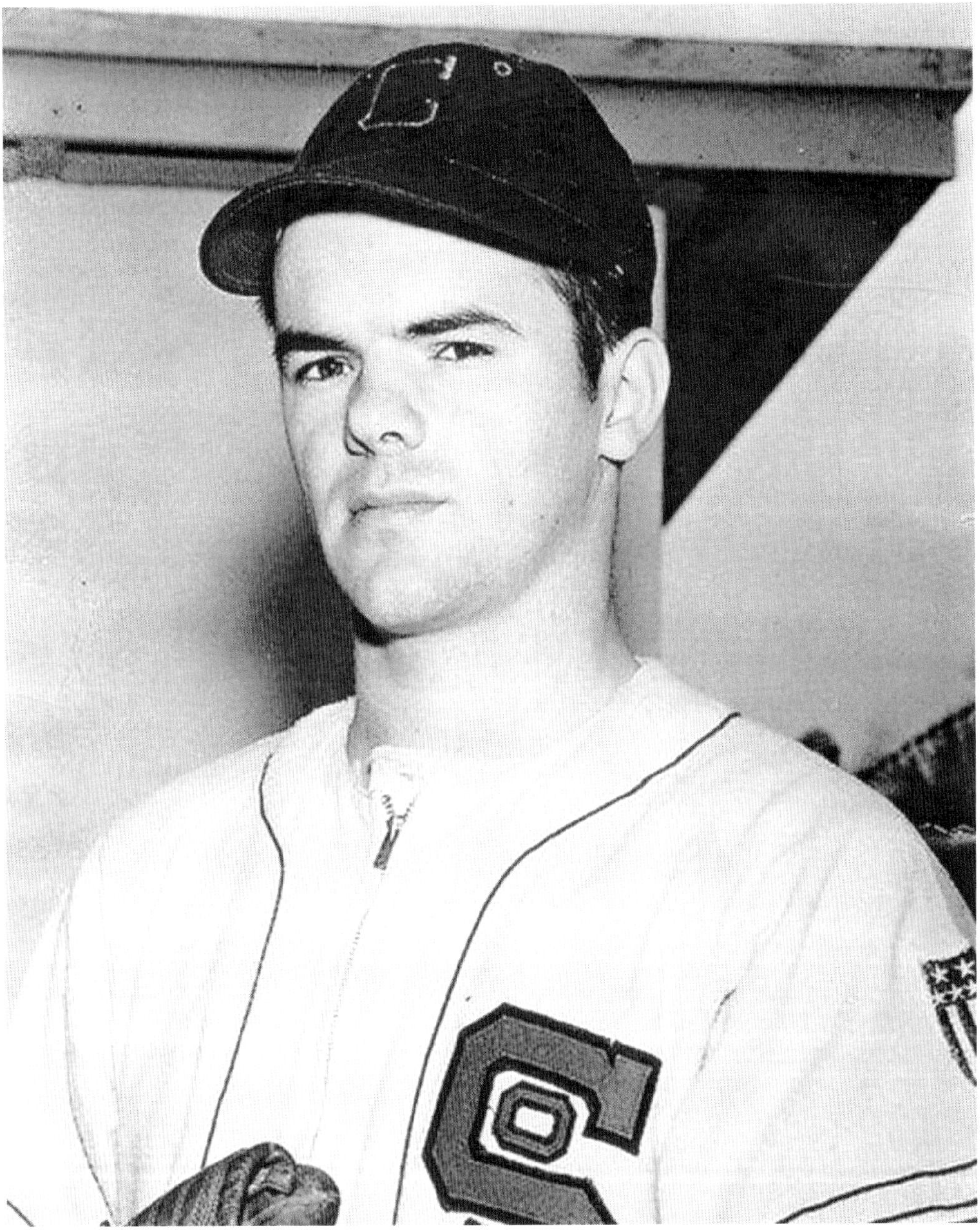

Billy Briggs played baseball at Collierville High School. At the tender age of 18, Billy signed with the Memphis Chicks. Later that season, in a game at Rickwood Field in Birmingham, he had the unpleasant misfortune of walking 15 batters in one game. The Chicks manager, wanting to show his confidence in Briggs, had him pitching the next game in relief. After serving in the Navy during World War II, Briggs came back to the Chicks for three seasons. He finished his professional career in 1952 with the Little Rock Travelers. After retirement, he coached youth baseball, leading the Kittle Pontiac team to the National Amateur Championship in 1958. (Courtesy of Susan Briggs Dold.)

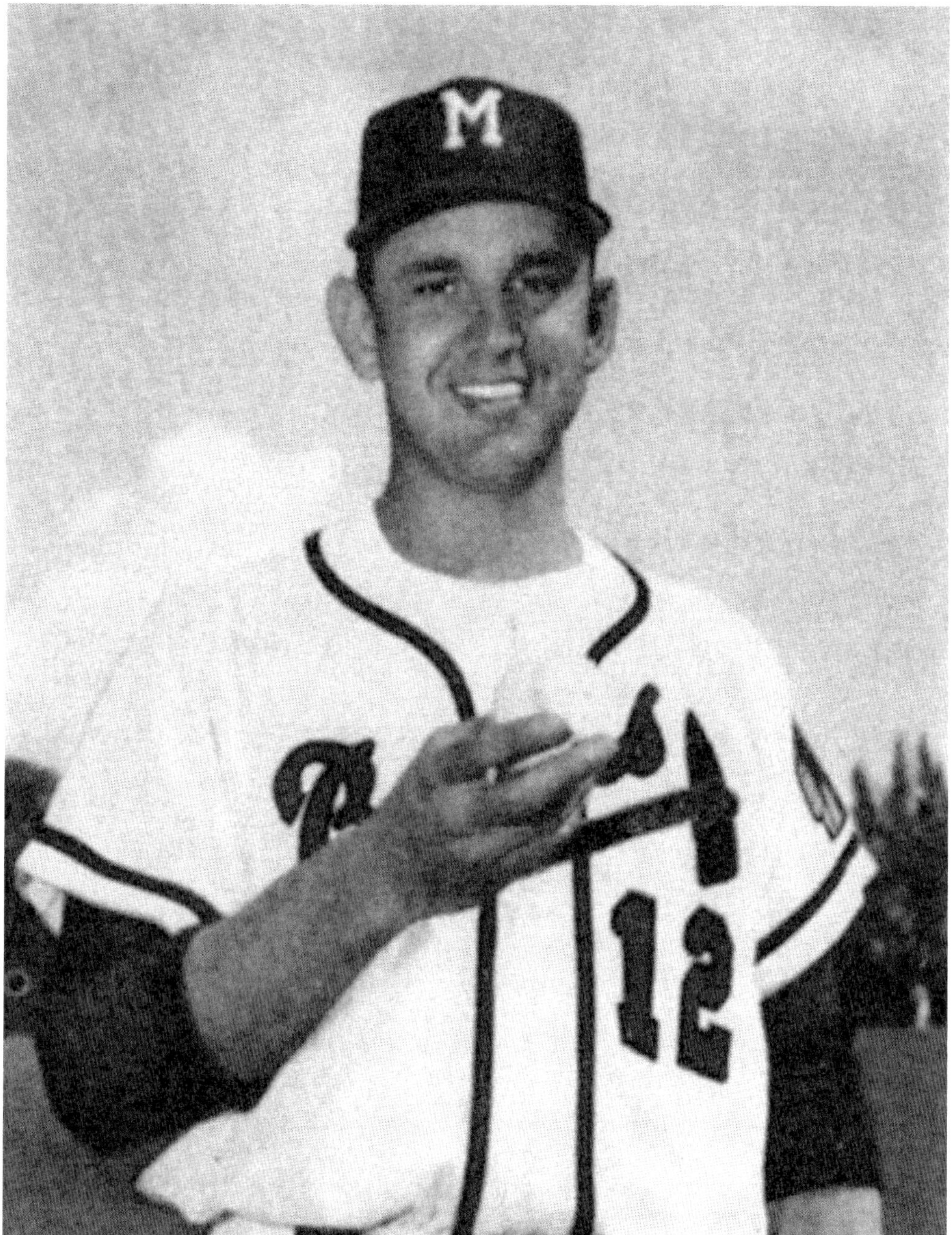

Ray Crone was one of many talented baseball players to come from Christian Brothers High School in Memphis. In 1946, Crone pitched a no-hitter in the Junior American Legion for Corbitt Motors. He signed with the Boston Braves straight out of high school in 1949. Crone pitched in the majors from 1954 to 1958 with the Braves and Giants. In 1959, he came home to Memphis to pitch for the Chicks. His last year in professional baseball was 1960. Crone retired from the game to become a successful major-league scout and now lives in Texas. (Author's collection.)

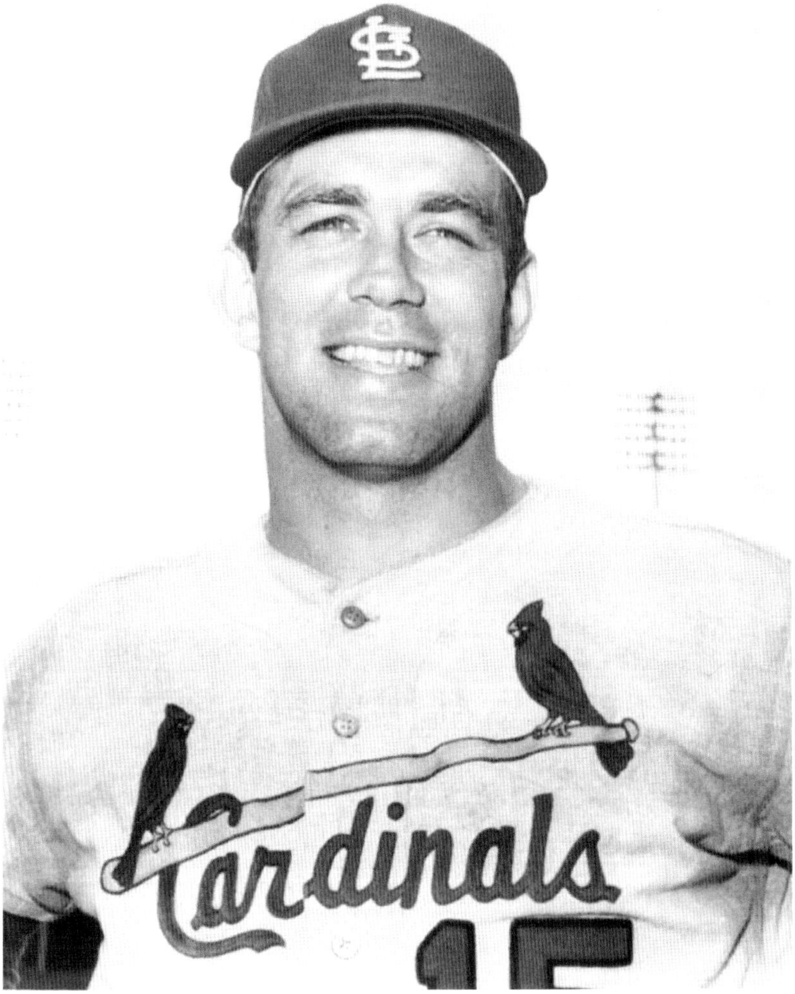

In 1959, Tim McCarver was named the outstanding prep baseball player for Shelby County by the Memphis Athletic Association. Turning down opportunities to play college football, McCarver signed with the St. Louis Cardinals. He played for the Memphis Chicks in 1960, the season Russwood Park burned. McCarver was familiar with Russwood, selling Cokes there as a boy. By 1963, he was with the Cardinals to stay. His home run in the 10th inning of game five of the 1964 World Series helped St. Louis to the championship. His playing career later included being personal catcher for Hall of Fame pitcher Steve Carlton. After a four-decade playing career, McCarver moved to the broadcast booth. His broadcasting career over the past 30 years has placed him as the lead baseball analyst for all four major television broadcast networks. McCarver also hosts his own television show for Chevrolet and has written several books about baseball. When the Chicks returned to Memphis in 1978 in the Southern League, Blues Stadium was renamed Tim McCarver Stadium—a fitting tribute to a favorite son of the Bluff City. (Author's collection.)

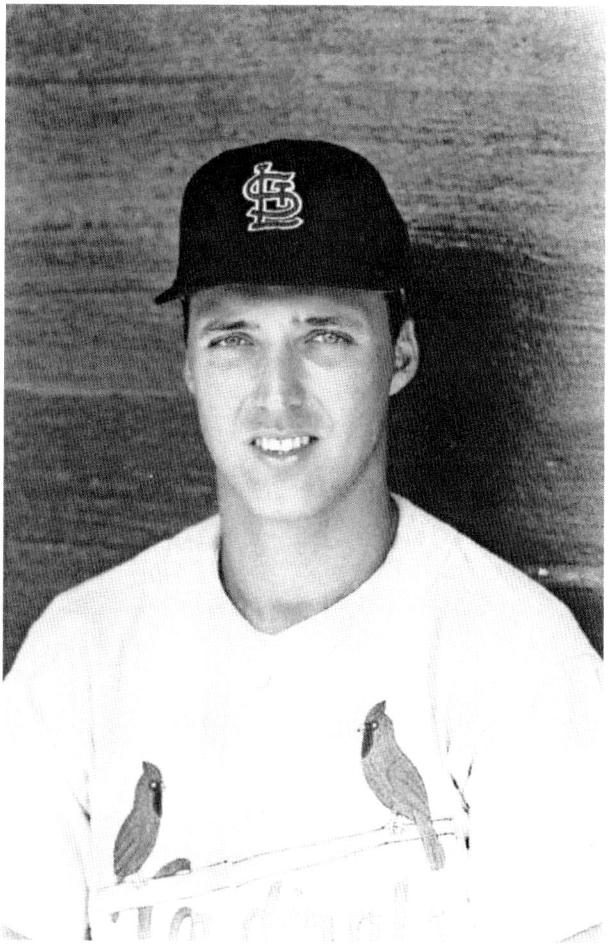

The Thornberrys were not the only Memphis brothers to play in the major leagues. From 1963 to 1974, Phil Gagliano (right) played in the big leagues; in 1960, he was a member of the Memphis Chicks. Phil's younger brother Ralph (below) played part of the 1965 season with the Cleveland Indians. Both men played baseball at Christian Brothers High School. (Both, author's collection.)

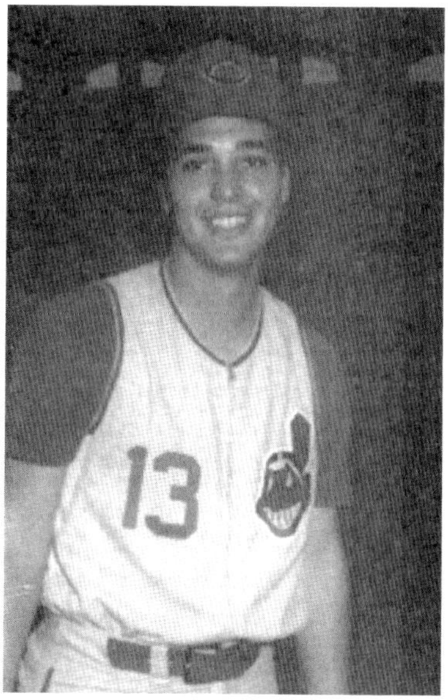

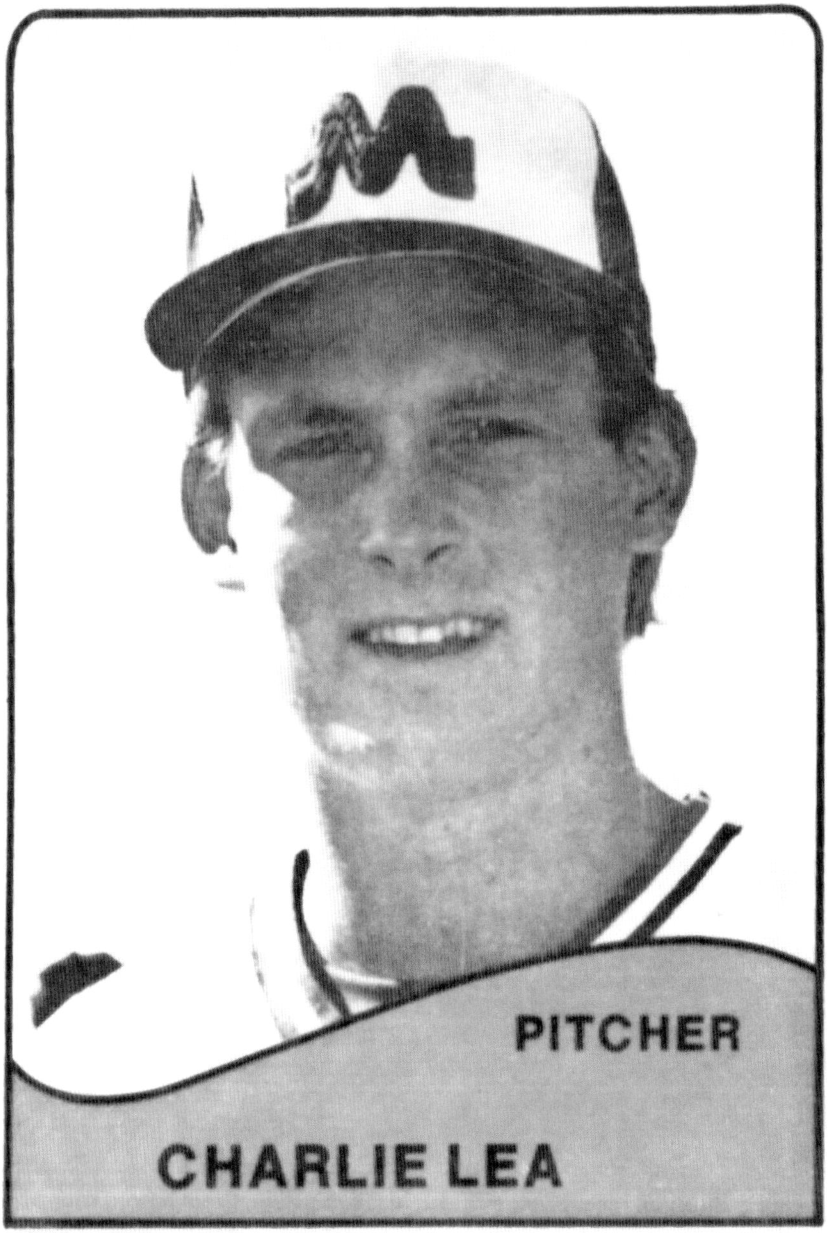

Charlie Lea was born in Orleans, France, while his father was stationed in Europe with the military. Lea was drafted three straight years while in high school but chose to attend Memphis State University. Finally drafted in 1978, Lea signed with the Montreal Expos. He pitched from 1978 to 1980 with the Memphis Chicks, becoming a Southern League All-Star in 1979 and 1980. Lea debuted in the strike-shortened season, throwing a no-hitter on May 10, 1981. Charlie now lives in Memphis and does Memphis Redbirds radio broadcasting. With Lea begins a long list of quality pitchers to come out of Memphis high schools: Ross Grimsley, David West, and Matt Cain. (Author's collection.)

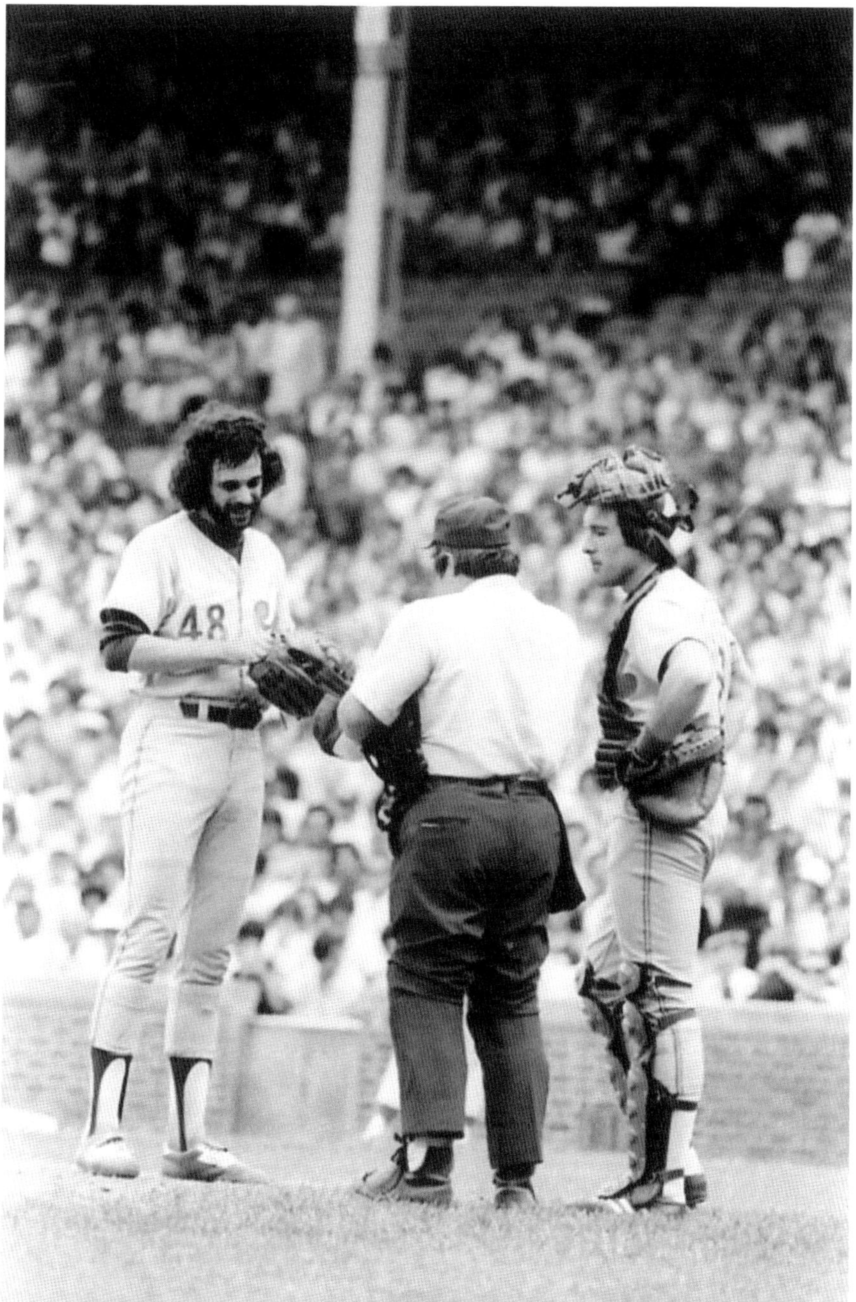

Ross Grimsley Jr., son of former Memphis Chicks pitcher Ross Sr., was an outstanding basketball and baseball player at Frayser High School in North Memphis. Grimsley played in the major leagues from 1971 until 1982. His best season was 1978, when he won 20 games for Montreal. Grimsley was known as a colorful man during his playing days. He was very superstitious and would not bathe during a winning streak. He was accused of hiding petroleum jelly in his large curly hairdo, leading to the nickname "Scuz." (Author's collection.)

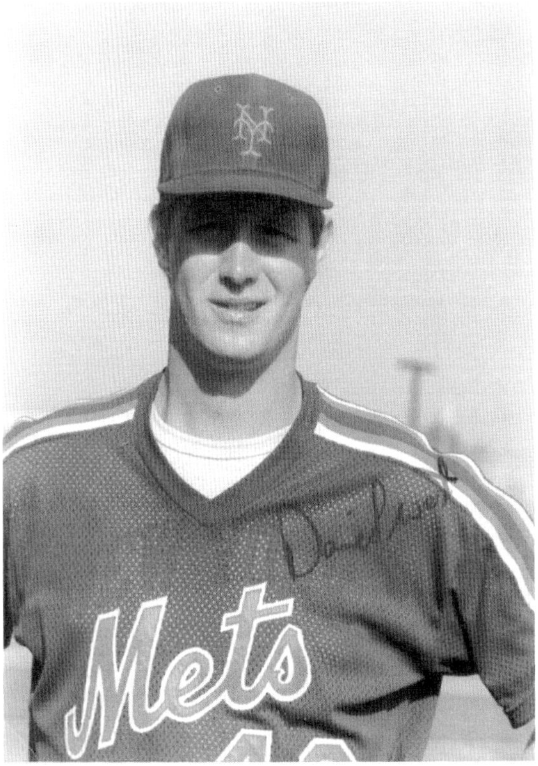

David West pitched for Craigmont High School in Memphis. After high school, he was drafted by the New York Mets. After two years with the Mets, West was traded to Minnesota in the deal that brought Frank Viola to New York. David pitched in the 1991 and 1993 World Series. He retired after the 1998 season with the Boston Red Sox. (Author's collection.)

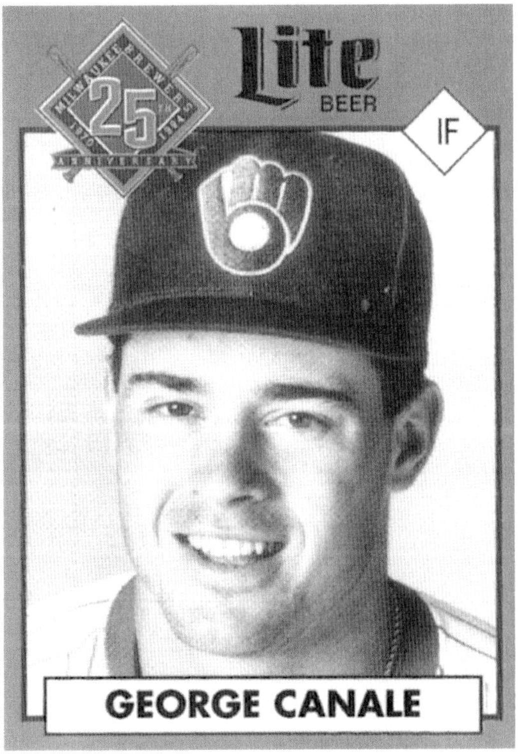

George Canale played three years with the Milwaukee Brewers (1989 to 1991). Late in his career, he played the 1994 season with the Memphis Chicks. Canale also is ranked seventh on the all-time college home-run list while playing at Virginia Tech. Canale played one year of professional baseball in Korea at the end of his career. (Author's collection.)

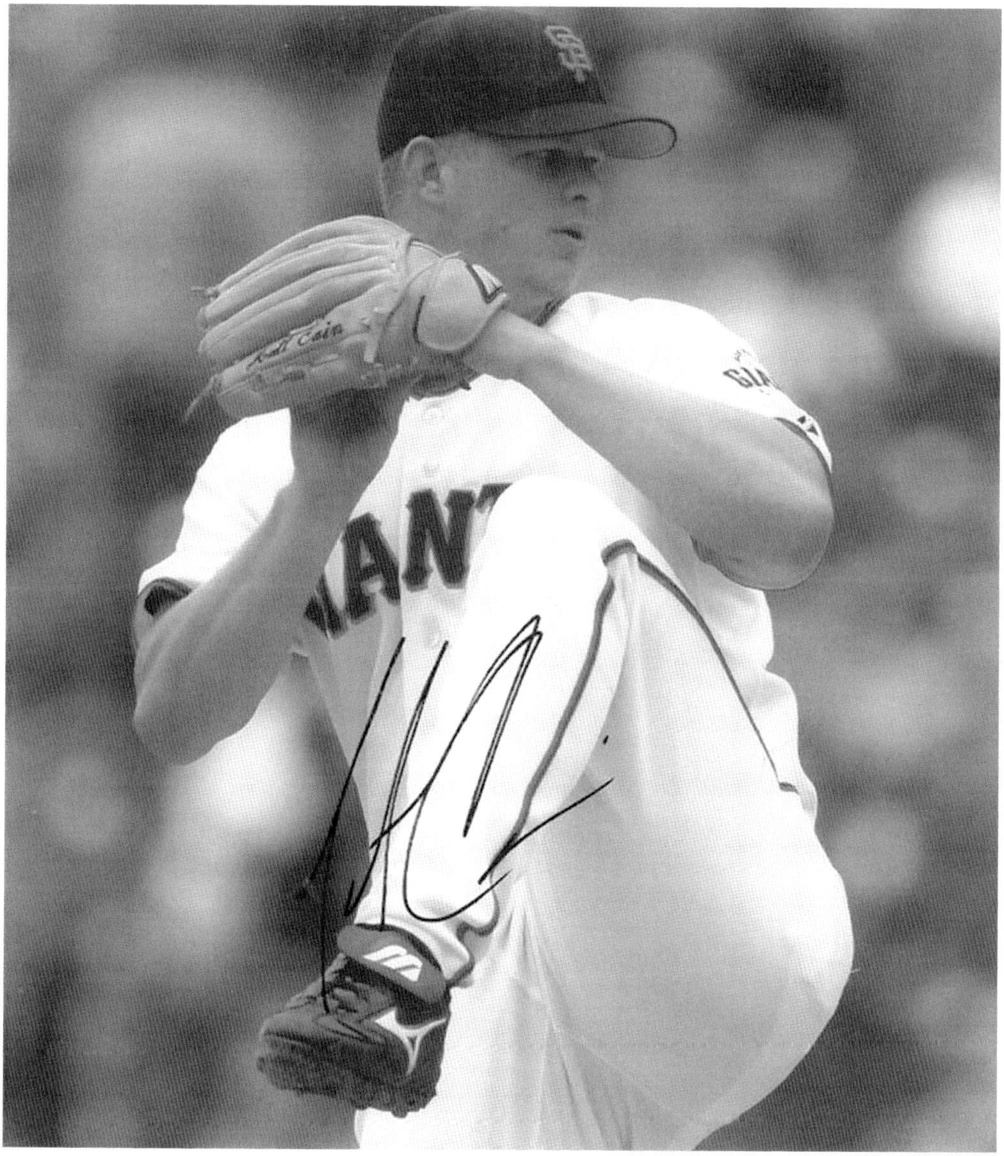

The latest in a long list of quality pitchers to come from the Memphis metro area is Matt Cain. Cain graduated from Houston High School in Germantown and was selected by the San Francisco Giants in the first round of the 2002 draft. He made his major-league debut in 2005 and has been mainstay of the Giants starting staff since 2006. Cain's manager during the 2006 Giants season was former Memphis Chicks manager Felipe Alou. (Author's collection.)

Consistent with our mission to preserve history on a local level, this book was printed in South Carolina on American-made paper and manufactured entirely in the United States. Products carrying the accredited Forest Stewardship Council (FSC) label are printed on 100 percent FSC-certified paper.